Reflections of a
Cat Whisperer

Reflections of a Cat Whisperer

Mary Ann Clifford

*I awaken to life
through
the eyes of a cat.*

Library of Congress Control Number: 2012920094
ISBN: Hardcover   978-1-4797-4055-0
                   Softcover   978-1-4797-4054-3
                   Ebook   978-1-4797-4056-7

To order additional copies of this book, contact:
Xlibris Corporation
1-888-795-4274
www.Xlibris.com
Orders@Xlibris.com
120445

Contents

Special Acknowledgments

Many thanks are given to Angela Davis for allowing me to use her picture of my handsome William's eyes on the cover.

Recognition is given for the excerpt from Josh Groban's song "You Raise Me Up," a paragraph from Irving Townsend's essay "The Once Again Prince," and a quote from Isaiah in the *Bible*.

Sketches of a select few of my thundering herd—my cats—are rendered by me, Mary Ann Clifford.

There have been many who have influenced my life, although one person I wish to recognize in particular stands out. I dedicate this collection to my husband, Pat, with deep gratitude. I want to thank him for putting up with me throughout the years by encouraging me to continue the devotion I have for the captivating four-legged creatures I so treasure—my cats.

Introduction

I was never fond of English when I was in school. The last thing I cared about was writing essays or papers on any subject. What was ironic, I enjoyed creating narratives about insights on life. Nonetheless, I wasn't brave enough to reveal them to others for the simple reason that I feared getting teased and having my peers laugh at me, assuming I had possibly gone off the deep end. In the years after my formal education, I fine-tuned these tales and added new ones. Even so, they remained inside my thoughts, though I did share them with a particular feline audience.

When I became older and a little more confident, I disclosed some of the tales with special friends. Eventually, they persuaded me to gather them together into a book. As a result, I started the process of placing what I was thinking down on paper.

It's doubtful I was ever intended to be a great writer. What I would like to see happen is the magic of looking at life and living it, which was passed on to me by my dad, will carry on after I am gone. More importantly, I hope each and every one of the cats who are part of my heart will be remembered.

I cannot take the entire credit for every idea in *Reflections of a Cat Whisperer*. The few selected inspirations and tales written by others are modified to denote my point of view. Furthermore, some direct quotes are appropriately included, although the vast majority of writings contain my own personal views and original ideas.

In these reflections, I share questions for which answers were never found and relate events from an unusual perspective, allowing them to appear as fantasies. Periodically, the regrets and heartaches I experienced are openly revealed together with the joyful moments that blessed my life and touched my soul.

Admittedly, all the expressed observations represent the wishes and dreams that are very much me. In addition, I confess that food for thought, alongside many tears and countless smiles, can be found throughout the pages.

CHAPTER 1

WELCOME to MY WORLD

Walking the path,
one step
at a time.

I was born different. By *different*, I mean I constantly walked a path that was not quite in step with the rest of the human race. Using an old cliché, I have definitely marched to the beat of a different drummer. In reality, I have marched to the meows and purrs of the domestic feline.

Since I formed a special bond with animals, cats in particular, I was destined to have them rule my whole being. Because of this bond, I walked on a path that would eventually lead me through a life filled with wonders, joys, and great sadness. For me, it certainly turned out to be an unusual existence, occasionally overflowing with special magic of perceiving the world in imaginary ways as well as including mischievous fairies playing tricks in it.

What's more, I was permitted to discover a deep sense of compassion that, at times, was quite overwhelming, almost bringing me to the point of losing my mind. Somehow I received the strength to cope, find my way, and proceed on an incredible journey.

I recognize my dedication to cats will always be a passion for me, and I am doubtful it could ever change. I feel the fascination I have for felines will keep me rooted on a curious course, allowing me to further develop and maintain deep attachments to these unique creatures. The magic of seeing life I have faith in and the fairies I perceive as a part of it will also continue to define who I am.

It doesn't matter how I am viewed in society. What matters is the love and devotion I sustain for cats for the reason that these characteristics provide me with the aptitude to be a caregiver not just for them, but also for humans as well. Periodically, I care for other creatures, too. From this compassionate ability of helping so many, I find deep satisfaction and great contentment.

Considering everything, I have come to the conclusion that my place here on earth was intended to be in serving the domestic feline and in helping others.

Now welcome!

Welcome to my world!

This Is Who I Am

From the moment I took my first breath, I have loved animals, principally cats. They were the center of my existence, and this has never changed, even to the present day.

As a young child, I dreamed I would someday be a doctor who saved every four-legged creature under my care. I played for hours, nurturing my toy animals. In this world of pretend, if any of them became sick or injured, I nursed them until they got better. I could heal them all. Nothing was out of reach or appeared impossible to accomplish.

When I got a little older, I made believe I was an animal doctor with the family pets. They were very tolerant patients. Sometimes they protested. To their credit, I have to say they were extremely forgiving every time I put a splint or wrapped a bandage on them. I probably had the only cat who came down with four different broken legs each week. It seemed there wasn't anything beyond my capacity to fix or cure. I felt positive I could perform miracles.

A few years later, I quickly learned the beliefs of early childhood were not that simple. I found out there was a beginning and an end to every living creature. Way too often, someone became ill or broken and was not able to be put back together . . . never made right again. Precious moments could stand still and permit life to remain the same, but not for long. The spirit then passed from this existence into the next.

Growing up at home, I was never without a furry companion. Beyond this safe and protected environment, I rarely came into contact with them. They were absent, primarily, in any work I acquired.

I lived in an area where jobs were extremely difficult to come across and far removed from the creatures I cherished. Entering my preteen years, I made spending money from babysitting to cleaning houses. For my first "actual" job at the tender age of sixteen, I was hired by a catalog company.

It featured men's clothing as well as woman's apparel. I quickly discovered women often fudged about their sizes, and men also did it more often than I would have ever guessed.

After graduating high school, I briefly worked for a book publishing company inside the mail order division during the summer before entering college. I spent many hours in the mindless sorting of incoming and outgoing invoices. It really gave me the desire to attain my goals of a higher education.

Throughout my college years, I earned money for my tuition from the salary I was paid as a savings teller in a bank. To keep my mind sharp, I took on the challenge of adding large columns of numbers in my head and soon became first-rate at it.

Following completion of the requirements for a baccalaureate, I received an art education degree. I was quite talented and more than likely could have made a sufficient livelihood in the field. Regardless, I found I possessed a slight problem. I felt little enthusiasm for the profession; and that kind of attitude, without question, appeared in my work.

For a short time after I married, I taught school until I became aware I never acquired a certain skill to make it a vocation. I determined I should possess a tremendous amount of patience when dealing with children to be a gifted teacher. Regrettably, I significantly lacked having that special characteristic.

My husband was an oil company executive for quite a bit of his career. Subsequently, we traveled to different locations around the country about every two years because of his changing positions. With each move, I sought out a number of different interests. In one city, I took on the task of tour guide in a historical museum park. Shortly, I advanced from docent to assistant art director. I definitely enjoyed the endeavor because I was fascinated with the local history and folklore of the region. I found ways to bring alive the past by relating local legends to visitors. Frequently, I had fun dressing in the fashion of the time. I also demonstrated and taught lost skills like quilting. I think it was mainly an escape since I didn't have to face any shortcomings of confidence and lack of courage to pursue what I really wanted from life.

It didn't matter what I did or accomplished for the simple reason that my heart was never really into anything I dabbled in over the years. I always obtained adequate positions, although I never found the satisfaction I longed from them.

Many years elapsed before I accepted the idea that I could do something about my dilemma. I went back to a part of a childhood dream and pursued my first love. I started working full-time with animals. I recognized I was at my best only when I was helping four-legged living beings.

In West Virginia, I was a registered lobbyist in the state legislature and fought for animal rights. I witnessed how sad it was that laws needed to be placed before mankind would ever be humane toward the animals under his care. I quickly realized all creatures, except humans, were considered property and definitely not always treated with the respect they deserved unless mandated laws were available to protect them.

I entered the field of animal control and observed situations I never realized could happen. It didn't take very long before I was overwhelmed with unbelievable sorrow. After a few years, I couldn't cope any longer with the never-ending heartaches and tragedies I encountered. Consequently, I walked away from its reality to keep some sanity. Even today, I wish shelters could be turned into centers for adopting pets and no longer existed for the primary purpose of correcting man's mistakes.

Over time, I taught myself how to groom cats and was exceptional at it. I shared this knowledge with others. I was always delighted to face the challenge of persuading a very determined cat to hold still long enough and endure the indignities that accompany the process of getting cleaned.

When I was trained to be a veterinary technician, I uncovered the part of the childhood dream closest to what I enjoyed most of all and something I was actually good at performing. A special doctor opened my eyes to the long-forgotten talents, which came naturally for me. I soon found my true gift was nursing animals; and I became an animal nurse, a veterinary technician.

Regrettably, some things were not meant to last forever. This happened at a point when I started to learn about my true talents. Very shortly, I would discover when one door closed another one does open. I just found it difficult grasping the knowledge at that exact moment.

Pat was transferred to a new location for a promotion as senior vice-president. Consequently, I left my job at the veterinary clinic. I moved with him and our group of hairball makers. I tried with little success to find employment at the animal clinics in the new town. As a result, I allowed the job to come to me. I turned my nursing knowledge toward home care of animals. It wasn't my first choice, but there was a need for it. I could assist animals desperately requiring help. Eventually, I devoted my skills and training to felines exclusively.

I started working with cats who could never be placed for one reason or another. They usually came with more than one problem. Their disabilities were either physical, emotional, medical, or any combination of conditions. Because their care consumed so much time, I lost count, long ago, of the number of hours I have devoted to these marvelous creatures. The endeavors also required a tremendous amount of love with even more patience, a very perceptive husband, caring veterinarians, and a great deal of money. With all of these support factors, the cats then received a quality life. Finally, I acknowledged the satisfaction and contentment I had been seeking.

My world at present revolves around very opinionated feline bosses. They are the center of it. I don't think there is ever an occasion I am not caring about them. It is a passion within me to understand and nurture these independent soul mates. Given that this enthusiasm runs quite deep, I repeatedly question my good sense. Funny, as I look back on my adventures, I recognize I have always been quite passionate about cats. Also, since I have such a deep affinity for these curious creatures, there is a part of me that questions the likelihood I could have been a cat in a previous life. If nothing else, it is an interesting concept to consider.

I share long days with various cats, belonging to me and others. I treat each one equally, although admittedly, a few take more than one piece of my heart. Some stay for an instant, and others remain for a lifetime. Even so, it is always too soon to say good-bye to any of them. Each time it occurs, my world is torn apart. Tears never cease appearing whenever I remember many are no longer here on earth. Frequently, I wonder if I have anything left in me to give . . . then another one comes along who needs some assistance.

A number of years ago, I posed some questions to a couple of friends. I asked, "What would you call what I do? What exactly is my profession? What is my title?"

After quite a bit of debate and many suggestions, a consensus was somewhat made. The new title for my vocation became "Professional Feline Consultant." Some felt "Cat Whisperer" was more appropriate.

Whenever I think of the titles, I can't help but chuckle, as I have reservations about exactly what I am. If someone asks me what my occupation is, I respond by saying I serve the domestic feline. I am also a caregiver for others. Actually, I do quite a bit in many areas it is hard to explain the tasks with a few words.

I have a limited home for cats, many with special needs. This requires a great deal of nursing skills and plenty of time. I teach techniques in home care for special-need cats to others who require the skills. I deal with feline behavioral problems and give consultations on the issues. I groom cats belonging to me and cats who are not mine. I also instruct other eager volunteers on developing grooming skills while dealing with different types of feline coats. Sometimes I lend a hand to the elderly in the care of their cats, and I help friends with their furry crews. Often I rescue and seek suitable homes for abandoned cats who cross my path. I do placing and referrals of cats belonging to strangers. I have assisted several caregivers in getting their cats spayed or neutered through a cat club program. I am a visiting cat nurse and, at times, a hospice caregiver for them. On occasions, I do cat sitting and have been teasingly referred to as a "cat nanny." I train human parents of diabetic felines how to measure their cats' blood glucose levels with meters. For many years now, I have been volunteering with a select few of my thundering herd in a pet therapy program. Whenever I have a moment, I write tales and verses I want remembered. Every now and then, I embark upon creative computer art and tackle the many houseplants inside my garden room.

It seems I am not sure if the things I do means very much to anyone else except for certain four-legged creatures and select others. After I am gone, I envision I will be referred to as "the crazy cat lady." I have no doubt with the passage of years, this will be long forgotten.

On the other hand, whenever I stop long enough to consider other possible careers, I know I love my chosen path. What's more, I guarantee I would never trade my place for another. Nevertheless, I admit that in a secret place tucked deep within my soul, I dream of being a special doctor—saving every broken and vulnerable four-legged creature who happens to come to me, making their life right again.

I Am the Cat Whisperer

From time to time, I think about why I am called the Cat Whisperer. I have never perceived it as an unusual or extraordinary talent. Basically, it's a way of life that has been a part of me for as long as I can remember and then some. I do recognize I have set myself apart from others by following this path of serving the domestic feline, the so-called tame cat. Thus, I sense it is the reason for the title.

The affinity I have for the feline began in childhood. I acquired a number of health issues I was forced to deal with during those years. Frequently, my sole companion was a cat. Perhaps that was when the close relationship with this creature started, although the love and devotion I have for the feline was positively instilled in me before I was born. Because of this belief, I've often been teased I was a cat in a previous life. Maybe I was. I definitely never ruled out the prospect it occurred.

Apparently, I never required any formal training to help guide me with insight into the nature of the worthy feline. In point of fact, this came as an innate attribute, giving me a very interesting and ever-expanding knowledge of the cat.

By viewing life from the perspective of a feline, I understand the distinctive reasoning power presented by the cat. With this ability, I then make an assessment of his thought process and respond accordingly.

Regularly, comments are offered by others about my capability of persuading the feline to do things that would be impossible for anyone else to accomplish. Yes, I achieve the objective by means of common sense. I alter behavior with the gift of tolerance and patience. I repeat desired commands and, occasionally, outsmart an opponent. Primarily, I reach my goal by having sufficient stubbornness to outlast a determined cat. Sometimes I step back and approach different situations with creative ideas, but I never surrender. However, every so often, I must concede and compromise when faced with a strong-minded cat.

With each interaction with the feline, I constantly exhibit a gentle touch. Then again, in certain circumstances, I have to demonstrate a great deal of firmness. I also use good judgment and regroup if a cat presents a very aggressive attitude.

It's repeatedly pointed out that I possess a unique way of communicating with the feline. I agree with this observation. I start by talking to the cat. He may not comprehend every word I said, but my emotions and body language are most definitely focused on quite intently. I then listen by watching his body language. Apparently, I was given a sixth sense that helps me reach the cat's inner soul. I admit there have been a few instances in which I was fooled since the cat can be most unpredictable.

The comment made that never ceases to amaze me is that I view life in ways others cannot visualize. I find this to be a very observant statement. It is the magic Dad shared with me in my childhood and which I never lost. I have the capability to imagine wonderful possibilities whenever I look at a cat. I open my mind to see, feel, and hear amazing things that for a normal person are not real or even conceivable.

Every cat I meet I find exceptional. I continue to perceive each encounter as a new and awesome adventure. Furthermore, I keep increasing wisdom from these exchanges with this magnificent creature, the domestic cat.

Now if the above mentioned comments make me the Cat Whisperer, then so be it—I am one!

CHAPTER 2

BEGINNING in CHILDHOOD

~∿~

Magic begins
as wonders unfold
in a perfectly
safe world.

~∿~

I thrived in the surroundings around me as a small child. It was a safe and secure place to grow up in during changing times. All the same, I was not completely protected from events outside of it.

Through trials and errors, I began to mature. I made mistakes and learned lessons from my newly acquired knowledge. I asked questions and occasionally found answers for them. I dreamed dreams I never forgot and added new ones to memory. I made friendships as well as close bonds that lasted a lifetime and then stretched into eternity. With each step I took, I ensued upon a long journey to become the person I am today.

Wisdom

When I was a baby, Mom said some of the first words I spoke were *pork chop* and *cat*. Pork chops actually were one of my most desired foods and still are up to this day. Cats, on the other hand, were my first love; and they unquestionably remained so throughout my entire life.

I did not acquire my first cat until I was four. Ever since then, rarely has there been a time I didn't have one with me. Better yet, rarely has there been a time a feline didn't have me with him.

When I was a young child, Dad was definitely my hero. I am sure my compassion and love for animals came from him. Dad was a very tall stern man of Irish descent with steel blue eyes that could put the fear of the Lord into anyone he felt deserved it. However, if you looked behind those eyes, there was a big heart; and I only saw that part of him. He possessed such tenderness for animals I can still feel it even now. It was because of that gift he opened my eyes and heart to the amazing world of animals, especially the wonder of cats. He also unfolded to me his magical observations of how to view life and the animals in it.

Dad quickly caught on whenever I saw a cat I would ask for one. It didn't matter if the kitty was a toy feline or a real one. If I wasn't talking about these marvelous creatures, I was drawing pictures of them. Dad promised a cat would be mine as soon as I was old enough to care for one. Meanwhile, I reasoned in my child's mind that I'd demonstrate the best methods of looking after my stuffed animals. I figured Dad would surely realize I was ready to take on an actual living cat.

I treated my stuffed animals as if they were real pets and took care of their every need. Shortly thereafter, I decided to be their doctor. I lined them up and obtained temperatures. I also placed bandages on every part of their body and feed them imaginary chicken soup until they got over a particular ailment. I believed I was an excellent animal doctor and dreamed I was going to be an outstanding one when I became an adult.

The town where I grew up in was in the Northeast. My family home was located on the side of a mountain. The view was most definitely breathtaking, looking down into the valley. Experiencing four seasons was certainly spectacular because they were painted in many different ways, with springtime the one I enjoyed the most. After long months filled of bitter cold, it was delightful to watch nature turn green and lush. Filling the air, the fresh smell of blooming flowers was everywhere. It also was the time of the year I acquired my long-awaited first cat.

On a sunny spring, although it was still slightly cool outside, I found out I would be getting a kitty. My fourth birthday arrived, and Dad happily announced I was finally ready to take on the responsibility of caring for a cat.

Dad took me to what I considered a strange place, which was located in another part of town. I remember riding through the city park before coming to a large square white building. The place was the local animal shelter. It was clean inside, but I thought it contained a weird smell.

A man in a uniform greeted us. He was average in height and very slender, almost too thin. He introduced himself as the Humane Society officer. Dad informed him we came to give a cat a good home, and the feline was for me.

While we followed the officer into the cat room, I held Dad's hand. I was scared. Consequently, I gripped it very tightly. Dad felt my uneasiness, so he quietly explained in a tender voice that I was there to pick out my very own kitty. The decision on choosing the right one was completely mine. The kitty could be big or small, longhair or shorthair, boy or girl. Dad also instructed me to look closely at each one before making a selection.

I felt it was an awesome responsibility and was very unsure if I could do it correctly. At first I was speechless upon finding a great many cats housed in a single room. All I saw were cage after cage filled with many different kinds, and I didn't know if I could pick one. More than anything, I was determined to make a proper decision. Much to my relief, the instant I peeked at the felines, any doubts I felt quickly left. I initially glanced at the enclosures. Slowly, I looked inside each cage, one by one.

As I proceeded on my quest, a loud noise kept exploding from a cage about halfway to the ceiling. I had a hard time getting a good look at the cat who was making the racket and kept reaching out for me. Seeing my frustration, Dad lifted me up in order to find the cat who desperately wanted my attention.

The kitty was a male with long legs. He was a juvenile with shorthair and dressed in a black-and-white tuxedo coat. His eyes were the color of gold, which quickly melted my heart. As I watched him, I thought he was the most handsome cat ever born. Softly touching his paw, I turned to Dad and said, "I would like this kitty!"

With the biggest smile, Dad asked me if I was certain since I didn't check out the remainder of the cats. I stared directly into his eyes and very seriously decreed, "Yes, I'm positive!" I also proudly proclaimed, "This cat chose me, and that's why I want him!"

Pleased with the decision, Dad set me down; and we walked over in the direction where the officer patiently waited. Dad spoke with him. Then pointing at the cage, Dad indicated the cat we wanted to adopt. The officer had been watching and agreed with the choice. He went over and reached into the enclosure. He took out the kitty and plopped him into a box with holes in it. After Dad finished the paperwork, we left for home. I was excited beyond words, and I couldn't wait to show Mom the wonderful cat I just acquired.

Dad put the box on the backseat of the car. During the drive, the young juvenile didn't seem frightened in the least bit. He was curious and stared at us through the tiny openings.

I opened the box in the living room, and the adolescent jumped out. He immediately butted and rubbed against me. He never stopped purring, not even for a second. I have to admit I was more thrilled about the cat than Mom at the moment. It didn't matter. I asked Mom anyway what she thought. Without much elaboration, she acknowledged he was cute.

The next big decision was choosing a name. Actually, that was easy. The men who worked with Dad called him Mick. Therefore, I decided to call the kitty Mickey. After all, it was because of Dad I finally acquired a cat.

Life was perfect. Somehow I think Mickey sensed he was special. Just before he came, I began to have health problems. After his arrival, I frequently came down with bronchitis and was then plagued by allergies with asthma. Frankly, it was irrelevant how ill I became because Mickey was with me and never left. I can remember days went by, and the only contact I had with anyone besides my human family was Mickey. He was my whole world.

At a time when no one really understood what secondhand cigarette smoke could do to young growing bodies, the effects of breathing cigarette smoke was not considered a contributing factor why I was sick so often. Everything else was blamed instead. Frankly, it didn't matter. I knew everything was going to get better as long as my best friend purred in my ear.

If I was under the weather and didn't move around very much, I curled up in a large living room chair. Mickey stretched out with me and stayed until I was ready to leave. I loved having him snuggle with me. He was a warm and soft comforter.

Over the years, I shared many secrets with Mickey only he appreciated. He was wise beyond anyone realizing it, except for me of course! Often I played for hours with Mickey and made believe he was the patient. As a result, it wasn't unusual the doctor checked on him and not me. At least, that was what I pretended and wished it could be.

When I was growing up, a doctor still made house calls. It wasn't uncommon to think of him as part of the family. If his services were required, he came. Not once did he take into consideration whether it was day, night, or the weekend. He was always on hand.

Dr. McDonnell was a very pleasant gentleman. He talked to Mickey and had fun with the idea of treating him. I then related exactly how Mickey was getting along. Essentially, it was the way I was feeling. I would listen closely to the doctor's instructions. Without question, I wanted to make sure I cared for Mickey properly. In reality, Mom was the one who received the information.

Gradually, I learned how to handle both allergies and asthma. It wasn't always easy, and there were many occasions I tested the waters. Each time I disobeyed my parents or the doctor's instructions, I definitely paid the price for it. One thing for sure, I could always depend on Mickey to help me get through my troubles. He was a lifesaver. I thought I was caring for Mickey. Truthfully, he was the one caring for me.

Life with Mickey ended much too soon, and one of the saddest moments of my childhood took place when I kissed him good-bye. He came down with an incurable illness. Even now I don't have a clue what it was. I think, possibly, the veterinarian didn't know either. I just remember it was something that could not be treated. With tears in his eyes, Dad took Mickey to the animal clinic for the last time.

I did not grasp what death was until I lost Mickey. At that moment, it meant my best friend was gone and would never return. My heart was broken, and I cried for days.

Dad's heart was also sad when he saw how lost I was without Mickey.

He made a suggestion, eager that I'd find consolation from his words. He said, "Mickey is an angel in heaven, but he will always be in your heart. You can still talk with him and tell him what you're thinking. He will hear your words and help guide you."

Honestly, I figured Dad was pulling my leg. I thought it wasn't possible to be in heaven and in my heart at the same time. Despite any doubts, I did listen and took Dad's advice. I talked to Mickey. Once again, I shared with him my secrets, wishes, and dreams.

Little by little, I started to heal. Then one day I asked Dad for another kitty. I explained, "Mickey feels I should have another cat to care for since he is now an angel in heaven."

Dad agreed.

I found the means to work through the grief and deal with the loss because of Dad's guidance. I never forgot his words I needed to hear at a tender age. It is still amazing to remember how wise Mickey was and how much more wisdom Dad possessed.

Do Animals Go to Heaven?

Both of my parents were Catholic. Therefore, I was raised Catholic, except I didn't attend any of the Catholic schools in the lower grades. I was a student in the public system. That meant every Wednesday afternoon throughout the school year, I walked to a particular Catholic school along with a number of other Catholic kids from the public system. We did this to participate in catechism classes. The group I was in headed for the Irish Catholic school directly across the street from the church where my entire family belonged as members.

The year I began catechism school, I was placed in the First Holy Communion class. I was in the first grade when I started. I was just six at the time. I should have been a second grader to enter the class and seven to receive the sacrament. Since my seventh birthday fell a few days before the official day of the Sacrament of First Holy Communion, I was put in the First Holy Communion group of students.

The First Holy Communion teacher was a nun whose name I have long forgotten. However, I remember Sister quite well. She was of the order of the Sisters of the Immaculate Heart of Mary. Back then, nuns wore the traditional habit. Sister was petite, although she looked like a giant in her starched-white head cover with a black veil over it and dressed in a long, dark blue robe. She definitely appeared quite intimidating to a six-year-old child.

I was small for my age and very shy. I tried my best to always be good and, for the most part, the perfect little girl. At least, it was that way until I met a particular First Holy Communion teacher.

Each week, Sister assigned different pages in the catechism book for reading homework. The following week she quizzed us about what we learned from the readings. During one session, Sister asked, "Do animals go to heaven?"

In the First Holy Communion book, it stated people entered heaven when they died; but there was never any mention of animals being allowed to go or not go there. It didn't matter. I already knew the answer. With a smile from ear to ear, I raised my hand.

Sister called on me to stand and answer the question. I obeyed and quickly rose to my feet. Pleased as punch, I responded, "Yes, animals go to heaven when they die!"

Quite flustered and with a shocked look on her face, Sister snapped at me: "Animals aren't given souls like ours, so they can never have eternal life in heaven!"

I looked straight into Sister's eyes. For the first time ever, I talked back to someone no child would have dared flipped off to in those days—a *nun!* In a loud clear voice, I proclaimed, "Sister, you are wrong because it's not heaven if animals aren't there!"

Not one of my classmates made a sound or even moved an inch in their seats. They just kept their eyes glued on Sister. I think they were amazed I dared talk to a nun in such a manner.

Sister was very annoyed with me. She was red faced and definitely passed the point of being reasonable on the subject. Her voice became high pitched and was teetering on the brink of erupting like a volcano. She looked at me and demanded, "Who told you such a story?"

With a stubborn streak I inherited from Mom, I stood my ground. I crossed my arms and replied once more, "My dad told me, and he knows everything!" I did not understand how any nun didn't realize this obvious fact, especially Sister. I thought everyone knew animals went to heaven when they died, and she must be just plain stupid for thinking differently.

The attitude I displayed was my downfall. Faster than lightning, Sister came toward me, taking two steps at a time. She grabbed me by my arm and escorted me out of the room. I was walking so fast I felt as if I was wearing roller skates on my feet. I had a sinking feeling I was in trouble for talking back to her, but it never occurred to me I was in trouble for what I said.

Muttering under her breath, Sister escorted me over to the rectory where the offices of the parish priests were located. The head priest was Monsignor. He was in charge of both the church and the school. Monsignor was quite elderly and very stern looking. Actually, he was very kindhearted. At the very least, I hoped he would be sympathetic to my predicament.

Sister ordered me to sit in the reception area and not utter a sound. I obeyed without question and sat in one of the large galley chairs. Sister burst into Monsignor's office, slamming the door behind her. Even with the door closed, I was able to hear what she said since her voice was booming. I suspected the neighbors who lived down the street could hear it as well.

There wasn't any misgiving Sister was very upset. She related to Father what I told her earlier inside the classroom. She finished her tale by snapping at him: "You must call this blasphemous child's parents and get them up here, immediately! They must explain how this child came upon such an idea!" She ended her tirade with one more order. She demanded he punish me for such arrogance before the devil got my soul.

Before Monsignor could respond, Sister left the office in a huff. She rushed past me with no further word, not even a look. Frozen and unable to move, I kept my eyes glued to the floor.

Sister failed to completely close Monsignor's door. Consequently, I was able to hear him dialing the phone and was pretty sure he was calling my home. At that moment, I recognized I was in major trouble. Needless to say, my heart sank.

From the way Monsignor talked, I was positive Dad answered the phone. I let out a sigh of relief. I figured Dad was the one person in the entire world who would understand what happened. After Monsignor hung up the phone, everything turned quiet. The only thing I heard was the ticking clock on the far wall. I waited for what seemed like forever and worried.

I started to understand the big mess I had gotten myself into for standing up to Sister and making her mad. Deep inside me, I still thought she was completely wrong by saying animals weren't permitted into heaven when they died.

All kinds of visions kept running through my head while I squirmed in the chair. I imagined there was a very good chance I would not be allowed back into catechism school. I pictured my friends receiving the Sacrament of First Holy Communion, except me! I knew for sure I was in deep trouble with Sister and, probably, Father for talking back to a nun. I assumed I would be thrown out of the church because I was a blasphemous child, whatever that meant. Finally, I had overwhelming feeling Mom would send me to my room for the rest of eternity because of such arrogance, whatever that meant, too.

About fifteen minutes passed before Dad arrived. As he entered, he looked serious. I was relieved and scared. He glanced in my direction but didn't take time to stop and never said a word. He went into Monsignor's office and closed the door behind him. Since they talked with low voices, I was unable to hear what was discussed. After a few minutes, Dad came out and gestured for me to come with him. Very quickly, I ran over and took his hand.

Upon leaving, Dad was quiet. I desperately wanted him to say something, but I was afraid to ask anything. At that moment, I felt my life was over before I had a chance to grow up to become an adult.

Dad opened the passenger car door, and I slipped inside. After he closed it, he instructed me to quietly wait until he returned. He went into the school and shortly reappeared with my book bag. Dad sat down on the driver's seat, shut the door, and turned toward me. He asked if I had anything to say.

Very meekly, I looked at Dad and related what transpired earlier. Lowering my head and speaking in a soft voice, I admitted I talked back to Sister and said she was wrong for saying animals couldn't enter heaven when they died.

Quite patiently, Dad listened to the entire story. He was holding back a smile while he stared out the window. He took a deep breath and composed himself before he spoke.

Dad explained, "Some people have different thoughts on what heaven should be like, and not everyone will ever agree on who can go there. Quite sadly, they will never see eye-to-eye on it either. Anyone who is good and loved definitely goes to heaven after death, no matter if they are a human or an animal. It just wouldn't be heaven if both aren't there."

With a very stern look, Dad also made it very apparent I should never have talked back to Sister. He requested I hold my tongue and mind my manners in the future. He insisted, rather firmly, I must respect Sister even if I didn't agree with what she said.

Dad assured me I would be allowed back into catechism class the following week on the condition I apologized to Sister. I then could receive the Sacrament of First Holy Communion with the other students.

Grateful for understanding my plight, I hugged Dad and gave him a kiss. Pleased with the outcome, I promised to tell Sister I was sorry.

I never found out what was said in the conversation between Monsignor and Dad or what was discussed between Sister and Dad. Whatever came to pass in the meetings fixed the trouble I had gotten into on that infamous day.

The following week, I returned to class. With my head slightly lowered, I sheepishly approached Sister and said, "I'm sorry." I didn't say anything else.

Sister accepted the apology and ordered me to take my seat. Sister never again brought up the subject about animals going to heaven. I was very relieved because I didn't want to tell her she was wrong one more time and then be thrown out of the class—permanently.

On June 16, 2006, my beautiful blue-gray kitty with the biggest green eyes was losing her battle for life to a cancerous growth deep within her chest. I was about to let Feathers go in peace when Kristin, a technician at the veterinary clinic, asked me, "Do you think animals go to heaven?"

Kristin never realized how thankful I was for the question. It gave me the strength I needed for dealing with the situation at hand. With tears rolling down my cheeks, I remembered my dad's words. I looked over at Kristin and smiled since I definitely knew the answer to the inquiry. From the belief Dad instilled in me many years before, I said,

"Yes, animals go to heaven when they die because it's not heaven if they're not there!"

Pennies from Heaven

When I was a child, Dad frequently took me along with him whenever he went on "errands." One of his hangouts turned out to be the local hardware store, which was a drugstore at the same time. He occasionally looked at tools and various other items. Often he was more involved in the conversations among his friends. They also came and did the same. Essentially, it was more of a gathering place for quite a few of the local men of all ages. I always sat at the soda counter, enjoying some ice cream. Regularly, there were other dads' kids sitting there, doing the same.

One time in particular, I wasn't interested in my ice cream. I just sat on a stool and picked at it. The owner noticed I was deep in thought and asked me if there was anything on my mind.

I told him, "Nothing."

That was far from the truth. Grandpa died two weeks earlier, and I was wondering if he was with my cat who already was in heaven.

Grandpa had been very special to me; and I loved him, although I didn't know him very well. I am positive the reason he meant so much was the fact he was my dad's father, and Dad was the most important person in my life. Dad was also my hero who could fix anything, and I was his little girl.

I can't recall very much about my grandfather. I barely have a few vague memories. I do seem to remember he was ill and had been living in a nursing home in the country for a number of years. I also recall that on Sundays, Dad drove up to see him, weather permitting. I went along for the ride every opportunity, even though I was young and not allowed inside the home. Usually, I stayed inside the car or sat close by on a bench and patiently waited until Dad was ready to leave.

Grandpa regularly appeared at the window on the second floor and waved. He threw me a kiss, and I sent one to him. Shortly afterward, Dad returned. When Dad arrived, he always carried five pennies in his hand. As Dad offered them to me, he told me they were pennies from Grandpa.

After a brief visit with his friends, Dad and I left the hardware store. We headed for the car when Dad pointed at the ground. I looked down and saw some pennies. Dad instructed me to pick them up and explained Grandpa sent them from heaven.

Dad knelt down in front of me and smiled. He said the pennies were Grandpa's way of showing how much he loved me. Dad further explained Grandpa promised to always take good care of my heavenly kitty angel just for me.

I threw my arms around my Dad's neck and hugged him. I didn't have any idea he understood what I was thinking. Somehow he did. Dad gently hugged me back and suggested if I saw any pennies on the ground in the future, I should pick them up, too. He said a special angel would be watching over me one day, and this angel might toss them exactly like Grandpa did. I was baffled by Dad's words because I never considered the possibility of ever losing him, but I agreed.

Years passed, and I became a teenager. Life was filled with so much potential. Then unexpectedly, everything changed. On a chilly April day, with a brisk northerly wind blowing, I was saying good-bye to my dad. I believed heroes were invincible; and since my dad was my hero, I thought he too was invincible—but he was human. As one, he could also get sick and die.

The cemetery where Dad was about to be buried in was actually quite a beautiful place. It was located on the topside of a mountain; the view was majestic, and a quiet beauty blessed the ground. Nevertheless, deep sadness echoed everywhere I looked.

The service was finished, and I was leaving Dad's grave. Heading back toward the car, I held on to Mom's arm while my brother and sister walked a few feet behind us. By chance, I glanced down and noticed two pennies on the gravel. I bent over and snatched them up with my fingers. Clutching them tightly with my hand, I stared at the heavens. Tears filled my eyes as I whispered ever so softly, "Thanks, Dad!"

In my heart, I knew it was Grandpa's way of reminding me how much he loved me; and I suddenly realized it was Dad's way. I also knew my heavenly kitty angels were purring beside Dad; and I was positive he would take good care of them, precisely like Grandpa had been doing for some time.

I never said a word to anyone about those pennies I found on that chilly April day, scarcely a few yards from my dad's gravesite. It was a special secret

Dad and I shared together. Maybe heroes really don't die; they just move into life in heaven while still keeping tabs on those left behind.

Presently, I am all grown and an adult. Each time I pick up any pennies I happen to come across, I securely hold them in my hand. With a warm feeling within my heart, I look at the heavens and thank my dad. I continue to find comfort from his words about how a special angel is letting me know he loves me and is taking good care of my heavenly kitty angels along with some other heavenly pets.

And yes, I kept those two pennies my dad sent on the day I said good-bye to him.

The Day the Chicken Flew

Somewhere around the age of twelve, I was delegated with the chore of learning the various preparations for dinner. Ordinarily, nothing unusual occurred during those times, with the exception of a certain day I will never forget. It took place one afternoon as Mom prepared a chicken for the evening meal.

I was sitting at the kitchen table, breaking toasted bread in small pieces for the stuffing. Mom worked at the other end, cleaning the chicken.

Dad came into the room and rested against the corner wall by the stove. He was paying half-attention to what was happening at the moment. I noticed Dad sported a gleam in his eye, and I wondered if he might be up to something. Sure enough, he was.

Shortly, Dad engaged Mom in a discussion about something irrelevant and silly. He found it amusing to watch her become so irritated with his opinions. I was positive he pursued it purely to attain her goat. Obviously, Dad failed to grasp that she reached the end of her patience and her Irish temper was getting the better of her. Out of the blue, Mom grabbed the chicken and threw the plump bird at Dad!

Stunned, Dad stared at the approaching chicken with wide eyes and the most startled expression on his face. Having no time to spare, he quickly ducked as the chicken barely passed over the top of his head. It slammed into the wall directly behind him, bounced off it, and took off in the direction of the open cellar door. While the fat bird sailed down the staircase with great ease, I would have sworn it was alive!

Still sitting in my chair, I stopped tearing the toast and watched the ongoing events quite mesmerized. Hardly a few seconds passed before I ran over and stood at the cellar door to watch the airborne bird.

In the meantime, my cat, a red-striped and very large tomcat, was peaceably catching forty winks on a step halfway down the staircase. Big Mick enjoyed his perch where the coolness from the cellar below came as a much-appreciated relief throughout the hot days of summer. It was definitely true until that particular moment.

Because of the commotion, Big Mick opened his eyes. He rapidly became aware a fat featherless chicken was headed in his direction. Possessing great feline dexterity, he jumped to his feet and quickly moved out of the bird's aim. The oncoming bird missed him by sheer inches. Big Mick was half-furious and half-scared. He immediately bristled into the biggest cat I had ever seen. The instant the chicken hit the spot where he had been comfortably sleeping just a moment before, Big Mick swiftly scrambled after the bird with all fours, ready for battle.

The chicken kept tumbling down the steps to the floor below. Big Mick ran after the bird at top speed and used unspeakable language, which definitely didn't need one bit of translation. The second the chicken arrived at its final destination, Big Mick attacked and killed the poor thing for a second time.

When Big Mick was positive the chicken was really and truly dead, this proud tom grabbed the unfortunate bird by the leg. He made sure it was well secured between his jaws before he slowly and diligently pulled the now-lifeless body back up the steps and into the kitchen. Showing the pride of a victorious hunter, Big Mick triumphantly laid the battered carcass on the linoleum, right in front of Mom.

Noticing the look on Mom's face, I recognized Dad was in deep trouble for the proceedings. I also suspected a particular brave feline was, possibly, inside the same boat! Without a second thought, I dropped the piece of toast I was still holding and scooped Big Mick into my arms. I cautiously set him on the floor close to Dad and me. At the speed of light, the three of us exited the kitchen. I followed Dad, and Big Mick trailed behind me. I headed for my bedroom with Big Mick and never looked back. I don't know where Dad escaped to in the interim to give Mom time to cool down.

I didn't have chicken that night. Memory fails me about what Mom finally served. I do remember I swore I'd never make her mad if she was in the middle of preparing dinner, especially a chicken, and never did. As for Dad, I am not sure how long he stayed in the doghouse before Mom forgave him.

After that incident, I do know Dad was much more sensitive about Mom's feelings because they really loved each other. Actually, Dad never intentionally meant to upset her. I also had a very good notion Dad didn't want another chicken thrown in his direction—ever again.

Childhood Rhymes and Prayers

It wasn't unusual that I changed the simple prayers and rhymes I learned as a child to have them reflect my thoughts. I rarely repeated them out loud since they were secrets. They remained with me throughout my life, hidden away within my mind. Yet they were ready to appear when I wanted to partake in them.

As an alleged adult, I continue to use these rhymes and prayers. I also fine-tune them whenever necessary, although I still keep them as secrets. I admit I share them with my cats because they never reveal any secrets.

I never liked hearing the nursery rhyme about a baby falling out of a tree, and I in no way considered thinking about my cat falling out of one either. Around the age of seven, I decided an angel should rescue the cat in this rhyme.

Rock-a-bye kitty on the treetop.
When the wind blows,
The cradle will rock.

If the bow breaks,
An angel will come,
And catch kitty,
Before he falls down.

I am not sure how old I was when I exactly understood the concept of death. At a very young age, I thought a loved one just went away and I never saw him again. Growing older, I believed one returns to the home in the heavens and reunites with the presence of the Lord Father. I now believe the latter, and I believe every loved one will be there no matter if they are people or animals. If, for any reason, they are not in heaven, especially my pets, then I do not wish to enter such a place.

> *Now I lay you down to sleep.*
> *I pray the Lord blesses your soul.*
>
> *If you should leave before you wake,*
> *I pray the Lord takes you home.*
>
> *Until the day I come to you,*
> *I pray the Lord keeps you safe.*

Throughout my youth, I played many different games with the other kids in the neighborhood. The game that was on top of my list of favorites was tag. To pick the child who was it—the one chosen to find the others after they hid—I recited this rhyme.

> *Eany, meany, miney, moe.*
>
> *Catch a kitty by his tail.*
> *If he growls let him go.*
>
> *Eany, meany, miney, moe.*

Currently, if I see my cats playing tag, I know they are using their own version.

> *Eany, meany, miney, moe.*
>
> *Bite a human on his toe.*
> *If he hollers let him go.*
>
> *Eany, meany, miney, moe.*

CHAPTER 3

*Insight opens up
from each interaction
with the astute feline.*

RED, WHITE, and BLUE

Many words and phrases have definite meanings. Much to my enjoyment, some of these words and phrases have represented to me other things in my life.

There are a few expressions that bring to mind very different thoughts from what they are supposed to symbolize. I take delight in reliving the special memories I have each time I think of the stories behind them. Two narratives are from my childhood, and one is when I became an adult. All three are adaptations of patriotic themes.

Old Glory

Whenever I hear the words *Old Glory*, I do not picture the American flag. Instead, a very unusual feline and the story behind his name pop into my mind. The kitty I am referring to received the name Old Glory.

Every summer throughout my grade school years, Dad rented a cottage at a local lake. It was a tiny structure with red shingles high upon a hill. It contained very little in the way of creature comforts. Inside there was only cold water. The stove dated back to the turn of the nineteenth century and burned coal. The bathroom was an outhouse located about fifty feet away from the side door. Downstairs included three living spaces. A small loft was tucked above the main area and contained a pair of double beds. Two rooms on the first floor were bedrooms; and the other large area was a combination of kitchen, dining area, and living room. There was also a small storeroom in the corner, which would eventually be converted into a bathroom. On the front a screened porch was situated, overlooking the lake.

Some of the happiest times in my childhood were spent at this vacation home. Each day was carefree, and I didn't have a worry in the world. I lived every moment to the fullest, never thinking about the future. Together with my best pal, a younger brother, we made our adventures, escaping from reality into make-believe where all things were imaginable.

Located not far from the summer retreat, a small dairy farm was nestled between a hayfield and a pasture. The farmer and his wife were scarcely making ends meet. Any extras, such as replacing worn-out stone fences, were certainly out of their budget. They could scarcely afford the cost of mending them. Quite often the cows broke through the weak spots and grazed on the front yard grass next to the cottage.

My brother and I were thrilled the cows appeared almost daily. We quickly learned the farmer would soon come and herd them back to the barn for early morning milking. After meeting the farmer, he allowed us to tag along with him over the following weeks and help gather the strays. In no time, we also became acquainted with the farmer's family.

The farmer was a small thin man. He looked somewhat older than his years because of the hard life he lived. He spoke few words. The times he did, it was always with kindness. I could also see he possessed a gentle nature as he cared for his animals. This special tenderness spilled over to the way he treated my brother and me.

It wasn't very long before my brother and I were shown the art of milking by hand, even though the farmer used milking machines. We were taught to assist on small chores around the farm as well. In quiet moments, the two of us could be found playing Tarzan inside the barn's hayloft or visiting with the farmer's wife in her kitchen.

Each morning throughout the vacation at the cottage, I opened my eyes to the sun rising in the distance and the sweet songs of birds nearby. I also heard the sounds of cows mooing outside the window by my bed. I then hastily changed from my nightclothes into shorts, shirt, and sneakers. I promptly woke my brother who was able to sleep through anything and everything. Barely half-conscious, he also put on a pair of shorts, a shirt, and sneakers. After grabbing a quick breakfast, my brother and I swiftly exited so as not to disturb our parents who were still sleeping while we started on the daily quest of gathering the cows.

The herd wasn't very large. The cows were quite docile and possessed different personalities from one another. My brother and I placed a name on each one. We had fun thinking of them as very large pets. They adored having their noses scratched and necks rubbed. Occasionally, if our backs were turned, a few came up and had fun nudging us until we paid attention to them.

The farmer's wife was as round as she was tall. She, like the farmer, looked older than she was because of all the hard times that she had gone through. In contrast to her life, she never acknowledged how difficult it had been since she was always cheerful and kept a smile on her face.

Some of the most delectable smells came from the farm's kitchen. The farmer's wife loved baking goodies and canning vegetables from her garden, although the best part for me was tucked in the corner of the room by the stove.

Almost hidden behind the stove, a cardboard box contained a mother cat and her newborn kittens. I was quite fascinated and spent hours watching them. Over the summer, I learned quite a bit from the farmer's wife about farm cats and the kittens I adored. When the kittens were about eight weeks old and weaned, the farmer's wife asked if I wanted one. Without an ounce of thought, I said, "Yes, I'd love one!"

I never stopped long enough to give any consideration to what Mom would say. Shortly, my conscience got the better of me. I realized I needed permission before taking a kitten home. Mom was tough. She maintained a hard and fast rule of not having more than one animal in the house at any given time. We recently acquired a dog, and the prospect of keeping a kitten was slim to say the least.

Later in the afternoon, I found both my parents on the screened porch. They were sitting on the glider, enjoying the quiet of the day. Figuring it was the best opportunity to ask about the kitten, I held my breath and meekly approached as my brother stayed behind me. I began telling Mom and Dad about the litter of kittens, explaining that the farmer's wife said I could pick one out and keep my choice.

Observing Mom's expression, I already knew her thoughts on the subject. Before she had a chance to say a word, I looked at Dad for help. Thankfully, he immediately jumped in and suggested we should get a cat because we currently did not have any. Grinning, he said, "Tell the farmer's wife it is acceptable to adopt one." I was amazed he never gave Mom an opening to put her foot down and stop the proceedings. Thrilled with the outcome, my brother and I started cheering while waving our arms high above our heads in victory.

Mom was quiet during dinner. But her silence was deafening. It didn't matter. I was too keyed up about getting a cat to let anything bother me.

Excited beyond words, I could hardly contain myself and felt the next morning took forever to come. When it finally arrived, I dragged my brother out of bed. After gulping down the juice and swallowing some muffins almost whole, we headed for the farm in record-breaking time. Once the milking was finished, I raced into the kitchen and sat on the floor with my brother alongside me.

I stared at the kittens while they played with each other. My brother kept pestering me about my selection. I ignored him as I carefully watched for some sign to help me choose one. I thought for a long time and contemplated about the decision. There were four. Two were black with white. The others were red-striped. They were so cute and cuddly. It was difficult making up my mind.

At long last, I picked the tiny black kitten with white feet. He was the smallest and the sweetest in the litter. Besides, when he became worn-out, he crawled on my lap and snuggled in for a nap. Once again, I was thrilled a cat selected me as his own special "purrson."

Looking at the farmer's wife, I asked, "Is the kitten a boy or girl?"

The farmer's wife bent over and lifted the kitten up with her hand. She hesitated before announcing: "It's a little girl!"

Proudly, I named the kitten Gloria after their daughter. It wasn't until a few weeks later I found out my little girl was really a little boy. I then altered his name a little since I wanted it to be a little more appropriate, and I dubbed him with the name Old Glory.

Old Glory grew up to be a very unusual cat. He never was very large in stature. As it turned out, he was more feminine than masculine and never acted like a real tomcat. Naturally, this made Old Glory ever so tender with all living creatures who crossed his path.

This tomcat looked after our dog, a mix between a terrier and a hound. He taught Black Jack to use the cat box in the same manner as any good cat should learn. The box was actually a large tin filled with coal ashes throughout the long weeks of winter and contained sawdust during the other months. Let me say, that was unprecedented—watching a male dog squat and never make a mess outside the box. If Black Jack came close at missing, Old Glory popped his ears and made him keep his business inside the tin.

One Easter, Dad came home with a white bunny he rescued from the mail system. Incredible as it may have been, the US Post Office, when I was young, allowed animals to be shipped through its parcel service. Occasionally, these animals were sent to bogus addresses. If that occurred, they usually landed in Dad's office. Dad found homes for kittens, cats, puppies, and dogs. He also placed chicks, ducks, rabbits, some exotic fish, crickets, and once two tiny goats. Over the years, he saved quite a few that I long ago lost count of the numbers and forgot all the different kinds.

The method Dad relied upon to get Mom's agreement in keeping the bunny was the logic he used before. Dad explained it was perfectly acceptable to adopt one since we did not currently have a rabbit. Besides, the bunny was for me and I would be in charge of his care. His reasoning did not settle very well with Mom this time, but she relented and permitted the bunny to stay. I then christened the little ball of fluff Pink Ears.

Dad built a hutch for the tiny bunny in the cellar, though Pink Ears did not stay inside the enclosure for long. Old Glory opened the hutch door, took the bunny out, and mothered him. To my total amazement, Old Glory decided he'd raise Pink Ears. He treated the bunny as if Pink Ears was a kitten. Old Glory then dutifully made sure the bunny was safe and never out of sight. He carried Pink Ears around the house in the same manner as a mom cat carries her young babies. He looked after the bunny and taught him to be a well-behaved cat. Eventually, Pink Ears was also cat box-trained by a very determined little feline, although I think the best part occurred at naptime. It was really neat to watch Old Glory, Black Jack, and Pink Ears cuddle together in a big ball and sleep very peacefully.

Old Glory took great pride in his family of a rabbit and a dog. He loved and accepted them both as cats. For this reason, he expected them to act like good felines. Remarkably, they did exactly what he taught them to do.

Since those days, I have observed additional male cats foster kittens in the same manner as Old Glory nurtured Black Jack and Pink Ears. Except for Old Glory, I have never seen another male cat raise a rabbit and train a dog to perform as felines. The only difference between Old Glory and the other two was quite unique—Old Glory's dog and bunny looked like very unusual cats! I give Old Glory a great deal of credit for having been a very exceptional cat by succeeding at feline parenthood.

Stars and Stripes

Over the years during my childhood, there was a succession of cats passing through. One in particular was a feline I never forgot, and I bet neither did my childhood friends.

I can still remember a very tough tomcat. He ruled the neighborhood where I was raised with an iron paw. His name was Big Mick, and I belonged to him.

Smokey, a stray cat, decided she'd have her babies in the cellar of my family home. She gave birth to four boys. The largest and most rambunctious was a kitten I fell in love with and wanted to keep, except Mom held firm none of them would stay, not even Smokey. Way too soon, the kittens were weaned and each one left for a new home, including my favorite. The kittens were placed with families across town, and some friends of Dad adopted Smokey.

The following summer my family and I were staying at a cottage on a local lake. It was the same summer home Dad rented each year for us to enjoy for the duration of the vacation break from school. Shortly after arriving and getting settled, my younger brother and I set out for the farmer's house.

Once again, there was a cardboard box containing a mother cat and her kittens inside the kitchen. The box was sitting on the floor, close to the stove. The new litter consisted of six babies of various colors. One was a big red boy. He was not only very rambunctious, but he was also very affectionate when I picked him up and held him. Because the little kitten reminded me so much of the one in Smokey's litter I wanted to keep, I asked the farmer's wife if I could adopt him. She smiled and highly suggested I should ask my parents for permission before taking him home.

I thought about the kitten the entire way back to the cottage. Before entering the side door, I put my brother on his word of honor to not mention anything about the kitten until I talked with Dad. Having Dad on my side, I felt I would stand a better chance of receiving Mom's consent.

Dad loved animals. Since we presently did not have a cat, I felt deep down inside Dad also wanted one. At any rate, I kept telling myself he did. The problem was Mom. Pets were not high on her list of things she liked. She accommodated the ones we previously acquired, but she never really wanted one any more. Besides, we already owned a dog and Mom preferred just having one pet at a time. If Dad, my brother, and I were in agreement, I thought there was a likelihood Mom would concede and allow the kitten to become part of the family.

After arriving home from work, Dad went down to the dock to try out his different fishing rods. It was early evening, a good hour before dinner, and Dad used the time for unwinding from a long day. It never concerned him he didn't use any bait. Dad aimed at catching fish anyway. I thought it was the best opportunity to ask if I could keep the kitten before my brother spilled the beans to Mom.

With great enthusiasm, I approached Dad. First, I said the farmer's cat gave birth to another litter of kittens. I then explained how much a particular kitten meant to me and the reason for it. I said no matter how hard I tried, I never forgot Smokey's red kitten. Sheepishly, I asked if it was possible to adopt the little one who reminded me of Smokey's baby.

Grinning, Dad patiently listened. He continued casting the fishing line and nodding his head at the same time. I stood there in silence, studying his expression. Dad definitely was thinking about the idea. I crossed my finger behind my back, eagerly waiting for a *yes* to the request.

It seemed like an eternity before Dad spoke. Finally, he put his rod down and turned in my direction. He admitted he didn't have any problem adopting a kitten, although the final decision was in Mom's corner.

I hinted Mom would have no alternative but consent if the three of us asked together. Dad chuckled and said he would give it his best shot during dinner.

Later at the table, Dad very diplomatically brought the subject of pets into the conversation. In a roundabout way, he snuck the subject of farm cats in the discussion. He related the story about the farmer's cat having a new litter of kittens and how much fun it would be to at least think about getting one since we didn't have any. My brother and I shook our heads, totally agreeing.

I was counting on the fact Mom was caught off guard and had her defenses down. Then again, from her demeanor, I had a sinking feeling she was suspicious. I was more than positive she knew quite well where Dad was headed next, but she didn't say much. Because she was outnumbered, Mom gave permission to look. Little did she realize Dad somewhat twisted her words by thanking her for saying *yes* to adopting a kitten!

Hearing this, Mom was not pleased she had been cleverly tricked. Still upset, she gave us a short sermon before she reluctantly accepted the new addition.

Immediately after breakfast the following morning, my brother and I headed for the farm so I could tell the farmer's wife the wonderful news. Excited beyond words, I informed her I was given permission to adopt the rambunctious kitten. Thrilled, I lifted the baby with my hand and let him snuggle under my chin.

I decided to call the kitten Big Mick since Dad's nickname at work was Mick. Once more, because of Dad's help, I thought the name was appropriate.

Big Mick was a red tabby with mackerel stripes. He was a Domestic Shorthair and grew to be a very large cat. He wasn't fat, just big. He weighed around twenty pounds and was entirely muscle. Big Mick acquired nicks in his ears from battles he never lost. He developed tough and thick skin. This prevented severe bites, which more than likely could have created deep wounds. His large tomcat cheeks and huge neck also protected him during scuffles. Big Mick never picked a fight, and he never backed down from one either.

The entire block I lived on in town regarded Big Mick with respect. Often he was referred to as the neighborhood bully, though he was gentle and loving with me.

This very protective cat perceived his human family as his personal responsibility. Big Mick included Black Jack (a small terrier and hound mix), the house, and surrounding property in the package. Big Mick unquestionably believed he was the great defender because of it. Most of all, he especially did not take kindly to anyone, either two-legged or four-legged, setting foot inside his turf without permission. Generally, Big Mick kept a keen eye on any visitor from a short distance, making sure the caller wasn't up to anything.

One day I observed a mailman foolishly throw a rolled newspaper at Big Mick. I can truthfully say that occurred just once. After the incident, Big Mick patiently waited the next day for the mailman's arrival. Big Mick remained concealed deep in the bushes located at the front of the house, watching. When the unsuspecting mailman approached the porch, Big Mick sprang directly at him. It sounded like a bomb blast! Having teeth bared and growling feline four-letter words, Big Mick leaped with claws aimed for the startled mailman. Frightened and unnerved, the mailman sprinted down the street for dear life. Big Mick rapidly "purrsued" the poor man, with Black Jack joining the chase.

Around noon, the neighbor brought over our mail. Mom thought it odd to have the letters accidentally delivered next door. I believed that in Big Mick's best interest, I needed to keep quiet about the reason for the mistake. As a result, I never said a word about what happened earlier.

The following morning, my brother and I waited to see if Big Mick would let the mailman back inside the yard. Being typical kids, we were delighted it never took place. Big Mick with his partner, Black Jack, once again chased the mailman. We cheered for the infamous duo when they ran after him and laughed as letters flew in just about every direction from his bag.

The mailman eventually recovered the fallen mail and delivered it to every house on the block except ours. It was left in the neighbor's box exactly as the day before. The moment the mailman departed, my brother and I retrieved ours and took it home.

During the day, the story spread about Big Mick, Black Jack, and the mailman among the neighborhood kids. Needless to say, they joined my brother and me the next morning. We quietly waited to see if the race would transpire yet again.

Sure enough, it did!

We watched the mailman run for dear life from a cat followed by a dog. Exactly like before, we kept out of sight until the duo began the pursuit. We then cheered with all our might while Big Mick swatted at the mailman's legs and Black Jack barked at him. They stopped chasing the flustered mailman when he jumped into his mail truck and slammed the door shut. After a few more growls and barks, the notorious pair returned home. Black Jack happily puffed from the excitement, and Big Mick proudly strutted with triumph.

Once more, after the fallen letters were recovered and delivered, the mailman quickly departed. My brother and I then recovered our mail and took it home. This commotion lasted for three days. Finally, the mailman was fed up and turned the entire situation over to his supervisor so it could be rectified.

That's when the secret was exposed.

The phone rang right before lunch on Friday, and Mom answered it. After explaining the mailman's trials when delivering the mail, the supervisor notified Mom no mail would be delivered at the house unless our viscous cat and dog were appropriately curtailed of their behavior. He also informed Mom the mailman had threatened to quit if something wasn't immediately done. Consequently, starting tomorrow, the mail would have to be obtained at the post office until the situation was corrected.

Mom apologized profusely. She promised everything would be resolved before the day's end and finished the conversation. After a stern lecture from Mom, my brother and I tiptoed upstairs to his room along with the two culprits. We thought it best if we stayed out of Mom's sight.

I have to say by the time Dad came home from work, Mom was really mad about the whole thing. Sure enough, I was convinced we would be grounded for life.

Very quietly, my brother, Big Mick, Black Jack, and I sat at the top of the stairs. My brother and I decided to eavesdrop on our parents' conversation. Since we were eager to catch every word that was spoken, my brother and I stretched over the banister as far as possible without getting detected. We intently listened when Mom explained the past events.

Mom retold the saga of the mailman's sprint each morning in order to escape from Big Mick and Black Jack while Dad patiently paid attention. Both Dad and the supervisor worked for the post office but in different divisions. Still, Dad knew the man quite well and liked him. For that reason, he informed Mom the supervisor was a reasonable person. After asking only a couple of questions, Dad called the man back.

Initially, Dad didn't say very much except an occasional yes or no. Then to my astonishment, Dad advised the supervisor he would have a talk with Big Mick and Black Jack when they came inside for the evening. Slightly grinning, he hung up the receiver.

Dad summoned my brother and me downstairs. Dad instructed, quite sternly, we must keep Big Mick and Black Jack inside the house until the mailman finished delivering the mail and then departed. We were more than willing to comply with the demands. We were also very grateful the mail came by eight-thirty in the morning.

Dad always took things in stride. He never let the small things bother him. Therefore, the actions of Big Mick and Black Jack weren't really that earth shattering. Dad probably suspected the mailman deserved what took place. Whatever he actually thought, he never let it known.

Over the years, Big Mick's obsession as the great defender of my family and our dog never ceased. I can recall one night when he saved Black Jack from getting attacked by a collie.

First, let me tell some details about Black Jack.

Black Jack was notorious for thinking he was a larger canine than he actually happened to be. He stood approximately about fifteen inches tall, and I am quite certain he regarded himself as a Great Dane. He also thought he was top dog and king of his turf. By having such grand thoughts, Black Jack tried holding his ground with canines much bigger than he was in reality. Predictably, that kind of attitude stirred up more trouble than Black Jack could ever handle. This was the point Big Mick rushed in and saved him from disaster. Big Mick always went to Black Jack's rescue the instant Black Jack barked from distress of possibly getting hurt by an aggressive dog. The problem was Black Jack never stopped challenging a dog who came inside the yard. Anytime one did, the dog chased Black Jack. Black Jack constantly scrambled at top speed and then ran for safety. Big Mick simultaneously charged from wherever he was and jumped the unsuspecting canine with claws extended. It was not unusual to hear a dog yelp with complete surprise and absolute fear after receiving a few scratches across his nose. Afterward, the dog quickly ran in the opposite direction, with Big Mick in pursuit followed by Black Jack.

At dusk one summer day, I was sitting on the top step of the back porch with Dad. In the distant field behind the yard, we noticed a boy walking his collie. The boy did not see us, although the boy spotted Black Jack.

Probably for the first time in his life, Black Jack was not instigating anything. In fact, he was contently chewing on a bone at the end of the yard. I suspect the boy assumed no one was watching when he approached our dog.

The boy suddenly said, "*Sic!*"

At top speed, the boy's collie charged right for Black Jack!

Little did either the boy or his dog realize Big Mick was concealed in the tall grass. Big Mick was catching forty winks while savoring the light breeze as well as keeping a keen eye on Black Jack. Let me say, I never saw any cat take after a dog quite so swiftly the way Big Mick did at that particular moment. Big Mick burst out of his camouflage and nailed the dog's nose with his front claws seconds before the dog reached Black Jack. Panic stricken, the dog rapidly exited the yard with a furious cat and a laughing dog hot on his tail.

We observed Big Mick continuing the chase. He hissed and growled at the top of his lungs while flying after the unfortunate collie. In Black Jack's usual manner, he carried up the rear, running and barking a short distance behind Big Mick. It's hard to imagine, but the collie actually climbed a bent tree as fast as his legs could carry him. He then balanced on the lower limb, trying very hard to avoid Big Mick's fury. Big Mick and Black Jack sat at the base of the tree, waiting. Both kept their focus on the collie's every move. I assumed they were daring the flustered dog to come down and receive some more punishment.

A few minutes passed before the boy walked into the yard. He was headed for the house when he noticed Dad and me. Upset and somewhat nervous, the boy timidly approached us and politely asked my dad to call off his cat.

Dad whistled to Big Mick. Obeying, Big Mick stopped the pursuit and returned with Black Jack. Both were exhausted, though I could see they were pleased with their accomplishment.

With a serious tone in his voice, Dad told the boy to take his dog home and think twice before giving such a command ever again. Dad also made it very clear he would not call off Big Mick the next time if the boy tried to hurt Black Jack.

After the boy and his dog left, Dad leaned over in my direction and lightheartedly stated, "The dog is probably still seeing quite a few stars from a very angry striped cat!" Looking toward the distance and half-talking to himself, Dad further explained his thoughts: "There's a good chance the boy might learn a lesson tonight since the actions he chose did have consequences. From watching what happened, the boy should take into consideration the welfare of his pet before giving such a command in the future. Hopefully, the boy will also treat other animals with respect. If nothing else, by remembering this encounter, the dog will not be quite so foolish to chase Black Jack any more!"

I am not sure who taught the lesson, Dad or Big Mick. Conceivably, they both did.

Dad never let the situation get out of control. He realized the dog was never in any real danger for the main reason that Big Mick was more terror than he was bite, or should I say, claw! Dad merely allowed the dog to receive enough feline rage and a few scratches so the canine would not go after Black Jack again.

By not stopping Big Mick, Dad permitted the boy to discover that hurtful acts really do have consequences. Then in the future, the boy might show better responsibility for his dog and be watchful of other animals.

Whether Big Mick maintained any idea about his role in the lesson, I wasn't sure. I did feel he was more than instrumental by teaching it. As for Black Jack, he never stopped chasing dogs out of the yard. It was Big Mick's love and devotion for a Great Dane in a small terrier body that kept Black Jack out of harm's way.

Throughout my life, I have thought about Big Mick and his brush with the collie. Human and canine saw a few stars from my striped feline on that warm summer evening. With any luck, both learned lessons from the encounter.

I definitely gained some insight and understanding from the event. After watching my very protective cat, I learned that not everything in life is exactly as it appears. If I set out to hurt someone, I may be the one who is ultimately hurt.

The Fourth of July

Summers in East Texas can be brutally hot, and the Fourth of July in 2001 was no exception. The temperature was headed into the high nineties, but it already felt like the heat reached the target.

I finished taking care of my cats around 7:00 in the morning and was headed over to visit with my best friend. For the longest time, we got together for coffee on a particular morning each week, even if it fell on a holiday. This gave both of us a chance to relax and play with her feline crew. It also allowed us the opportunity of catching up with the weekly events in our lives.

A short distance from Cheryl's home, I noticed a police car traveling in front of me. The car was about half-a-block away from my vehicle. By the direction the officer was headed, I was pretty sure he was on his way back to the police station since in all likelihood his shift had ended.

The officer suddenly swerved to avoid something on the middle of the road. Apparently, it had been thrown from a car, which was about twenty-five yards ahead of him. I slowed down because I definitely didn't intend to hit whatever he missed. After the officer drove passed the object, I noticed it was a tiny kitten. The little one was alive and struggling to get on his feet.

Not having a second thought, I slammed on the breaks and immediately stopped. I jumped out of the car and raced over to the kitten. Ever so gently, I scooped up the bundle of what appeared to be skin and bones. It was obvious the tiny feline was a little girl. She seemed scared and unquestionably confused. As I tenderly cradled her in my arms, she settled down and purred.

One thing for certain, I have always been passionate about animals, especially cats. For this reason, I couldn't help but feel anger at the officer. I thought he showed little regard for the feline's life by totally ignoring her plight and proceeding on his way. The kitten definitely needed help or else it wouldn't have been long before she became road kill. Sadly, the officer merely left her to face such a horrible fate, except the kitten was safe with me.

It was a weekday, Wednesday to be exact. It also was the Fourth of July, so the veterinary clinic was closed for the day. I was pretty sure one of the doctors would be there caring for the boarders and patients in this early hour. For how much longer, I wasn't sure. Aiming to enjoy the holiday, the doctor elected for hospital duty diligently worked on finishing the chores and then promptly left. With any luck, maybe I'd find one still there; but that meant I had to hustle and get there as soon as possible.

I proceeded to Cheryl's house. In less than a minute, I arrived and stopped just long enough to explain where I was headed with the injured kitten.

Since it wasn't a workday, I didn't have to deal with heavy traffic that came with it. Thankfully, I made the trip to the clinic in about eight minutes. I let out a sigh of relief the moment I noticed a doctor's car parked at the back of the clinic.

When I burst through the unlocked rear door with the injured kitten, I discovered my cats' doctor present with her husband, also a veterinarian at the clinic. Kathy wasn't completely surprised at seeing me as I was already quite positive she wouldn't have been . . . just curious. This wasn't the first time I arrived unannounced with a very sick or injured cat, and it would never be the last time either. All the other doctors were aware of the possibilities of this occurring, too. To their credit, they were always very patient and thoughtful of me whenever it happened.

Kathy first looked at me and then the kitten. She grinned and inquired, "What do you want me to do?"

Kathy already had a very good idea what I was about to request, but I asked anyway. I just wanted her do whatever was needed for the little one in my arms.

While I tenderly placed the kitten on the exam table, Kathy patiently listened to the details of the kitten's plight. First, I explained where I found her. Then I further related the saga about the policeman who failed to stop and render aid.

Carefully, Kathy checked the bundle of skin and bones for injuries. She determined the kitten was malnourished and dehydrated. What's more, the little one could not stand on or use her back left leg. Sadly, the kitten dragged it behind her tiny body.

Kathy decided that when the kitten was a little more stable, x-rays would be taken to see if anything was broken. Until then, she gave the tiny little one some fluids to help the hydration and an injection for the shock. Afterward, Kathy gently placed the kitten inside a hospital cage with fresh food and water. The kitten ate everything and settled down on a towel. Shortly, the little one fell into a deep sleep.

Realizing the kitten was in good hands and would receive the necessary treatment she desperately required, I was relieved. I departed and went over to Cheryl's residence before going home.

The following day, I returned to the clinic and checked on the kitten's condition. I was anxious to find out when or if she could be discharged. During the kitten's stay, she was examined and tested for everything. Any possible health issue, which could prevent her from coming home with me, was eliminated.

When x-rays were taken of the kitten's leg and pelvic area, nothing broken was found. There weren't any apparent tears in the muscles or ligaments either. Yet the kitten could barely move or rest weight on her back left foot. Kathy was betting it was a severe sprain due to the trauma she underwent. If that was the case, the kitten would eventually get back the use of it. Time would certainly tell the possibility of it occurring. The kitten did have ear mites, coccidia, and tapeworms. Obviously, I left with the essential medications to take care of these nasty parasites.

Kathy believed that what the kitten required more than anything else was home care with plenty of TLC. For me, those were easy orders to follow. I gently placed the little one inside the carrier with a soft blanket and took her home.

While settling the tiny feline in the guest bathroom, I kept running through my mind what to call her. Then the thought hit me—name her July but spell it Julie. Almost two years earlier, Julie, a very dear friend of mine, died. The last time we spoke, I informed Julie I would name the next female cat who adopted me with her name. Julie laughed and confided there would probably be a lot of Julie cats in the future since a number of her friends wished to do the same.

For a long time, Julie was a special person in my life. A close bond developed between us, and I am convinced it was because both of us loved cats. Even though the years took us in different directions and many miles apart, we remained steadfast friends.

Julie was an ordinary person just like me, except she was so much more. Julie was a devoted daughter, a loving wife, a caring mother, a wonderful friend, an enthusiastic coworker, a person of deep faith, and a dedicated caregiver. She never met an angry cat or a mean person, only someone having an off-day. Julie found good in everything around her. Needless to say, it was really hard saying good-bye to such a compassionate friend. The one thing that made letting go somewhat easier was the pledge I made. I also found myself smiling whenever I'd glanced at my Julie cat, remembering my friend's enjoyment of the idea of naming a cat after her.

However, I've always believed every creature on earth deserves a unique name. For this reason, I decided to pronounce the kitten's name July. I'm positive Julie smiled down on me from heaven with delight, seeing the humor in the twist of words. The kitten's entire name became Kitten Julie (July). Eventually, the name was shortened to Kitten.

Kitten did get the full use of her back leg. She also grew into a stunning longhair brown tabby. It never ceased to amaze me: the large, beautiful golden eyes and the huge feet Kitten was given since her stature remained quite petite. I sometimes speculated Kitten's eyes were meant as windows for me to see Julie, and Kitten's feet allowed a part of my friend to still walk with me.

If nothing else, Kitten Julie matured into one of the happiest and most loving cats. By coming on the Fourth of July, Kitten remained a very special link to a good friend. Even now I think of how special Julie was whenever I say Kitten Julie's (July's) name.

CHAPTER 4

THOSE TENDER YEARS

*How wonderful
to gain imagination
from the antics
of the mischievous cat.*

As I spread my wings, I then flew to new places. I reached out for new experiences with great zeal and expanded my knowledge of a bold and uncertain world. Through every adventure, I was also completely aware that the safe surroundings of home would always be there to comfort and guide me if I fell.

Yes, I Promise!

Summer flew by and it was late August, scarcely two weeks before the beginning of school for the coming year. I turned fourteen a few months prior and was looking forward to becoming a freshman in high school. Secretly, I was much more excited about getting a Siamese cat. After reading a book about the adventures of one some years previously, I wanted a Siamese kitty. Finally, I was about to get my first one and was thrilled beyond words.

On a beautiful sunny day, I accompanied my dad when he drove down a country road in the Pocono Mountains. We were headed for a small white inn deep in the woods and close by a stream. The owner's wife raised blue point Siamese cats. Shortly, it was going to be my introduction to the breed and the start of a lifelong love affair with these intelligent and devoted felines.

Earlier in the day, Dad asked me if I saved enough money to buy a purebred cat. I was very proud of myself because all summer I saved my extra babysitting money. Thinking I attained more than sufficient funds, I proudly announced, "Yes, I have ten dollars!" At that precise moment, my aunt walked in and heard the conversation. She stopped by to say *hello* and chuckled as she listened to the proclamation. Knowing better, she reached into her purse and took out a five-dollar bill. She handed it to me and said I might possibly need it.

Mom, after catching wind of what was transpiring in the living room, was not very pleased. She did not believe anyone should buy a cat, more specifically a pedigree one. She was mad at Dad for encouraging me, mad at my aunt for giving me money to help purchase one, and lastly, mad at me for wanting one. Nevertheless, it didn't bother me because the only thing I could think of was getting a Siamese cat. Nothing could change my focus. Therefore, what Mom thought wasn't in the slightest way going to burst my bubble of enthusiasm.

Upon walking into the inn's office, I noticed a woman standing by her husband. She too was looking for a Siamese kitty. She was holding the prettiest blue point Siamese I thought ever existed. The kitty looked quite feminine. For that reason, I felt the little one had to be a girl. As soon as our eyes met, the kitten sweetly meowed. It was at that exact moment I realized she was the one I had been hoping would come to me one day.

There were two other kitties present, except in my mind, I already made a choice. When the woman set the kitten down, I looked at Dad and quietly explained she was the one I wanted. Dad didn't say a word as he reached for the Siamese and gently set her in my arms. The little one's warm body was sleek and soft. She had deep blue eyes, which were definitely crossed. While I cuddled her close, she didn't stop purring or licking my face, not even for a second. I'm absolutely sure that was what stole my heart. Obviously, my decision was firmly made. Better yet, I was positive she too made her choice on which human she "purrferred" from her response.

Dad suggested I should at least look at the other two, but his request was in vain. I refused because I believed the kitten and I were meant for each other.

I never gave the other couple a chance to choose the tiny female. Without any further delay, Dad spoke to the owner's wife and said, "My daughter will take the kitten she is holding." It was obvious Dad surprised everyone in the room by announcing such a quick decision, especially the other couple.

Dad asked the owner's wife the price and she replied, "Twenty-five dollars."

I froze and tightly held the kitty. I was worried since I had just fifteen dollars in my wallet and not a penny more. Conveying a desperate look on my face, I turned toward Dad and pleaded with him to come to the rescue.

Calmly, Dad inquired if the fee was negotiable. The owner's wife never batted an eye when in a firm voice, she stated, "No, it's not." Without further negotiating, Dad reached into his billfold, took out a ten-dollar bill, and laid it on the desk. He motioned for me to get my fifteen. I handed Dad the Siamese and put my fifteen dollars on top of his ten. Dad then placed the kitty back into my arms.

The owner's wife wrote out a receipt and asked if I wanted a copy of the kitten's pedigree. I smiled and quickly responded, "Yes, please!" In a monotone voice, she said it would cost another fifty cents. Dad rolled his eyes in disbelief. Once again, he reached into his pocket, took out two quarters, and handed them to her. She slipped the papers into an envelope and passed them to me.

My heart bounced with joy. I didn't think I could be much happier. After placing the Siamese on my shoulder, the three of us left the office.

When Dad started the car, he turned in my direction and asked me to promise not to tell Mom the amount paid for the cat. Dad put me on my honor to never mention the fact that he aided me with the finances. I found no problem promising Dad. I felt we would both be in trouble with Mom if she discovered what ensued.

I kissed Dad's cheek and said, "Yes, I promise!"

Years later, I stopped at the post office to buy some stamps while in my hometown. During the few minutes I was there, I ran into one of Dad's old friends I hadn't seen in years. He had been close with Dad for a long time, so it was good running into him again.

We started talking about my dad, and the friend admitted he still missed him. After asking about the rest of the family, he inquired, "Do you still have the Siamese cat? It's the one your dad took you to buy in the Pocono Mountains."

I smiled and said, "Yes, I still have the precious Siamese cat." I then proudly acknowledged, "She is my absolute pride and joy, too!"

The friend laughed and said he had a story he wanted to share with me about the kitty. He took a moment to collect his thoughts before he spoke. It was as if he was remembering an almost forgotten memory. Then he said, "You know your dad really loved you because the money he used to help purchase the Siamese cat was his lunch money for the rest of the month . . . and it pleased him to no end being able to do it for you."

I was stunned. With tears of gratitude filling my eyes, I exclaimed, "I didn't have any idea! Dad never said a word about it! I really wish I could have told him in person how much his sacrifice meant to me."

The friend hugged me and whispered, "He knew. He definitely knew."

A Thanksgiving to Remember

All through my youth, I always loved the holidays. Those special occasions were merry and full of surprises. They were the joyful times when immediate family, along with other special relatives, gathered together to celebrate and have fun.

One notable childhood Thanksgiving started like every other one, but it became one of the most memorable.

Early in the morning, immediately after breakfast, Dad and I gave our dog his bath. He was squeaky clean and smelled like the Ivory soap we used. My siblings and I got cleaned and dressed in our good clothes. Dad wore a nice casual outfit, and Mom put on a pretty dress.

A short time later, my aunt and uncle came in from out of town to join us for the festivities and to stay until the following Saturday. My aunt was always very pristine and proper. My uncle was easygoing and loved to laugh. Every time they came for a visit, Mom flew into a thither for days before they appeared. She endlessly cleaned and made sure everything was in its place. The house looked like it had never been lived in by the time she finished. She also put everyone on their honor to be on their best behavior. That meant a certain Siamese cat, Cackie, and a particular fox terrier dog, Bobby, needed to obey the same orders as well.

Around midday, I was assigned the task of setting the dining room table with the best china, linens, and silver for fifteen guests. The kitchen bustled with Mom and my aunt working on the final preparations for the feast. The aroma of the cooking food filled the entire house and was positively enticing. It made my stomach hungry. Saying it mildly, I was more than eager to begin eating.

At 5:00 p.m., the guests started to arrive. The men and children gathered in the living room while the ladies joined Mom and my aunt in the kitchen. Finally, the food was ready and Dad was summoned. It was a family tradition to have him carve the turkey a few minutes before dinner. Serving dishes were filled and positioned on the table. A turkey leg was placed on Dad's plate and the other one on a cousin's plate.

I thought everything was perfect.

Without an ounce of warning, a sneaky cat made her way into the dining room and jumped on the seat of a chair, which happened to be directly below my cousin's dinner plate. Bobby was suspicious Cackie might be up to some mischief, so he quickly followed the cunning feline. He sat on the floor next to the chair she was occupying and kept his eyes glued to her every move.

Before I could chase either one away, my aunt walked into the room. She was too busy with her assignments that she never noticed Cackie and Bobby were hiding under the dinner table. Needless to say, I purposefully stayed quiet. I watched the spot where the duo were concealed, hoping she would never catch a glimpse of them. She disapproved of having pets in the house and defiantly would be annoyed to see the two residents too close to the table upon which we would be very shortly eating our meal.

My aunt looked over the delectable spread one last time and made sure nothing was missing or needed rearranging. She seemed satisfied and proceeded to make her way back to the kitchen. I was much relieved, thinking two certain troublemakers went undetected.

Suddenly, it happened!

An unexpected movement of the tablecloth caught my aunt's eye. At that point, she realized it was Cackie reaching from beneath the table for the turkey leg on my cousin's plate. The instant this sneaky feline grabbed it, the leg flipped off the plate and sailed to the floor below. Having pretty good athletic ability, Bobby caught it in midair. Quicker than lighting, his feet moved but they scrambled a few times prior to shifting into the correct gear. Finally obtaining his traction, he promptly raced for the kitchen and headed for the cellar. In a split second, Cackie was hot on his heels.

Watching the expression on my aunt's face, I thought it best not to move or say a word. I held my breath and stood very still, pretending to be invisible. Then out of the blue, my aunt shrieked at the top of her lungs. It surprised not only me but also the rest of the family. Each person stopped whatever they were engaged in and stared at my aunt, wondering what on earth was wrong that caused her to react in such a manner. Startled, Mom let go of the items she had in her hands. As the utensils plummeted to the floor, Bobby and Cackie flew by Mom with the turkey leg.

Unable to maintain his grip any longer, Bobby dropped the leg before darting down the cellar steps. Cackie paused for a second and sniffed it. Afterward, she also dashed down the stairs. Mom remained by the kitchen stove, conveying a markedly shocked and embarrassed look on her face. Everyone else slowly chuckled and then broke out into full laughter.

Dad walked over and closed the cellar door. The two thieves were undeniably secured in lockup. Next, Dad cautiously bent over and retrieved the turkey leg. Mom instructed him to throw it out. However, he ignored the order and went to the cabinet on the far side of the table. He took out a piece of foil and wrapped the leg. He placed the bundle in the refrigerator and never said a word. I was almost positive he was saving the lost prize for the culprits, although at that particular moment, I was not about to ask any questions.

While each person took their place at the table, the laughing continued. Mom even showed a slight smile on her face. Somehow I think she was trying very hard to make the best out of the situation. Nonetheless, I knew she was still quite upset with two bold bandits for misbehaving in front of my aunt and the other guests.

It took a few minutes for my aunt to calm down. Once she finally composed herself, she joined us at the table. Without any more fanfare, my uncle said the blessing. Whenever my brother and I glanced at each other, we started giggling. Each time we did, Mom shot us a stern look to remember our manners or else.

The food was fabulous, and everyone enjoyed themselves. My cousin wasn't in the least bit upset over his missing turkey leg. He thought what transpired was rather humorous. Even so, my aunt hardly ate any of the food on her plate and remained quiet for the rest of the evening.

When the main course ended, desert was served and savored. Finally, everything was cleaned and put away. Guests said their good-byes and departed. In a short time, those left behind went to bed, including my aunt and uncle. With full stomachs, sleep was rapidly approaching. The house then became silent.

Somewhere in the distance, I faintly heard someone rustling around. It sounded as if it was coming from the kitchen, and I wondered if perhaps it was Dad. Of course, curiosity piqued my interest. I wanted to find out what was going on at such late hour. I slipped out of bed and tiptoed halfway down the staircase, just far enough to glance around the top of kitchen door. I noticed Dad was opening the cellar door. I assumed he decided it was time for Cackie and Bobby to come out of lockup. I also observed he already had taken the turkey meat off the stolen leg, divided it, and placed it in their food dishes.

The two thieves, realizing everything was safe, slowly emerged from the cellar. They sauntered over to their bowls as if nothing ever occurred earlier in the evening. They first checked out the meat and then took big bites, acting like they were starved.

Dad sat down on a kitchen chair near the two thieves and bent over in their direction. In a hushed voice, he cautioned them that the trouble they caused earlier certainly was not in their best interest. He requested that in the future, if they thought of helping themselves to a turkey leg, at least not do it in front of a particular aunt.

I smiled, feeling everything was handled. I was pleased with the way Dad dealt with the situation, and I was relieved Cackie and Bobby were safe from Mom's anger. Mom was never mean to them, but there was a good possibility they might have stayed a tad longer in confinement. Actually, it was comfortable for them in the cellar with soft warm beds, a dish filled with fresh water, and plenty of dry food.

Except, it still was lockup!

There was another possibility that occurred to me. The thought also passed through my mind that both Cackie and Bobby, more than likely, would never have gotten a chance to eat their prized turkey meat if it was Mom' choice. With gratitude, I looked at Dad and thanked him in my thoughts. Having my curiosity satisfied, I quietly returned to bed without saying a word.

The Flying Squirrel

I grew up in a small town in Pennsylvania. During better days, the region was well known for its anthracite coal. Over the years, production of the lucrative mineral waned and then ceased. Mines closed and were abandoned. Left to decay, they turned into environmental hazards that required attention or much of the countryside would become unsafe. Unique methods were created to stabilize the collapsing shafts and extinguish the underground fires. Eventually, the smoldering column dumps, which were mountains of mining waste, were dismantled and removed.

Throughout those days, life kept a slower pace and seemed less complicated. Computers, for the most part, remained in science fiction. Internet was unheard of, Facebook was possibly a book in the library, and television was definitely not a priority. On my neighborhood block, everyone knew each other and formed lasting friendships. When the weather was warm, young and old enjoyed getting together, particularly in the evenings. Porches often turned into meeting places for the adults, and backyards became magical playgrounds for the children. The grownups took pleasure in chatting about anything and everything while sipping from tall glasses of iced tea. The kids enjoyed drinking Kool-Aid, playing games, and catching fireflies.

All through those years, the wooded area directly behind my family home was untouched. The city hadn't bulldozed it down in the name of progress—yet. Many different kinds of small wildlife still made it their habitat, especially the flying squirrels. Those cute creatures were some of my favorite animals. I could gaze at them for hours. It looked as if they flew like birds. In truth, they perfected their ability to glide in the air currents.

I always enjoyed summer nightfall at my family home. As dusk approached, the heat from the sunshine rapidly gave way to the coolness of the awaiting twilight. It was the special time of the day that was filled with anticipation when reality turned into make-believe. Following sunset, fairies appeared after hiding and resting the entire day to play tricks on us kids. Even as a young teenager, I never lost interest in the magic of the coming darkness and regularly looked forward to the arrival of the little mischief makers—the wonderful fairies.

During a typical midsummer evening that was no different from any other, a scrupulous feline, Cackie, was on the loose. Shortly after sundown, she made a successful dash out the back door of the house. I immediately tried catching her but found it impossible. She "purrsisted" in staying a few feet ahead of me. By doing so, I couldn't get a hand on her. Having very little success, I was getting quite frustrated. Dad recognized my predicament and eagerly volunteered his help in the capture of the illusive feline.

Without any further delay, the two of us rushed in Cackie's direction. We were hot on her heels. Nevertheless, she raced away with great speed. We rapidly lost sight of her and decided to stop the pursuit.

Suddenly, I heard a slight noise on my left side. I turned my head and stared in its direction, and so did Dad. At that point, I happened to see my cat stretching over the edge of the second-story balcony on the neighbor's house. Cackie took a soaring leap before I could say a word. As Cackie's legs extended in opposite directions, a breeze caught her slender body in flight. She fluently glided in the sky above my head. I was stunned, but I marveled at such grace.

Time seemed to stop and everything became quiet while Cackie effortlessly sailed through the heavens. Frozen in place, I still gazed at my cat with complete wonder. I think I was totally spellbound by the event. The flight appeared to go on forever. Actually, the journey lasted for less than a minute. Then Cackie's tail, acting as a rudder, gently steered her toward the soft moist grass below. She landed on four paws with delicate ease. Not having a second to waste, she darted into the nearby field. She instantly disappeared in the midst of the tall weeds and the looming darkness.

I looked at Dad and noticed he was laughing. I had to acknowledge it was funny to observe a flying squirrel navigate through the sky in the disguise of a blue point Siamese cat. I couldn't help it either; I too laughed. Like my dad, I never saw anything like it before.

Both Dad and I realized we were outsmarted, so we ceased our quest and walked to the back porch. We sat down on the top step and waited. We both were pretty sure it would only be a few minutes before a certain flying squirrel would make an appearance and demand to be let inside the house.

Sure enough, Cackie slowly emerged from the distance and approached us. The instant she reached the bottom step, she came to a standstill and sat down. I sensed misbehavior flaring in her thoughts as she looked at us with regal pride.

Staring into her deep blue eyes, Dad asked, "Did you enjoy being a flying squirrel?"

I noticed Cackie understood every word Dad spoke. Very quickly, she replied with her deep Siamese voice, *"Most empathically, I did . . . thank you!"*

Laughing, I scooped Cackie up and hugged her. With her secure in my arms, I advised the fairies they did an excellent job of turning my cat into a flying squirrel and keeping her safe for the duration of her flight. Dad laughed and nodded his head in agreement. After saying good night, Cackie and I stayed in the house for the remainder of the night.

There was never a chance Cackie could ever have gotten hurt from the height she took off from since it was only a little over eight feet tall. Plus, the grass was thick and soft for her subtle landing. To me, it was incredible to watch a cat soar in the air currents as if she was born to accomplish it.

Another thought also passed through my mind: Perhaps the fairies protected Cackie by sprinkling fairy dust over her body, allowing Cackie to turn into a flying squirrel for that one spectacular moment in time!

Catnapped

Cackie, my blue point Siamese cat, was infamous for attempting to flee into the great outdoors. This notorious feline was quite clever and sneaky about her plans on how to accomplish it, too. Typically, Cackie "purrtended" the idea of longing to be in the open air never entered her mind, except that was furthest from the truth.

I did not permit Cackie to have the freedom of the outside world. Even as a young teenager, I understood quite well the many hazards that were waiting in the forbidden land. I wanted to protect and keep Cackie safe from these lurking dangers. Nevertheless, Cackie definitely maintained other views on the subject; and teaching the benefits of staying inside the house was difficult because of it.

Cackie was very smart and definitely used her intelligence to a great advantage. She received the ability to work through any situation in record time. For Cackie, escaping was simply another challenge and an easy problem to solve.

This devious feline loved to lie in wait for either the front door or the back door to barely come open. In a split second, she would then dash at full speed and bulldoze her way through anyone's legs to escape into "freedom!" Everyone who knew her was aware of these tactics. Mostly, the plans were foiled and Cackie never made it past anyone coming in or going out of the house, although there were occasions this cunning feline accomplished the mission.

Normally, if Cackie escaped, she did not stay very long in the forbidden land. She also remained close by the house for the duration of the wandering. The entire neighborhood knew her and made sure she headed back home whenever they caught sight of her.

One day, it was different. After a breakout, Cackie failed to return home.

Around 3:30 in the afternoon on that infamous day, I arrived home from school and walked into the kitchen. Since Cackie failed to greet me upon my arrival, I asked Mom if she had any idea where my cat was hiding. Mom was occupied with preparations for dinner and never noticed Cackie was missing. She did admit she hadn't seen her all day. Hearing this, I went to my room and promptly changed from my school uniform into everyday clothes. As fast as lightning, I checked outside, trying very hard to locate the wayward feline. I called and called, but Cackie never answered.

Dad came home from work at 4:30 p.m. and became aware of the situation. Understanding how panicked I was, Dad joined me on the search. The two of us looked everywhere one more time. Still, there wasn't a trace or a clue to Cackie's whereabouts. We ended our quest and returned home.

I was quiet at dinner. I really didn't feel like eating because I was positive Cackie vanished. I tried not getting upset but found it difficult to accomplish. Seeing my distress, Mom asked me not to worry. She felt Cackie would sooner or later put in an appearance. I didn't believe her, and then my imagination took over any reasoning. I feared something terrible happened to my precious cat and I would never again see her.

Dad accompanied me the following day right before school in the early morning hours, helping post signs about my lost feline. A reward was offered with the expectations for a safe return. Dad also took one with him when he left for the post office.

Nothing. Not even a response!

Two days passed and I remained somewhat optimistic, but it was rapidly fading because there wasn't one word about Cackie's whereabouts. Finding Cackie was the only thing I was able to concentrate on both day and night. I just wanted her back with me. Since sleep seemed the best way to relieve the anguish, I went to bed early in the evening.

Later, around 9:00 p.m., Dad was sitting at the kitchen table, reading the evening newspaper. By chance, he heard a car drive into the field behind the house and come to a stop. He looked outside, wondering who it was. Since the hour was late and darkness filled the sky, it was unusual to notice a vehicle without any discernible headlights to light the path. The proceedings captured his curiosity so Dad kept watching. In a short time, the light from inside the car temporarily came on when the passenger door briefly opened. After the door closed, the car was dark once more. Slowly, the car took off, still without any lights to guide the way.

Often teenagers parked in the field and did things they were not supposed to do. Understandably, Dad assumed it was kids playing around. But in a few minutes, he came to another conclusion. From the distance, Dad thought he perceived a faint cry, which sounded like a Siamese cat. He wasn't sure because the voice was raspy. Very shortly, Dad was positive what he heard belonged to a Siamese cat—and the screaming cat was Cackie. The missing feline sat on the back porch, demanding to be let inside.

Dad got up and opened the door. In her special way of greeting, Cackie looked at him and gave a kitty wink. Wasting not a second more, she dashed over to her food dish. It was quite apparent she just wanted to eat and drink. She was totally famished and made no bones about it. Dad had a hunch it was the first meal she possibly consumed in days.

With great enthusiasm, Dad summoned me. Not hearing what occurred, I wondered what he wanted. I felt groggy from sleep, but I obeyed. When I entered the kitchen, Dad was sitting in his customary chair with a big grin on his face. He pointed at the corner where Cackie was feasting. I definitely lacked enthusiasm as I gradually turned my head in the direction. Suddenly, I grasped the reason for his reaction.

I almost didn't believe my eyes—there crouched down at the food dish was Cackie!

I was surprised and speechless. Tears of happiness swelled in my eyes as I ran and grabbed Cackie with my arms. She dropped the kibble she was chewing when I hugged and kissed her. In turn, she licked my face and butted my chin.

Reluctantly, I gently put Cackie down on the floor to finish the food. When every last crumb was swallowed, including the fallen morsel, she stretched out and started talking. Hearing her voice, I was shocked and wondered what on earth made it hoarse. I asked Dad, "What happened to Cackie's voice? Why does it sound so rough?"

With a serious look on his face, Dad shook his head and shrugged his shoulders, acknowledging uncertainty.

I then inquired, "Where was she?"

Dad admitted he was mystified and didn't have an answer.

At that moment, I didn't care. Cackie was back, and that was all that mattered. I carried the precious bundle to my bedroom. I closed the door and climbed back into bed. Cackie settled down next to my pillow. Shortly, she fell asleep, probably for the first time in days. I put my arm around my kitty and snuggled my head on her warm body. Almost as a reflex, she purred. I kissed her and thanked the Lord Father for my cat's safe return.

Dad came to the conclusion Cackie had been "catnapped." The abductors were the people in the pitch-black vehicle. These people assumed the cover of darkness protected them while they dropped Cackie off and then exited. They were somewhat right about their disguise since Dad was unable to see any details. He could only distinguish two passengers when the inside light briefly flashed on them.

Because Cackie was a purebred Siamese cat and possessed an outgoing "purrsonality," Dad assumed it was the motive the captors maintained for wanting to keep her. What they absolutely never realized, Cackie would never go quietly with them. More than likely, she never calmed down for any length of time in their custody.

Dad had a good hunch Cackie probably screamed with her loud, piercing Siamese voice from the minute the catnappers laid hands on her until they let her go. The nonstop howling hurt their ears and literally drove them to the brink of losing their minds. At that point, they decided to return her home for the simple reason that they preferred having us driven crazy and not them.

I admitted the theory was interesting. Whatever the reason for the "catnapping" didn't matter. I was most thankful the captors weren't coldhearted to do something drastic. I was also grateful beyond words they were compassionate enough to return her home.

Cackie finally understood the security of home was a heck of a lot better than the possibility of getting abducted again. She unquestionably showed no desire to go outside or approach an open door after the trauma—at least, for a little while.

Oh yes, Cackie's voice did return to normal in a couple of days after the abduction, the "catnapping."

The Game of Statue

Statue was a game I played during my childhood. My blue point Siamese cat, Cackie, also enjoyed participating in it. I'm not sure if she learned this unique game from watching me whenever the neighborhood kids and I engaged in this pastime. Possibly, she discovered the game from observing other felines when they also played it. I have a sneaking suspicion this particular activity was shared by cats throughout the ages and children just copied them. That's the reason I thoroughly believe the game came naturally to Cackie

Cackie, a highly intelligent feline, sharpened her skills of the statue game at an early age. She was pleased to execute it anytime she felt the "purrfect" opportunity presented itself, and she was even more delighted to demonstrate this master ability on some of the most inappropriate occasions.

It happened to be a typical school night, no different from any other. I was diligently preparing my homework on the dining room table for the next day at school. Dad was out in the kitchen where he enjoyed reading the evening paper spread out on the kitchen table. Mom was upstairs, helping my sister get ready for bed. My brother was watching television in the living room. Bobby, our toy fox terrier dog, slept on the floor by Dad's feet. Last but not least, Cackie was curled in a ball on a living room chair where she found pleasure from one of her most desired activities, cat snoozing.

Around 8:00 p.m., Dad's friend and his wife stopped by for a short visit. They parked on the driveway at the back of the house and entered by way of the kitchen door. It was the first time the friend's wife came to our home, even though Dad's friend had been over many times before.

Hearing strange voices, Cackie perked up and ran for the top of the television to position herself. That way she could have a better view. She sat upright and wound her tail around the front of her legs. She then glared directly into the kitchen with wide eyes. Cackie kept "purrfectly" motionless and never twitched a muscle. If I didn't know better, I might have thought she wasn't breathing.

I smiled because I understood Cackie quite well and speculated on the possibility she was up to something. Rather quickly, I concluded she decided she'd play the statue game and turned into a cat statue. At that point, I definitely suspected she was in one of her mischievous moods.

When the friend's wife walked into the living room, the first thing she noticed was Cackie. While looking at my cat, the wife remarked she couldn't believe how lifelike the statue appeared. Then wanting a better look, she walked toward Cackie. Before anyone could say a word, she reached out to touch my cat. Once her fingers came within inches of Cackie's head, this devious cat let a loud Siamese cry. The friend's wife instantly pulled her hand away as she simultaneously walked backward at a very rapid pace.

I wanted to laugh but realized it was inappropriate. From the expression on the woman's face, I sensed she almost had heart failure by nearly touching a living cat. She certainly was quite flushed and appeared very scared in her retreat into the kitchen.

The friend said his wife did not like cats. He further explained she was very afraid of them since she was a small child and never went near any. I thought the story enlightened us on the reason of her reaction—somewhat. I still had a hard time understanding the whole concept, but I remained extremely quiet and very polite. Eager to prevent any more frightening encounters, Dad then asked me if I would take Cackie to my room for the remainder of the visit.

Carrying Cackie on my shoulder, I went upstairs. I closed the bedroom door and put Cackie on the bed. Slowly, I stretched out beside her. While gently petting my cat, I burst into laughter. It was hard to imagine how anyone could be afraid of cats, particularly Cackie. Purring with satisfaction, Cackie looked at me and agreed.

The friend's wife never again entered the living room during the visit. She stayed close to the exit, actually gluing herself to the kitchen's back door. I was positive she was watching to make sure the cat statue didn't decide she'd return. Then if by chance a certain cat did make her way inside the room, the friend's wife could take off through the back door in a flash and flee into the safety of the outdoors.

I was thoroughly convinced Cackie's sixth sense informed her about the woman's fear of cats, and that's why this very cunning cat decided to play the game of statue. In classic cat behavior, Cackie took immense pleasure in tormenting anyone who was afraid of cats or didn't care for them!

CHAPTER 5

*Learning independence
just like a cat.*

GROWING UP

I always felt as long as my parents were living, a part of me was able to remain a child. For this reason, I believed I was safe and protected. After both of my parents died, I was forced to let go of the childhood section of me and become an adult. Then for the first time, I stood completely alone since neither parent was around to retreat to for comfort, support, or guidance. Not that I necessarily did—it was the idea that they were there if I needed them. It didn't matter I maintained a life of my own with a loving and supportive husband. I was unsure inside me. Essentially, I found a loss in direction and the security my parents provided me.

With the help of my felines, one cat in particular, I slowly relied upon inner strength to meet the challenges I faced. However, I've gone through moments in which I wished to go back in time and have my parents with me once again. I have longed for the element of a child in me to return so I could recapture those special feelings I experienced when I was one.

Never Examined the Small Print

Pat and I were married in the month of September. With the time of the year being fall, our honeymoon at Cape Cod remained quiet. The tourist season was over until next summer, so the entire area was mostly ours to enjoy. Much to my dismay, the week ended way too soon. Then a few days later, Pat flew back to the army base where he was stationed. Three more months of active duty were required before Pat would receive a discharge.

Stemming from a practical upbringing, I stayed with Mom and kept my job at the bank until Pat was released from the service. Afterward, Pat and I planned on moving to New Orleans since Pat's engineering job at a large oil company was put on hold as he served in the military and he was obligated to return to the position.

Following the departure from Cape Cod, we returned to my family home. The first night back was awkward, saying it mildly. It was the first time Pat stayed with my family; and my cat wasn't pleased, not even somewhat, over the idea. Because of it, Cackie glared and growled at him with total disdain every opening she found. Occasionally, she swatted at him if the mood hit her.

I belonged to Cackie. She was my protector, confidant, and companion for almost six years when Pat and I started dating. Cackie was a highly intelligent and beautiful blue point Siamese who possessed definite opinions. Consequently, she never missed a chance to comment on any subject she thought required some input. Therefore, the moment Cackie caught wind Pat was still here, she began a protest that lasted the entire night.

It had been a long day, and I was tired from the traveling. As a result, I retired early in the evening. Cackie followed me. She always slept with me, and there wasn't any exception to the routine in spite of the addition of a particular roommate.

Cackie snuggled next to me until Pat came to bed. When Pat stretched out on the far side, Cackie sat at full attention between us, totally annoyed. If by chance Pat moved a muscle, she growled, hissed, and swatted at him. Sometimes she leveled a nip or two before I stopped her. She firmly believed he had no business being there and tried everything in her power to get rid of him.

Pat was a sound sleeper and nothing disturbed him. I'm positive it was the reason that Cackie wasn't been booted out of bed. Pat apparently didn't hear a sound or feel any of the pops from her paw. I was even more than thankful he never felt her nips. Despite that, I wondered how he could accomplish it. Then again, I speculated he was just pretending to ignore my staunch protector's mischief to avoid a problem during his stay. I admit there was a part of me that wasn't completely sure.

Early the next morning, after receiving little to no sleep, I dragged myself out of bed and went downstairs into the kitchen where Mom was in the midst of the morning chores. I was exhausted from keeping alert and trying to prevent my staunch defender from beating the tar out of Pat. Cackie, in her customary fashion, sauntered right behind me as fresh as a daisy. She tiptoed over to the food dish and ate her breakfast. She then jumped on the window ledge and groomed her face—very content. After finishing, she curled into a ball to enjoy a morning nap while basking under the rays from the warm sun.

Still tired, I described the events from the endless night while Mom intently listened. I was quite panicky and feared Pat would be angry with my very protective feline. After I finished the details of Cackie's conduct or misconduct, Mom made the offer to keep Cackie when Pat and I moved. Of course, I was both shocked and upset at the thought of being separated from my cat and quickly responded, "No way . . . that's not an option!"

At that moment, Pat walked into the kitchen. He was in a very good mood and all smiles from what seemed a restful sleep. I figured he must have been oblivious to Cackie's shenanigans. At least, I hoped it was true, although I noticed he was curious about what Mom and I were discussing because we looked serious.

Before letting Pat say a word, I asked him if he heard Cackie during the extremely long night. He stared at me with a blank look, which said everything I wanted to know. I was definitely reassured he really didn't have a clue of what I was talking about. Grateful for the reaction, I then recounted the story of Cackie's mischief.

I explained about Mom's offer, and Pat almost said something. Here again, I stopped him. I looked at him and decreed, "Cackie will be coming with us, period!" With a twinkle in my eye and a very stubborn look on my face, I suggested he should have examined the marriage contract much closer, especially the small print, if he had any reservations. I just said, "The contract states quite clearly when you marry me, you agree Cackie is also part of the package deal!"

Pat laughed as Mom rolled her eyes and shook her head in sympathy for my new husband. Without a doubt, both of them realized I wasn't joking, I wasn't going anywhere without Cackie, and I wasn't about to change my mind either. Pat sat down and ate his breakfast, sensing the discussion was over.

Two days later, Pat returned to the army base in Kansas, pleasing Cackie immensely!

On that early morning inside Mom's kitchen, Pat definitely understood I would never consider living apart from Cackie for any reason. I also wasn't certain I could cope with the upcoming changes without Cackie with me to bring some stability in the approaching new life halfway across the world.

I don't know at what moment Pat grasped the depth of my attachment to Cackie and vice versa. Possibly, he already accepted the relationship as ours became serious. It didn't matter at what point it happened. I was grateful Pat never questioned my feelings about the matter.

Can a Cat Ever Get Horse?

During the final months of my husband's enlistment, I remained with my mom in Pennsylvania. When the military obligation ended, Pat arrived at my family home shortly before the Christmas holidays. Immediately after New Year's, we planned on moving to New Orleans, which seemed so far away from my hometown. Pat had been on leave from his position at a large oil company in this southern city and had to return to it.

On January 3, we packed everything we could cram into our small car. We arranged to have the other possessions shipped at a later date. Somewhere around 7:00 in the morning the following day was our departure time. We planned on everything except dealing with a never-ending serenade from a very vocal Siamese cat that was about to occur and continue throughout the entire trip.

After Mom and I said our good-byes, I lifted Cackie in my arms and headed out to the car where Pat was patiently waiting. The minute Cackie caught sight of the car stuffed with her belongings, including the litter box, she categorically became suspicious of what was about to transpire. Cackie had always been leery of car travel, and she rapidly realized she was about to face one. This certainly wasn't something she wanted in the slightest possible way.

Carefully, I put Cackie on the backseat containing a bed placed inside a very large carrier for her comfort. I positioned food, water, and more importantly, the litter box close by the retreat. However, my blue point Siamese cat wasn't enthusiastic with the attention to every detail. She thought I was ridiculous, assuming the accommodations would meet any approval and placate her.

Pat started the engine as soon as the car doors were closed and locked. It was at that exact second Cackie started screaming. In protest, she bellowed at the top of her lungs with her deep Siamese voice. I thought for sure she would stop after a short period of time.

Silly me!

Little did I ever grasp Cackie would have the ability to keep it up for the next sixty hours and forgo very little rest by doing it. Before long, I was about to find out how great her endurance could be.

As we gradually made our way through each state, Cackie sustained the protest. She went from deep moans into ear-piercing yowls. Without a doubt, Cackie was determined to make life miserable. She definitely felt we should dearly pay for inflicting this horrendous car travel upon her.

I tried holding my obstinate cat, playing the radio, and giving treats. Sometimes I put Cackie in the carrier with the door closed and a blanket over the enclosure, giving her some quiet time. I was eager to see if she would settle down.

Foolish me!

Nothing I did appeased this very strong-willed cat. She was given a stubborn streak that ran back to the beginning of time, and she unquestionably knew how to use it. As a result, Cackie howled even louder!

The few times Cackie succumbed to a nap, I was thankful beyond words for the silence. Of course, I never moved a muscle or spoke a word, trying hard not to stir the never-ending bellows. Following my lead, Pat remained quiet during those brief times, too.

After a very long day of travel, we pulled into a motel for the night. The last thing Pat wanted to hear was they did not accept pets. Holding his breath, he never told them about our Pennsylvania bellows.

I carried Cackie, wrapped like a baby, through the lobby and down the hall to the room. With each step, I prayed she would keep quiet long enough just so I could safely get inside before she began the caterwauling all over again. Amazingly enough, Cackie held her tongue until the door was closed. After checking out the accommodations, she resumed the protest in earnest. To counteract Cackie's loud voice, Pat turned on the television and put the volume on high.

Through the night, I tried sleeping with a pillow over my head while Cackie sat on the foot of the bed, intensely glaring at me. If I made the slightest move, she took up the serenading with a vengeance.

The next morning I was still tired due to lack of sleep and had the worst headache from having my ears assaulted by a piercing Siamese voice for a little over twenty-four hours by then. All the same, I again carried my very peaceful cat, wrapped like a baby, through the lobby and out to the car.

Apparently, I got the idiotic notion Cackie possibly surrendered and accepted the situation; but that wasn't true, not even faintly. Inside the car with the doors closed and locked, she started screaming with extra vigor. She was more determined than ever to make sure we paid, *dearly*, for this torture bestowed on her.

At the end of the second day, we were finally approaching New Orleans. The only thing I cared about was finding an apartment as soon as possible before my nerves were completely shattered. Regrettably, locating a suitable place was put on hold until the next day. Unfortunately, the three of us were required to spend another night in a motel before the search could launch in earnest.

True to form, nothing changed. Cackie was an angel when it benefited her, and she threw away the halo the second the mood hit her. Sorry to say, nothing altered and the second night copied the first one.

Bright and early the next morning, Pat enlisted the aid of an apartment finder. The agent lined up a few choices to preview a short time later.

Cackie was sequestered inside the carrier as the agent took us to look at a small complex located in the uptown section of New Orleans. It had everything we requested. It even accepted pets. Totally worn out, we jumped at the prospect and moved in the same day.

When I let Cackie check every inch of the apartment, she quickly understood it was her new home. Satisfied, she stretched out on the carpet and meowed, "I am finally home, so I guess there's no need to complain any longer!"

I didn't mind the three of us slept on the floor the first night since I was too exhausted to really care. Happy in her new home, Cackie curled beside me and contently purred.

Pat made only one comment after two days into the adventure. He calmly asked, "Does a cat ever get horse or lose her voice form screaming?"

The question didn't require an answer. By day three, Pat concluded a certain cat, namely Cackie, never would. Beyond a question, Pat should have been awarded the Purple Heart for enduring those long days inside a very small car with a Siamese cat screeching nonstop in his ears.

Thank-You

My mom died when I was in my twenties. I had a difficult time dealing with the situation. The main reason was that many mixed emotions ran through my mind from the strained relationship Mom and I developed with each other.

I dearly loved my mom, but I was angry with her for not letting me understand where she was coming from on many things she did. I thought I knew who she was, except I didn't know anything about her as a person. I took care of my mom, although I was never allowed to be a part of her life. For these reasons, I always felt as if she kept me at a distance; and I was very upset these matters were never resolved when she was alive. In reality, this perception wasn't the complete picture of Mom and our relationship. Unfortunately, I just became aware of these facts after her death.

My husband could not help settle Mom's estate after the funeral. He had no choice but return to his job in New Orleans since his allotted time-off was coming to an end.

I did it alone.

I remained in my family home located within the small town where I was raised. I needed to go through Mom's possessions, clear out the house, and settle her financial affairs. Slowly, as each day passed, I started piecing together Mom's life and the person she really was. I learned more about her during those few months than I ever knew about her while she was living. As the days slipped into weeks, I discovered who Mom really was and the reasons for the many things she did.

In dealing with Mom's life, I kept a gift my father had given me three years before he died close to me. The gift was Cackie, and she turned out to be a much-needed lifeline. Cackie was a wise and intelligent blue point Siamese cat. I swear she could read my mind because she always sensed almost before I did what I was thinking or feeling. Cackie listened to my troubles throughout those long days when I sought someone's TLC. She sympathized and never criticized me for being silly. Cackie just snuggled on my lap and purred. It was something I dearly treasured. This deeply sensitive feline helped me sort out the pieces of my relationship with Mom as I gradually put closure to Mom's life.

When the day came I left my family home for the last time, I realized I would never return to a place that meant the world to me. I thought my heart would never stop hurting. Not only did I say a final good-bye to Mom, I also found myself closing the door on my childhood. I recognized for the first time with both parents gone, I was no longer a child—I was an adult. I felt alone and somewhat scared. It was a ridiculous reaction, but I was leaving my comfort zone; and everything I believed would never end was headed into memory.

Finally, I returned to New Orleans after many months of putting Mom's estate in order and to rest. I was tired and numb. Throughout those long months in Pennsylvania, I had gone through a lifetime of possessions, finances, and memories and still had to deal with my feelings.

During the first couple of nights after arriving back, I was restless and didn't sleep very well. I awoke often. On one particular night I couldn't get comfortable in bed. I kept tossing and turning. Eventually, I went into the den to watch some TV. I relaxed on a cozy chair and looked at the screen in silence. I didn't want to disturb Pat since he had to get up early the next morning. In about an hour, I turned off the television and tiptoed back to the bedroom.

The room was dim, although I was still able to see details. The moment I entered, I stopped and stared at the far side of the bed. I noticed Cackie was curled in a ball on the blanket at the foot. I also saw my mom. She was sitting on the edge next to Cackie and softly stroking Cackie's head. Cackie, in turn, was purring and looking at Mom. I froze with disbelief and kept telling myself this couldn't be true! I thought I was imagining it for the reason that I was overly tired and, more than likely, dreaming. It didn't matter. A part of me wanted to accept the vision was real.

Mom looked at me and tenderly smiled. She said, "Thank you!" After a short pause, she continued, "I've always loved you and will for the rest of time." Before I could say a word, she was gone.

Half asleep and groggy, Pat mumbled, "What are you talking about?"
I replied, "Nothing."

When I settled back in the bed, Cackie came and nestled close to my face. Satisfied, she gently licked me. I gently rubbed her head and then quietly asked, "Was Mom really here?"

After giving me a kitty wink, Cackie intently stared into my eyes and purred. It was loud and strong as if to say, "Yes, Mom really did come!" I closed my eyes and slept soundly for the first time since returning.

I didn't mention anything about what transpired to Pat. I was positive he would have thought I was foolish or conceivably went off the deep end.

Over the years, I have thought about that night. Each time I asked myself if my mind was just playing tricks on me since the whole thing was perhaps a dream. It doesn't matter how many questions I've had. I still come to the same conclusion it did happen because Mom recognized my longing for her words so I could find peace within me.

Through Mom's final good-bye, I did finally let go of the anger that still lingered. I accepted my mom for who she was. Whenever I have misgivings about what I saw, I remind myself Cackie was there and she too saw Mom. From Cackie's manner and her response, I feel it did take place.

Sometimes I think my mind plays tricks on me and allows dreams to appear real in order to handle the painful events I must deal with in life. Then another part believes the ability is more than a coping mechanism. It is the magic of seeing beyond reality and accepting remarkable moments in time can actually occur. It is the magic of wonders within my soul from which my dad wanted me to perceive and live by each and every day.

TNT

My husband and I were sitting out front of our first home in Kenner, Louisiana. It was a Friday evening, a few hours before dusk and emergence of the dreaded mosquitoes. Cackie, my blue point Siamese cat, accompanied us. She was savoring the many smells emanating from the lake on the other side of the levee less than two blocks away. She was also listening to the different sounds the outdoors offered her keen hearing.

Before long, Pat rose and strolled along the edge of the lawn by the road. He periodically stopped and remained motionless, thinking he heard a small cry; except he couldn't pinpoint exactly where it was coming from, at least for the moment. Since the sound bugged him, he wanted to find the source. He walked across the street toward the vacant lot, seeing if he could possibly track it down. Suddenly, he spied something and called me to come and take a look.

I ushered Cackie back into the house and closed the door. Swiftly, I flew to the spot where Pat was kneeling and intently watching the object. I bent over and peeked into the tall grass. About three feet away, a small black-and-white kitten was sitting. Whenever Pat reached for the kitten, the little tabby moved and maintained a position a few inches from his grasp.

I instructed Pat not to budge and just keep an eye on the kitten until I could get some smelly cat food for bait. Then hopefully, the kitten would come close enough to let me catch the tiny ball of hair.

As fast as my feet could take me, I raced back home and grabbed a can of kitty tuna fish from the pantry. I opened it and returned. Carefully, I bent down and held the food close enough for the kitten to get a good whiff of the fragrant aroma, which was all that was needed. The little one couldn't resist the delectable smell and came toward it. I slowly pulled the can, with the kitten following close enough to catch her by means of my other hand. Because the kitten was quite skinny, I was able to circle a grip around the young one's entire body and hold on to her. It wasn't difficult since she was a heck of a lot more interested in the food than in me. The moment I lifted the kitten out of the grass, she immediately took a chunk from my finger. When Pat reached over to pet her, this determined kitten bit him, too.

Even though my hand was wounded and bleeding, I never let up on my grip. I just walked back home and went directly into the guest bathroom before letting the tiny dynamo loose. I arranged a comfortable area with the required necessities until the next day when it would be possible to have her checked by the veterinarian.

The kitten didn't find any problem settling into the new surroundings. I think she assumed it was a new and fun adventure. When I put some food down, she rapidly devoured the morsels to the point where I thought she would burst. Warm and finally full, she snuggled upon the soft blanket on the floor and contentedly drifted off into a deep sleep.

While I tended to the kitten, Cackie stayed glued outside on the bottom of the bathroom door. She wanted an explanation about what I was doing behind the closed door. This very astute feline was not pleased that she had been excluded and made quite a racket about her displeasure by alternating between pulling and banging on the door. Cackie also didn't hesitate to protest with her loud Siamese voice. She merely relented when I exited the room, but she remained suspicious about what was left inside of it.

Early the following morning, I took the kitten to be examined. The doctor certified her in good health after giving a thorough once-over and started the first round of vaccinations. A few weeks later, boosters would be given. In thirty days, she would be rechecked before the introduction to Cackie.

I named the kitten Shamrock after quite a bit of deliberation, thinking it was quite appropriate for the reason that she was found in a field of wildflowers and weeds. Shamie was the name she was addressed with if she was good, and Rock was the one I christened her with when she was a holy terror. In time, the kitten's nickname became TNT, which matched her explosive personality.

Shamrock attained a way of testing my patience, beginning with her stint in isolation. What's more, it didn't take the little one very long on finding different ways to accomplish it.

As it turned out, I discovered life was very interesting, to say it mildly, having one very spoiled resident cat and acquiring a very rambunctious kitten. Cackie, my cat for nearly eleven years, thought she should be an only child and kept her nose completely out of joint with the notion that there might be another feline inside the house. Cackie could not see the kitten but knew the little one was in the guest bathroom. Needless to say, she complained, loudly, with her Siamese voice over the prospect of sharing her home with anything that came with four legs, especially an unruly kitten with too much energy. The kitten teased Cackie by sticking her paw under the door and swatting at Cackie. After receiving some whacks on her nose, Cackie walked off in a huff and ignored the kitten's tomfoolery. Shamrock promptly got bored without anyone around to pay any attention to her. Being a typical kitten in her situation, she investigated the surroundings before demolishing them.

Nothing was an obstacle for this tiny ball of fur. She soon learned to climb the shower curtain and pierce holes in it at the same time. Then she could stand on top of the shower rod before sliding down to the floor, shredding both the curtain and the liner with her baby claws on the way. As for the toilet paper, it quickly turned into confetti and was easily scattered everywhere.

For Shamrock, a wonderful game was finding out the closed closet door opened if wiggled. Afterward, she took it upon herself to bite holes in the bags of new litter. Next, this mountain climber scaled to the top of the pile, creating more holes, and watched litter rain onto the floor. It was even more entertaining for the great adventure seeker to fling litter in every conceivable direction.

A small airplane plant sat on the windowsill above the toilet. It was thriving in the morning sunshine until a certain kitten spotted it. At first, the plant was out of Shamrock's reach. With plenty of determination and using the toilet's handle as a step, she acquired the means to reach the top of the toilet. Then she swatted at the defenseless plant until finally grabbing hold of it. The poor thing flew to floor, sending dirt and plant pieces in every direction. I counted my blessings it was in a plastic container and not in a ceramic pot. That's all I would have needed—a kitten with cut paws!

I shortly realized to never put it past the capability of a one-pound twelve-ounce feline to flush a toilet. This happened with little Shamrock.

Shamrock was fascinated that the toilet handle made water noises when it moved. Even with the toilet lid covering the water, she could hear the rushing water. This definitely intrigued her. Having her curiosity piqued, she sat for the longest time, pulling the handle and then intently listening to the water swirling under the lid. When it stopped, she did it over and over again. How long this continued I am not sure since I was not in the room when she acquired this skill. Somehow I feel this tiny terror not only flushed it once but also flushed it at least two dozen times at one sitting.

As the day went on, I did chores in the front part of the house and periodically thought I heard water running. Strange, every time I went looking for the source, I could never locate it. This kept going on until I walked past the guest bathroom when the toilet flushed. I knew no one was in there at the time except the kitten, and I presumed a problem developed with the toilet.

I cracked the door slightly open and stared inside. On the floor in the middle of the disaster, the tiny kitten sat with a ring of dirt around her mouth, glancing up at me and purring at the top of her lungs. I slowly looked around the rest of the room with complete awe. I first saw the shredded and very dirty shower curtain. I caught a glimpse of the new cat litter bags containing more holes in them than I wanted to count and still pouring litter onto the floor. I noticed the very pitiful plant with its wet soil plastered on every conceivable surface. Even so, I had no idea the kitten was responsible for the toilet's problems.

I spent quite a lot of time on hands and knees cleaning up soil, plant pieces, confetti, and litter. Muttering under my breath, I threw the unusable shower curtain, the torn liner, and the destroyed plant in the garbage. I then taped every hole in the litter bags and locked the closet door. Finally, I gathered the kitten's overturned food and water bowls. Still grumbling to myself, I put fresh ones down. During the entire time I was in the bathroom, the toilet never once malfunctioned. Because of the other distractions, I plainly forgot about the problem.

Later that night, I again heard water running in my sleep. Reluctantly, I dragged myself out of bed and stood outside of the guest bathroom door, waiting in the darkness. Cackie followed me and sat on the floor by my feet. Half-asleep, I kept quiet and listened. It wasn't long before I heard Shamrock scampering around and playing with the small ping-pong ball; then there was silence. The next sound I recognized was the handle of the toilet jingling. The kitten let out a joyful "eeee" as soon as the toilet flushed.

This time, I swiftly opened the door. Sitting on top of the toilet lid, the kitten was reaching for and pulling at the handle. She was very proud of her ability and eagerly demonstrated how a very tiny ball of energy had the dexterity to flush a toilet. I giggled and thought how clever. As for Cackie, she was annoyed her sleep had been disturbed. She hissed at Shamrock before returning to her warm spot on the bed. Obviously, I turned off the toilet's water valve before following Cackie back to bed.

Finally out of isolation and free to run throughout the house, Shamrock's antics took on another trick. She quickly learned to scale any and every vertical object within her path. Shamrock promptly mastered the art of using her talons for traction in ascents and leaving behind her signature claw marks with descents. It didn't matter if it was a leg of her human caregiver, a door jam, a wall, a piece of fine furniture, or a cat tree. Everything that happened to be in a vertical position soon had fallen victim to this mountain climber's scratches.

Clipping Shamrock's claws didn't deter the climbing, and declawing was not an option. Out of desperation, I took on the art of repairing woodwork via sandpaper and wood putty followed by either stain or paint. I attained upholstery perseveration through strategically placed throws. Pat and I also learned never to get caught in anything except long pants for self-protection even on the hottest days of the first summer with the questionable addition.

With age, Shamrock's destructive ways mellowed. She did settle down, at least most of the time. Shamrock's explosive personality occasionally emerged; and when it did, *look out!*

Through quite a bit of persuasion on my behalf, Cackie and Shamrock became the best of buddies. They bonded after Cackie finally accepted the fact that I wouldn't consider the idea of donating Shamrock to the Salvation Army. The moment Cackie recognized Shamrock was "purrmanently" in place, together, both were *holy terrors!*

Crystal Cats

Years ago, I fell in love with the beauty of crystal—crystal cats more precisely. The fantasy with these works of art really originated when I was introduced to an artist who helped me visualize and feel things inside crystal cats some might not consider real or possible. Ever since that moment, I have shared this wonder with a few special friends.

At an exhibit of fine crystal many years ago, an artist held in the light a crystal cat. With a gentle touch, he rotated the piece with his hand ever so slowly. When he did, it sparkled as if it was alive. The different lines and angles took on a mystical quality that reflected a beauty I never before imagined.

Almost closing his eyes, the artist explained what he envisioned. He said, "Just looking at this cat, you will only see a piece of crystal. By allowing your imagination to be your eyes, you will observe the spirit of this wonderful creature! If not, all that you will ever have is a glass object."

The artist lowered the piece of crystal and handed it to me. With a grin of a Cheshire cat, he asked if I would lift it into the light. He had a secret he wanted me to discover.

I did exactly as the clever artist requested.

The artist inquired, "What do you see?"

For the first time, I felt the magic the artist spoke about in the crystal. From the light's rays, a sparkle appeared within the crystal cat I held; but there was more. I realized how right he was. It was truly the cat's magnificent spirit inside it! Thrilled with what I learned, I related the find to the artist.

Beaming with pride, the artist stared at me and proclaimed; "Now you will always feel the wonder!"

Since then, each time I am given a crystal cat, I hear the words spoken by that curious artist. I no longer have merely a piece of crystal within my hands—I am holding the spirit of the cat!

At present, when I give a crystal cat to someone special, I share the wonder that special artist created for me. The difference is . . .

Now I am the one smiling and asking the question—"What do you see?"

A Cat of Many Different Coats

When I was a child, I saw the movie *The Wizard of Oz*. In it there was a scene that took place in the Emerald City, which captivated me. A horse of many colors appeared. Each time I caught a glimpse of the magnificent creature, the color of his coat was different. It was fascinating to count dozens of horses but realize there was only one.

I just moved into a rent house in the capital city of West Virginia with my husband and cats: Cackie, Shamrock, Corkie, and Clara. It was temporary, as the home we would eventually move into was under construction. It was difficult finding a short-term place to lease fitting our requirements. It was even harder locating one that allowed pets. When a dwelling on Skyline Drive came available, Pat and I jumped at it.

The small house was located in the hills above the capitol. I considered the hills the same as steep mountains. Roads were narrow and lacked shoulders. Then the land dropped off, and the fall to the valley below was nerve shattering. I have to say it took me quite some time to get comfortable with these cliff-hangers.

The landlord of the rent house maintained one restriction. He permitted just one pet. When Pat went to sign the lease, the landlord inquired if we had one. Pat acknowledged, very honestly, "Yes, a cat." He didn't add any more details. Since the landlord's question wasn't more specific, Pat never admitted we were owned by more than one.

After moving into the house, we became friends with the neighbors. On warm evenings, Pat and I took advantage of the outdoors and frequently visited with many residents on the street. Hearing familiar voices, our cats jumped on to a windowsill, one at a time, in order to keep a close eye on us through the glass. Being typical felines, they wondered what we were doing and didn't particularly care they had been excluded.

The neighbors noticed the cat seemed different each time they observed the feline through the window. At first, nothing was said. Finally, out of curiosity, a neighbor's wife asked if we had more than one cat.

I remembered the story in *The Wizard of Oz* about the horse who sported a different colored coat each time he appeared. Grinning, I responded to the question by saying, "I am pleased you noticed we have a cat of many different coats!" Everyone laughed and never again inquired about the number of cats we housed.

To this day, I am not sure if the neighbors thought I was serious or just pulling their legs. Perhaps they thought I was a little out of my mind. All I know is I still love the story about the horse of many colors. Even better, I still love the tale about the cat of many coats!

The Magical Cat

I was living in the capital city of a state in the Blue Ridge Mountains during the late eighties with my husband and feline crew. The capital itself was attractive and quite progressive. However, not far outside city limits, poverty persisted to flourish. West Virginia was advanced in many ways, and others remained backward. It was also a beautiful state, even though both mining companies and chemical plants took their toll on the land throughout different areas.

Before long, I obtained a job I loved, centered inside one of the capitol buildings. I accepted the position of lobbyist for the local animal rights organization. My boss had been a professional lobbyist for quite some time. On the contrary, I was a novice. My boss frequently didn't know what to expect from me, being new, but he quickly realized I was an asset to his company. I was quiet, intelligent, and very respectful. I followed instructions flawlessly and could be relied upon to be present at different places always on time. I did each mission to perfection. Truthfully, it was easy because I had fun at performing the tasks. Nevertheless, it was eye opening when I discovered what really went on behind political doors before a bill ever came up for a vote on the house floor.

Given the chance, I loved walking through the long hallways of the main capitol building in the lower level during the early morning hours before the day's business started. It was a slow time, usually without anyone else around except an occasional member of the housekeeping crew finishing the night shift. It was certainly a silent time when the fairies sought their chance to do a little mischief and not be seen. It was also a time when a poster appeared around the neck of a stuffed bear, which stood in front of a particular senator's office. The inscription said, "If hunters have guns, why not give bears some, too!" Even though I hated looking at the old grizzly, I never let any feelings show as I passed by it. No one maintained a clue who hung the sign on the bear, apart from, possibly, a certain boss.

I definitely sensed my boss wondered if I was the culprit of the act. I gave him a tremendous amount of credit for never asking outright if I was the one responsible. He may have been suspicious, although no one else considered it was me. If anyone asked, I felt the act was accomplished by the mischief makers, the fairies!

While I lobbied in the legislature, I also did volunteer work at the local animal shelter. The Humane Society ran the facility, which included city animal control along with county animal control under the same roof. For the number of animals dealt with on a daily basis, they really did an adequate job.

Occasionally, I handled adoptions and became known for my affinity for cats. Whenever a special cat came in needing either foster care or placing in an exceptional home, I was called upon for help. Eventually, I was elected to the board of directors and started a visitation program to local nursing homes.

It was a Saturday morning just after the shelter opened to the public. I was sitting in the office, checking the cards of the newest arrivals, when a kennel worker approached. She carried a little ball of fur and put the tiny cat on my lap.

The kitty was petite with very unusual black-and-white markings. She looked more like a Persian than a Domestic Longhair. The one difference between the two breeds: this little cat tooted a nose like others of her kind, and most Persians lacked having much of one. She also had large green eyes for such a little thing. Best of all, her purring was interrupted only by her wonderful cooing!

Rolling my eyes, I asked the worker what she wanted me to do with the cat. She smiled back and said, "Find a home for her." Without another word, she exited and left the feline with me.

After the worker left, I sat in the chair, muttering under my breath. Finding a home during that particular time of year was hard to do, almost impossible! It was springtime. And for the most part, prospective owners wanted a kitten or puppy, not an adult cat or dog. Knowing this, how was I going to place a grown cat?

Before I could get the list of potential homes out, the kennel worker came back and mentioned almost under her breath the cat was pregnant. At a shelter that sometimes took in close to a hundred animals in a day during the spring and summer, a pregnant one was not put up for adoption.

This time, the worker couldn't escape before I requested she take the cat to the shelter clinic and have the cat spayed without the director finding out about it. Pleased, she did exactly as I ordered.

While searching for a home, I found absolutely no luck at locating a placement and was feeling frustrated. Throughout the hunt, the ball of fluff was getting into my heart. Needless to say, later that night at dinner, I told Pat about the little cat the shelter workers were calling Oreo. After listening to the details, Pat made just one comment. He asked me when to expect her arrival.

There have been times a cat came to me and I never intended to adopt the little one. For some reason, I could not turn away the cat and ended up taking the feline into my care. It happened with this little, black-and-white kitty.

Following work on Monday, I went to the shelter and did the paperwork for the kitty's adoption. The next stop was at the veterinary clinic for a health check. If she passed, then it was home.

On the way to the clinic, the first thing I did was ask the pretty feline if she minded if I changed her name. I explained she should have a much more dignified one than the name the kennel worker had given her. I inquired if it would be acceptable to call her Megan. She looked into my eyes and cooed. I happily took it as a *yes!*

Megan passed the important tests with flying colors, but she did have coccidia and ear mites. Both could be easily treated. She also developed a fever from an infection from the surgery. Armed with the necessary medications, we headed home.

I put Megan inside a large playhouse located in the library with the necessary amenities. I then closed the playhouse door and the library entrance to keep the other cats from direct contact with her until the quarantine period was over.

Ha!

When I awoke the next morning, Megan was fast asleep at the bottom of our bed to everyone's surprise. I quickly realized this very tiny cat, no bigger than seven pounds, possessed the ability to open the playhouse door along with the library one since the library door didn't have a lock and could easily be released with a little rattling at the bottom of it. Then Megan didn't have any trouble finding her way upstairs to the master bedroom. She figured out the comforts of sleeping on the bed with both Pat and me, not mentioning the other cats, too. What Megan didn't count on was that I kept a strict rule of not introducing another cat into my established household of felines until the cat passed the next set of medical tests after thirty days. Needless to say, Megan returned to the library for the rest of isolation.

This, Megan did not agree to in the least!

The next night, I secured the door of the playhouse with a small piece of cord. I tightly tied the latch with a box knot, thinking I was very clever and through. Obviously, I wasn't too bright since the following morning Megan was again asleep at the bottom of the bed when I awoke.

To my total amazement, Megan did not chew through the cord but took the knot apart. It must have taken her hours, except the little Houdini seemed quite adept at the puzzle. Then that evening, I once more secured her playhouse door with the cord. This time, to my utter stupidity, I made about six knots in it.

Well, guess who was at the bottom of the bed the next morning after taking apart every knot?

To foil Megan's endeavor the proceeding night, I went to the local hardware store and purchased a metal kennel latch. That night I secured the door with it. In the morning, much to her bewilderment, Megan was still in the playhouse.

The thirty days flew by and it was time for the final health check. Megan passed, and she didn't have a problem mixing with the resident cats because she was both a cat's cat as well as a people's cat. From then on, every morning when I awoke, Megan was in her rightful spot at the foot of the bed with the other felines.

Megan was a magical cat for many reasons. Not only could she escape from anywhere, this tiny cat was able to fly through a room with delicate grace and never knock over any item in her path. She made everyone smile by curling her tail forward over her back and touching the end of her nose with it. What's more, Megan was the most nurturing kitty. She adopted and raised a kitten. Megan nursed the baby as if she had milk until he was three pounds heavier than she at the time. Then Megan decided to wean Jayme since he was also over a year old and should be on his own.

I could count on Megan during the good times as well as in the bad times. She possessed a sixth sense, giving her the aptitude to always recognize how much I benefited from her comfort. Whenever she cooed and purred, any problem I dealt with seemed much easier to face.

The one thing Megan sensed better than anything else was whenever I enjoyed some ice cream. Without question, Megan's most treasured treat was an ice cream cone. Anytime I munched on one, she would come from wherever and climb upon my shoulder. Gently, she would reach around to snitch her fair share with an unrelenting tongue.

With neither of us realizing it, years went by way, much too rapidly. One day as I was tickling Megan, I found a small lump on her stomach. It turned out to be cancer. Chemo followed surgery, but Megan's time was limited. Throughout her final weeks, it was my turn to nurture Megan.

It's been years since Megan went to heaven. Even so, if I look around, I can still catch a glimpse of the tiny black-and-white fluff-ball gracefully flying through the room while cooing and purring.

It broke my heart when I said good-bye to Megan. In the end, I could only offer to hold my little one and tell her how much I loved her.

On the afternoon I let Megan leave in peace, I whispered this to her.

Megan, my little one . . .

Shortly, we will say good-bye and you shall leave,
For the time has come to return to the heavenly home.

Forever enjoy great peace and happiness in your new life,
While rejoicing with complete freedom from earthly sorrows.

But please take a moment to remember the special times we shared together,
And never forget you will forever be a part of my heart.

Now, little angel, my last gift to you is some wings.
Please take them and quickly fly home!

March 4, 1987–February 23, 2001

How Cats Got Their Purr

There is an old spinning wheel sitting upstairs in a corner of one the rooms. Every time I glance at it, I think about a certain legend of how cats acquired their wonderful purring ability. If I quietly listen, I can hear it spinning long forgotten dreams of great feline accomplishments as well as purring songs of wishes for new tomorrows.

My great aunt quietly whispered a tale about the way cats obtained their purr the night before my tonsils were removed. I was four at the time and frightened. Wisely, she figured it would help ease my fears a little.

I long ago forgot my aunt's tale until one day when I was working at a historical museum park. My boss, who has since become one of my dearest friends, related another variation of it. When she recited her tale, my thoughts traveled back to that night in the hospital. Once more, I was four and very scared. Then I heard my great aunt tell her account.

Now with warm recollections of the two similar tales, it's my turn to deliver my version of the legend.

Many years ago in a far away kingdom, there lived a beautiful princess. When she grew up, she met a handsome prince and they fell in love. On the eve of their wedding, the prince was kidnapped by soldiers from a land across the sea. The soldiers told the princess if she wanted her prince safely returned, she had to spin ten thousand skeins of yarn for them by the next day. What's more, not one other person in the kingdom could aid in the task. Then without any further words, they departed.

The princess ran into the castle and sat near the fireplace. Needless to say, she couldn't stop crying. She knew there wasn't any possible way she could achieve what the soldiers demanded. As a result, she feared she'd never again see her prince.

From all over the castle, the cats came and watched the tears fall on to the floor from their mistress' eyes. Quietly, they sat and talked among themselves. Shortly, one stately cream-colored Persian by the name of Sean Patrick walked up to the princess. Staring at the princess with his big copper eyes, he boldly inquired, "My lady, what upsets you so much?"

The princess sadly explained to Sean Patrick and the other cats what just transpired. Still sobbing, she sighed. "It is impossible for me to meet the soldiers' demands. I will never see my prince ever again!"

The handsome Persian calmly sat and pondered the assignment given to the princess. After a few minutes, he proudly spoke his thoughts on the matter. With a very large grin on his face, he proclaimed, "The soldiers stated no person can help you spin the yarn, but they said nothing about us cats!" In grand feline manner and somewhat boasting, Sean Patrick continued, "Each one of the royal cats will assist you, given that we know how to spin yarn!" The princess stopped crying and smiled with gratitude.

Throughout the realm that night, the lone sound heard was the sweet purring song of the spinning wheels. Early the next morning, ten thousand yarn skeins were piled into baskets and carried outside the castle doors.

The soldiers from the faraway land promptly returned. Surprised and dismayed at finding the task completed, they accepted the yarn. Still quite amazed, they released the prince as promised. The soldiers left the princess' kingdom, never again to be seen.

Overwhelmed with great happiness, the princess turned to Sean Patrick and the other royal cats. She then lovingly bestowed the gift of purring upon each one. It was a special reward, thanking them for the help. She explained it would be theirs to keep and shall be passed unto their future decedents. Ever since that day, cats have purred, feeling contentment by remembering a great accomplishment from long ago.

Senior Cats

I describe a senior cat as a feline who is over the age of twelve. I define a super senior cat as a feline who is past the age of sixteen. Over the years, I have cared for and adopted senior cats along with super senior felines. These special cats resided with me in comfort for the rest of their lives. Each one of the wonderful elders gave more to me than I can ever say with words. Their spirits touched my soul and continued to do so even now.

When I met Skittles, I fell head over heels for senior cats. Skittles was twelve years old at the time. She was a brown tabby and slightly pudgy. This elder cat received an outgoing personality and used it to her advantage. Skittles was positively delighted to talk to anyone and everyone she met, though a tickle on the head topped her list of choice pleasures.

Sarah was this kitty's caregiver. Sarah was in her eighties, except she appeared much younger. She was a devoted grandmother and enjoyed traveling. What I remember most about Sarah is that she was such a warm and caring person. She always made me feel as if she could be everyone's grandmother.

Sarah loved Skittles dearly and took wonderful care of her. However, Sarah cultivated one weakness with her kitty: she overindulged Skittles with a little too much food. In any case, Sarah stayed on top of her kitty's needs, from premium cat litter to proper medical care. Skittles cherished Sarah because of the attention showered upon her, and this could easily be seen in the way Skittles responded to Sarah.

Over the following two years after our first introduction, I became acquainted with Sarah and Skittles. I grew quite fond of Skittles since Sarah occasionally had me sit for her kitty when she was away. It wasn't difficult falling head over heels for this cat since she was adorable. As a result, Skittles quickly acquired the position of favorite senior. During Sarah's absence,

Sarah was pleased with the exceptional treatment Skittles received. As a result, she never thought twice about leaving her kitty in my care.

The afternoon I found out Sarah died, I called the family to give them my sympathy and inquire how Skittles was getting along without Sarah. The son answered the phone and related he took Skittles, a couple of hours earlier, to the Humane Society. I didn't say much of anything after hearing the news, except I was sorry for the loss of his mother. Hanging up the receiver, I was still in shock and disbelief over the thought he didn't want Sarah's pride and joy, Skittles.

The next phone call, which I quickly made, was to the Humane Society. Since I did volunteer work at the place, I was well acquainted with the director. I inquired about Skittles, and the director informed me he placed her in the backroom. Understanding what that meant, I realized Skittles didn't have a chance of getting adopted because of the age factor so her time was limited. I asked the director not to do anything and said I would be over in a few minutes to adopt her.

I arrived at the shelter and flew into the backroom where I saw Skittles sitting in a cage. I opened it and gently lifted her out. I put her inside a carrier, which I borrowed from the clinic where I worked, and filled out the paperwork. After making a donation to honor Sarah's memory, I left with Skittles in tow and returned to the clinic.

Skittles was given a complete once-over. She was fine, though her weight issue still needed addressing. The solution was a reducing diet, which would find a trimmer figure. Skittles didn't care seeing as it was food, and she definitely loved eating.

The rest of the afternoon, I kept wondering how I was going to explain the fact about taking on another cat to my husband, and more to the point, one who was fourteen years old.

I left work a little early and settled Skittles in the study before Pat arrived home. I was anxious about introducing this elder to him.

That night at dinner, I meekly told Pat the story about Skittles and finished by saying she currently was in the study. Before he could lecture me about taking on an additional cat, I ushered him into the room to meet this very endearing feline.

Skittles immediately walked over to Pat and purred so loud I sensed she figured an outstanding presentation was needed to win him over in order to stay. It definitely worked. Very soon she succeeded in melting his resolve with her big heart and then wrapped him around her paw.

In the following days, every time Skittles meowed around Pat, it sounded more like a quack than a meow. He called her Quackers for this reason, although I think the quack was the name Skittles used to address Pat.

Skittles became a "spokespurrson" for the Humane Society with the dream other people would adopt senior cats like her. She made appearances on radio and TV. This senior cat even made the newspaper, promoting the concept of adopting older animals. I retired Skittles at the age of sixteen. She lived her senior and then super senior years as a member of my feline crew. Skittles also faced many more adventures until the age of twenty-four, when Lord Father decided it was time for her to be a heavenly angel.

In my heart, I feel Sarah is proud of Skittles for the accomplishments Skittles achieved. I also believe Sarah is thankful I came into Skittles's life and rescued Skittles when Sarah could no longer be there for her kitty.

In the same year I adopted Skittles, I met another senior cat who also stole my heart. This time, the cat was a tiny blue-gray Domestic Shorthair with white.

When I arrived at the clinic one day, a petite kitty sat in a cage watching me. Since I wasn't familiar with the little feline, I went over and looked at the chart on the front of the enclosure. I was curious and wanted to find out the instructions for her care. It simply stated, "Euthanize."

Very curious, I asked my boss, Linda (the veterinarian): "What reason did the owners give for wanting this kitty euthanized?"

Linda promptly responded, "They said she was old, and they didn't want her any longer."

I couldn't believe it! The kitty was fourteen. Yes, that was old; but I didn't believe it was a justification to end the cat's life!

Then I noticed the kitty had been brought in late yesterday afternoon after my shift finished, and I had left. I wondered why Linda kept her and didn't follow through with the caregivers' wishes. I thought, possibly, she was hoping the caregivers would change their minds and come back for her. Sadly, they never did.

As the morning went on, this kitty attempted to get my attention. She was bossy and opinionated. I tried hard to not let her get under my skin because I realized I would be upset when her life ended. Very cleverly, the kitty used her kitty ESP quite well. By morning's conclusion, I took the instructions off her cage and put my name on it instead.

I then looked at my boss a little suspiciously since she dragged her feet and didn't carry out the original instructions. I wondered if, perchance, she had a notion I would be interested in this cat and give her a home. She was correct with the assessment if that was her intention. Somehow I think she was putting off the inevitable, as she also didn't want to see the kitty's life ended.

Linda laughed when she noticed the new sign on the kitty's cage. She asked, "Do you have any idea how you will explain to Pat you acquired another senior cat and one who is vocal and bossy!"

Walking in the direction of the treatment area, I grinned and said, "I don't have a clue what I'm going to tell him."

The following four days, I kept the kitty, renamed Precious, at the clinic. I needed time to figure a way of explaining this little dynamo to Pat. I especially didn't want to hear any lectures about how many cats we already maintained under a certain roof. Actually, it was only a baker's dozen. I figured that by adding one more, the number would round off the household and we would no longer be at the bad luck figure of thirteen. Deep down inside, I really did understand my limits. I fully recognized that by adding Precious, I would be completely maxed out on how many cats I could adequately care for at home.

When I found enough courage, I brought up the subject about Precious. To my utter amazement, Pat didn't give a sermon and said he was looking forward to the cat's arrival. I was dumbfounded by the reaction. I expected I'd have to sell my soul just to get his agreement on keeping Precious. To my complete surprise, there wasn't a call for such extremes. In the back of my mind, I had a hunch Skittles paved the path. Since both Pat and I adored Skittles, I felt Pat developed a soft spot for senior cats in his heart, too. He accepted Precious into the family without a question—or a sermon.

Precious came home with me and joined the feline crew. Soon she acquired the nickname the Boss for obvious reasons. She was an eight-pound dynamo who easily obtained her way, procuring attention with a very loud voice and curled lip. Precious took great feline pride putting either cat or human in their place if necessary.

This bossy cat could also be a clown. It was humorous to watch her carry a much-loved ball in her almost toothless mouth wherever she went and present it with a smile to special ones. She also found delight in supervising me whenever friends came over to play board games or cards. Each time this little senior cat sat on my lap and instructed me which move I should make next. Even though she was rather demanding, Precious was also quite loving. She was definitely thankful for her new home and family. She certainly lived her senior days in contentment and happiness.

Skittles was a celebrity while Precious filled the role of boss in the household. Both kitties were very special elder cats with their different ways. Because of this, it was difficult comprehending why the former caregivers were unable to see the beauty of these senior felines. It has even been harder to understand why they discarded these special cats after they had been a part of their lives or a loved one's life for a long time.

The Ultimatum

In the early nineties, I was living in West Texas when my husband accepted the senior vice president level and was transferred to the eastern part of the state. Pat worked for oil companies the majority of his career, so it was not unusual to move to a new location when he received a promotion. Once again, because of job advancement, I was faced with the stipulation of relocating and wasn't very happy with the prospect.

At the time, I lived in a house I really did like, acquired a job as a technician at a veterinary clinic, established good friends, and was owned by an adorable feline crew. I knew I would have to give up the house and job but not any friends or my cats. This was going to be our eleventh move in twenty-two years, and I was tired of starting over once again. I just wanted some place to put roots down in that was permanent.

What worried me most about the upcoming move was the idea of driving between twelve and fourteen hours in a car with my felines. I was responsible for some special care cats, a few seniors, along with a number of juniors. I realized traveling confined in carriers for that length of time would be extremely hard on some of them, and I did not want any to become seriously sick because of the duration.

I thought and thought of every available option. Finally, the idea of having the corporate plane at Pat's place of employment transport us hit me. I figured it would take twenty minutes to get to the airport. Tack on another twenty to thirty minutes for loading the cats in the passenger cabin and the takeoff. The air flight was scarcely an hour long. After the final descent, unloading, and journey to Pat's apartment, another forty-five minutes was required. The total estimated duration of the journey should, approximately, come in around three hours to accomplish. I thought the plan was so much better than driving the same distance.

When I mustered up some courage, I gave Pat the ultimatum. I frankly told him if he wanted me to go to East Texas, he needed to enlist the company plane for transporting the cats and me. If not, I wouldn't move and basically explained the reasons. He listened but never said a word. From his reaction, I wasn't sure if he understood how much I meant everything I just said.

A couple of days passed before Pat called me from the corporate office in Houston. He explained arrangements were made to transport him from West to East Texas by means of the corporate plane for business. If I accompanied him, I was required to pay my way, and the cats would be listed as my baggage.

It completely amazed me Pat really listened. For Pat to think of a way of having his company plane fly the cats, I understood how important I was in his life along with the cats. With travel arrangements made, I felt a little more at ease. I then prepared for the departure.

I asked a young teenage boy I worked with at the veterinary clinic to accompany me on the trip. I required his help with the cats. I also required him to watch them when either Pat or I could not be present. I especially didn't want the cats alone in a strange place—the apartment—while the movers arrived to unload the household items at the new home. For Peter's valuable assistance, I promised to pay his trip on a commercial airline so he could return home.

Peter agreed. Actually, he was thrilled to be asked. Not only had he never been on a private plane, he never flew a commercial one either. Peter unquestionably looked forward to the adventure.

On the day we left East Texas, the corporate plane arrived at the airport somewhere around 6:00 a.m. It was definitely large enough to accommodate us since it sat twelve passengers and two pilots very comfortably in large leather seats. The pilots stayed at the private hanger while the plane was serviced. They called the house, informing Pat everything was on schedule.

Around 7:00 a.m., the young boy came over with another friend, Dolores. They assisted me in getting the cats ready and helped escort each one into various taxies. Most of the carriers contained one cat, and a few others enclosed two kitties. I recognized some of the cats would feel more secure with their best buddy next to them.

Pat, Peter, Dolores, and I loaded the crew into my station wagon and Pat's car. The caravan pulled out of the driveway, with Pat leading the trail. Peter and I followed. Last but not least, Dolores pulled up the rear in her car. Driving away, I glanced back at the house for the last time and felt sad leaving. I realized I would miss a life I really enjoyed and a home I felt totally comfortable in for the first time since I was a child.

We arrived at the airport around 7:30 a.m. and drove directly to the private hanger. The company pilots didn't say much as Peter, Dolores, and I strapped the carriers into the passenger seats and arranged a few taxies under them. With the final cat safely on board, Dolores and I said good-bye. Pat stayed behind to drive one of our vehicles to East Texas that day. In a week, he would return and retrieve the other one remaining at the private hanger. Dolores left for her home after the plane closed its doors.

The pilots prepared for the takeoff. There were a few meows when the plane started its ascent into the skies, although not much else occurred. I was ready for any event—from airsickness to accidents—and carried all the necessary cleanup items if needed.

The plane leveled off in the blue skies, and I relaxed. In contrast, Peter, looking out the window, was thrilled and fascinated. It was the first time he had ever flown, and he was excited beyond words. After living his entire life in West Texas, he couldn't believe his eyes. The terrain went from vast brown fields and pump jacks to a lush, green terrain with hills and lakes. Peter was quite amazed at the view because he had never seen so much water before except on TV.

Approaching the final destination, the plane launched a slow descent. The air was slightly turbulent, though not too bad. As for the cats, they didn't like it in the least little bit. Without hesitation, some complained. The landing only lasted a few minutes. Then the plane taxied down the runway and finally pulled in front of another private hanger.

After coming to a complete stop, I popped out of the seat and checked on each kitty. One had been airsick, and another had an accident. Before the door of the plane was opened, I turned my attention to the two carriers that needed to be cleaned. One at a time, I handed Peter the distraught cats. He held each one in turn and softly gave comfort as I worked at getting rid of the messes. When I finished, Peter placed both back into the appropriate carriers and latched the doors.

The pilots were patient and didn't rush me. They helped unload the precious cargo into another friend's SUV. I thanked the pilots and said good-bye and then climbed inside the friend's vehicle. The friend drove us to Pat's apartment and graciously helped unload the crew and baggage.

Peter and I entered the apartment with the cats. The first thing on the agenda was to check the place and make sure there was nothing that could harm the felines before allowing them the freedom to roam. Next, Peter helped arrange litter boxes. Diligently, he also placed food and water dishes close by their area. Finally, Peter and I opened the carriers and let the cats out to investigate. Both of us closely watched as each cat checked out every nook and cranny.

It was late evening before Pat arrived at the apartment with a to-go-order of food in hand for the three of us to enjoy. He asked how the flight went, and I related the details of the trip.

Peter stayed with the cats when Pat and I went to the new house. It took the entire day for our possessions to be unloaded. After the movers left, we settled the guest room for Peter as well as the master bedroom for us before returning to the apartment.

Early the following morning, the cats were once again ushered into the appropriate carriers and loaded in the friend's SUV. This time, the drive took fifteen minutes. Safely inside the new home, the thundering herd inspected everything. By early afternoon, each cat was completely relaxed. On Sunday, Pat and I took Peter to the airport and he returned to his home in West Texas.

Over the Christmas holiday after the move, I was at the corporate Christmas party with Pat. The pilots were there, too. They came over and inquired how the cats were getting along.

I smiled and said, "Wonderfully!"

They teased me that the felines were, without a doubt, the most unusual passengers they had ever flown and enjoyed having the chance to help out. I laughed and replied, "I bet they were quite different from your customary passengers!" I also thanked them for all they did.

My cats made the journey with the least amount of trauma to their lives, even though one cat did get airsick and another one had an accident. They also needed to stay in a strange apartment for two nights before going to the new home. These events were really minor since none of them had any major problem. With the belongings somewhat arranged, they settled into a normal routine rather quickly. I was delighted that none of the crew had any major problem from the adventure, and I was pleased that everything turned out as planned.

The Counting of Cats

Often I am asked the question "How many cats do you have?"

I answer by responding, "More than one."

Adding nothing further to the reply, the subject is then dropped with a giggle or two—most of the time. If anyone continues to inquire about the *precise* number or tries ticking me into releasing the grand total, I am consistent with the comeback. I state, "I have more than one feline. If you want an accurate number, you are more than welcome to come over and take your best shot at counting them!"

The reason I don't acknowledge how many I have is, mainly, I am quite aware public reaction would regard me as a crazy cat lady requiring professional help. Then they would unequivocally take stock in the assumption at the same time!

It is not that I don't know the number, although it can change on a daily basis with visiting cats coming and going. The numbers are categorically not staggering or beyond my limit of care. Even with a varying population, the house is most impressive and quite immaculate, too!

With a number of regal ones apparently present at any given time, I find it absolutely feasible to provide individual attention to every one of them. The love I have for each one is, certainly, a given. Each of the fur makers is unquestionably made to feel special. It might be very probable these felines are spoiled. Never in my opinion is it possible! Still, the total is never admitted.

I find it amusing some friends have referred to my home as "heaven on earth" for the kitties and wish, after they die, to return as one of my charges. Regardless of their kind words, they cannot get me to come clean on the number in attendance.

All kinds of figures are offered, but no one has a clue. I am no help because if someone says five, ten, or two, I tell them they are most definitely right. On the other hand, I might say, "Really? How can that be possible?"

Thus far, not one person has guessed the number. I somehow doubt anyone will ever figure it out either. A few have come close—conceivably, right on target, except it was never acknowledged by me. Nonetheless, with a smile in my voice, I always validate any answer in the end—whatever it might be. Still, there remains uncertainty; and I can't imagine why.

When it comes to the counting of cats, somehow I feel I might possibly be the only one to know for sure how many reside inside my home. Well? Perhaps that statement is true. Now let me see. I have one, two, three . . . maybe four?

Better Be Running

A while back, I saw a show about what transpires on the Serengeti when life awakens at dawn. I chuckled as I watched it. I thought it perfectly described the feeling I experience each day by reflecting the mad rush in the early morning hours in my home.

Thankfully, I don't have to worry about getting devoured by a lion or having to run after my dinner to survive. Essentially, what happens is that the alarm goes off at 3:00 in the morning and I fly out of the warm bed along with my husband. We do this to keep up with the feeding, medicating, cleanup, and litter box detail of the thundering herd—my feline crew. Therefore, when the sun rises, I am most definitely running in order to stay one paw ahead of the thundering herd.

On the African Serengeti, at the brink of dawn each morning,
A slender and petite gazelle quickly awakens,
Sensing she must outrun the fastest and strongest lion,
If she intends on keeping her life for another day.

On the African Serengeti each morning,
A proud and majestic lion slowly awakens,
Knowing he must outrun the smallest and slowest gazelle,
Or in brief time, he will surely starve to death.

In my household before dawn each morning,
It doesn't make a bit of difference,
Whether I am a lordly lion or a delicate gazelle.
When the sun rises, I better start running,
To stay ahead of my thundering herd!

I Am Persian

Never in my wildest dreams did I think I would ever be owned by a Persian cat. It wasn't I didn't like the breed. I really did not want to deal with taking care of the long fur that came with the feline. Little did I ever envision I would be owned by one, but many more of these wonderful creatures would eventually pass through my door.

Clara-la-belle captured my heart when she was a young kitten. She was a scrawny, little tortoiseshell with large round eyes. It wasn't too long before she matured into the most beautiful Persian ever imagined. I informed her on a daily basis she was gorgeous, and she knew exactly what I meant. She "purrformed" a little two-step with her chin tilted high into the air, agreeing with these thoughts. It wasn't long before I gave Clara the nickname of Miss New York City for such theatrics. She danced with extra vigor when presented with the esteemed title.

Sean Patrick was a little fuzz-ball kitten when I was introduced to him. He wore cream-colored fur and had deep copper eyes. Sean was as handsome as Clara was beautiful. He pictured himself as a sleek and agile ballet dancer who wore slippers on his feet, except little did he realize he put on large clodhoppers instead. Sean acquired more sprained legs by taking great leaps and then missing his footing the more agile long-legged cats could accomplish without an ounce of difficulty.

Upon our first meeting, Clarissa-la-bell was a baby kitten. She was Clara's gift from heaven when Clara passed on home. Clarissa was cute and pretty, dressed with a tortoiseshell coat. She was not Miss Sophistication, not even slightly. Clarissa was more the flower child and free spirit. She definitely remained kitten-like throughout her life.

Next, Precious, a very tiny tortoiseshell adult, arrived. She came from a home where her caregivers could no longer deal with her behavioral problems. When I discovered the misconduct was caused by an underlying medical condition and it was treated, she blossomed into a loving and sweet little kitty who was well mannered. As it turned out, she was mentally challenged, although she was happy as a lark inside her own special world.

Roten Kotzen was a flaming red elder with copper eyes. He entered into my care because he required medical attention his human mom could not provide at home due to her own physical handicap and medical issues. Kotzen instantly stole my heart. Because of him, his human mom and I became close friends. In a short time, Kotzen went from a lonely and grumpy old man into a happy and content elderly gentleman. He made strong friendships, discovered girls, and relished eating baked chicken.

Pepper was a tiny black-and-white ball of fur. She entered my friend's life after Kotzen passed on home. Unfortunately, at the age of six, Pepper developed a medical condition that ultimately took her life. As a result of Bettie's own constant health problems, Pepper lived her final months with me.

Coco Puff happened to be the prettiest chocolate Persian I had ever seen. I acquired her as a gift for Betty after Kotzen and then Pepper died. When Betty passed on, Coco also became one of my thundering herd. Coco possessed a blazing personality that gradually mellowed, and she turned into a sweetheart who demanded attention and tickles.

Every one of my Persians retained characteristics of their breed, but they possessed their own personalities and intelligence levels, too. I loved each one because of it.

As the friendship with an acquaintance developed, we became best friends. Cheryl loved Maine Coon cats and raised them. I, unlike Cheryl, kept a special place in my heart for the Siamese breed. However, I loved and adored all felines. For this reason, my home was opened to many different breeds over the years, especially the Domestic Shorthairs and the Domestic Longhairs.

At the first meeting of my crew, Cheryl did not think very highly of the resident Persian cats, Clarissa and Sean. Consequently, Sean ignored her, and Clarissa ran from her. The more Cheryl professed Persians to be dumb and stupid, the more Sean ignored her and the faster Clarissa ran in the opposite direction from this silly human.

One afternoon, Cheryl again started in on her dissertation about dumb and stupid Persian cats. Sean was sitting in a cat tree, listening to every word said. I could see from the expression on his face he was fed up with the prejudice.

The instant Cheryl walked by Sean, this very handsome Persian stiffened and demanded Cheryl's full attention. In no uncertain terms, he proclaimed in a loud clear voice Persian cats were neither dumb nor stupid in any categorical way! Sean also insisted that Cheryl stop calling him such because he was far from it and would not put up with the broadcasting such nonsense another time. Finally and without any qualms, Sean proudly stated he was a full-blooded Persian and was quite proud to be one!

Cheryl froze in her tracks. She couldn't believe what just happened. She realized she had been told off by Sean, a Persian cat, for thinking and saying he was dumb and stupid. Suddenly, Cheryl appreciated how wrong she was in such an assessment. She then apologized—profusely. She humbly asked Sean to pardon her for being the one who was dumb and stupid. Cheryl also realized how she hurt his feelings by acting so insensitive, and she asked for forgiveness.

In catly manner, Sean forgave Cheryl for the foolishness.

After hearing the apology, Clarissa decided to stop running from Cheryl. She concluded this silly human finally acquired some good sense and learned the lesson that Persian cats were most definitely intelligent.

Clarissa, like Sean, forgave Cheryl in catly manner.

Since that day, Cheryl has not once thought or said Persian cats are either dumb or stupid, especially Sean and Clarissa. I am pleased to say these two highly intelligent and deeply sensitive Persian cats taught Cheryl the lesson quite appropriately.

Lucille

Years ago, my best friend worked as a nurse for a home health care agency. Occasionally, she called upon my services when some of her patients needed help with their cats. Quite often these patients were elderly and didn't have anyone else to aid them. Gladly, I volunteered my assistance many times. In the process, I met some wonderful people and their cats.

In the spring of 1997, Cheryl asked me to help out a patient by the name of Lucille. Lucille was in her late seventies. She had white hair and beautiful blue eyes, which sparkled like jewels. Lucille was very tiny and barely weighed ninety pounds, if that. Because of it, she appeared quite fragile.

Lucille was recovering from a serious operation due to an intestinal ailment. She returned home from the hospital no more than a couple of days before I met her for the first time. The morning I arrived at her place, Lucille introduced me to her kitten by the name of Tigger. In a short time, I became very fond of Lucille and, particularly, Tigger.

Tigger was a scrawny, six-month-old brown tabby with a somewhat long coat. He required vaccinations and neutering. Obviously, there wasn't any way possible Lucille could afford to do either since she was living on very little. Through a cat club neuter program, I was able to have both done at no charge. Shortly, I made an appointment at the veterinary clinic and took Tigger for both matters. Everything went smoothly, and Tigger was released the following day.

After returning Tigger to Lucille, I continued helping with his care three times a week. I stopped by to clean Tigger's litter box, check on the cat food, trim nails, comb, or do any combination of necessities. I did whatever Tigger required to keep him healthy and happy. I also supplied Tigger's food, feeding dishes, litter, litter box, and flea control. I mainly spent time talking with Lucille. She told stories of what it was like as a sharecropper's daughter and marrying at a young age.

Lucille's husband died years ago. He too had been a sharecropper and didn't provide Lucille with very much to live on during their life together. Lucille struggled throughout her life, trying to make ends meet. She never owned a great deal of anything, but she was content with what she did have. For the attention I gave Tigger, she was grateful beyond words.

Periodically, Lucille was admitted to the hospital with ongoing problems with her intestine. During each absence, I went over every day and took care of Tigger. I made sure he had fresh water, food, a clean litter box, and, most definitely, a tickle on the head.

It was a Thursday afternoon and Lucille was rushed to the hospital with severe pain. This time, nothing could be done. She was dying. Lucille went into a coma during the night and passed in the early hours of the following morning.

At 7:00 in the morning, Cheryl called me. She had accompanied Lucille to the hospital while Lucille had been admitted. It was late in the evening when Lucille was settled into a hospital room. Shortly afterward, Cheryl left for home to get some rest. Since Cheryl was listed as Lucille's home nurse, the hospital notified Cheryl and related Lucille had died.

Around 9:00 a.m., I went over to Lucille's small house to take care of Tigger until I could contact one of her children about his placement. I promised Lucille that if anything ever happened to her, I would make sure Tigger found a good home. On that day, I did exactly as requested. I placed Lucille's kitty with a very familiar couple.

When I entered Lucille's house, it had been ransacked. Everything was thrown in every direction. Even the mattress and box springs were pulled off the bed and tossed on the floor. Nothing was in its place, nothing at all. It was difficult believing my eyes, and it upset me to the point I began to cry.

I was quite concerned about Tigger since I didn't see him anywhere. I quickly called his name. Tigger recognized my voice. Out from under a small nook between the mattress and the wall, he came running to me. I scooped him up and hugged him. He was trembling and shaking. I knew by his reaction that what happened earlier scared him. As a result, he remained hidden in a protected place. With me, Tigger felt safe. He purred and purred. He was definitely happy I came to his rescue.

At that moment, a neighbor of Lucille's came from across the street. Standing there and cuddling Tigger, I asked, "What on earth happened?" I assumed the house had been burglarized in Lucille's absence.

The neighbor explained that Lucille's children came earlier and ransacked it, looking for anything of value, particularly money. I knew Lucille didn't have anything of value, especially money; so it bewildered me why anyone would do such a thing, particularly her children. I looked at the neighbor, astonished and in disbelief, and asked, "Why?"

The neighbor didn't have an answer. She said that when she noticed my car outside, she wanted to find out about Lucille and make sure Tigger was all right.

I explained Lucille passed on a few hours earlier, but I didn't have any more details. I said I was taking Tigger and wasn't giving Lucille's children an option about keeping him.

Stepping over Lucille's possessions, I went into the kitchen and found Tigger's water bowl, which had been tipped over on the children's hunt for valuables. It was easy to see the dry kibble had been scattered in every direction from the frenzy. I grabbed the empty food dish. I also took the case of cat food. Last but not least, I retrieved the litter box with an unopened bag of litter.

The neighbor helped me out to the car. I was about to leave when she said, "Lucille was very fond of you, and she would be pleased Tigger is in your care." In my heart, I agreed with what she just said.

I climbed into the car with Tigger and left. Tigger settled on my lap and never stopped purring. He received a good home as promised. Tigger joined my thundering herd.

In the following days, Lucille's children didn't even notice Tigger was missing; and I never let on where he was. I don't think they were even concerned. If they were, it didn't matter. Tigger would remain in his new home where he was safe and happy.

I was unable to attend Lucille's funeral. It was planned at a time there was a conflict in my schedule. Perhaps it was for the best. I did not want to face Lucille's children after discovering what they did to her house. I was also angry with the way they treated and frightened Tigger. Lacking any consideration, they left this kitty without any water and his food thrown everywhere. Because of these feelings, I really didn't want to go, although Cheryl did make it to the service.

Before the service at the gravesite, a gentleman approached Cheryl. He was big and burly in appearance. He had been a member in the same church Lucille belonged to for most of her senior years and had been acquainted with Lucille for a long time. The gentleman inquired if Cheryl had any idea where Tigger could be found and asked if he was okay.

Cheryl looked at the man and said, "Yes, he's fine." From Cheryl's response and the expression on her face, the man fully understood Tigger was in safe hands. He didn't question Cheryl any further. He smiled with gratitude and walked away.

Over the years, I have thought about Lucille and her children. What took place after Lucille's death still upsets me. To this day, I have a hard time understanding why the children behaved in such a manner. If by chance I ever find the reasons, I still can't condone such actions.

I am positive Lucille is resting in peace, knowing I followed through with the promise. I undeniably kept my word to the sharecropper's daughter with the sparkling blue eyes.

The Great Escape

There were a few times I participated in questionable activities that could have brought more trouble than I could have imagined, but these deeds didn't. The great escape was one particular event that definitely fit into this category.

In the latter half of the nineties, my best friend and I rescued a number of abandoned cats and kittens around the neighborhood where she lived. The two of us arranged the room above her garage into a so-called "cat house" or cat apartment (less controversial, less speculative) for the felines until arrangements could be made to have them adopted out into forever homes.

It was springtime and the weather wasn't in the sweltering heat of the summer yet. It was quite pleasant outside, so the windows of the cat room could be opened. This permitted the cats the opportunity to enjoy some fresh air through the screens. They loved looking out, talking to the wildlife, and sleeping while surrounded by the sunshine and the fresh air. Neither Cheryl nor I ever gave it a thought that any of the cats would push a screen out, which would allow the group to partake in a great escape, except one vixen did.

Early one morning, just before sunrise on a beautiful weekday, the apartment crew jumped through a broken screen on to the top of Cheryl's car and then to the ground below. For them, it was a great adventure, exploring the outdoor surroundings with their newfound freedom. Afterward, it became our mission to search, capture, and return them home.

It wasn't difficult catching most of the kitties. One cream-colored boy, namely Garfield, sat on the porch and patiently waited to be let back inside. He absolutely didn't have any particular desire to leave the safety of his home and miss out on dinner. Most of the others came when either Cheryl or I called their names. Nevertheless, we had a difficult time getting our hands on two six-month-old twin sisters dressed in blue-gray fur, at least momentarily.

Cheryl left for work around 8:00 a.m.; but I stayed, attempting to find the wayward duo. Somewhere around 9:00 a.m., I noticed Windy, the blue-gray kitty with white, had somehow climbed on the apartment roof. I tried everything I knew to coax her in my direction as I stood on the apartment porch railing, with one arm tightly holding on to the wooden pole. I reached on the rooftop using the other one and tried to grab hold of her, but she never came within reach.

Out of desperation, I shimmied up the pole and pulled myself on to the roof. Windy finally decided she'd approach me at that point. I sat on the warm shingles, with Windy curled on my lap, and tossed over in my mind about getting both of us off our perch. I needed help, but it would be hours before Cheryl left work and returned home. If I yelled, there wasn't anyone around who could hear my plea. After questioning my sanity, I decided to put a lock-hold on the back of Windy's neck and slide back down the pole with her in tow. Much to my relief, Windy never flinched as I carefully swung both of us on the porch.

Having my feet safely back on the deck, I was more than happy to return Windy to the apartment with the other kitties. When I stopped shaking from facing my fear of open heights, I spent the next hour pulling a number of splinters from my legs since I had been wearing shorts and the wood pole was more than generous by supplying them.

Still, there was one lone feline left to find and capture—Feathers.

Feathers was a very tiny and slender kitty with solid blue-gray fur and large green eyes. Her father had been a feral cat, and she certainly received his genes. Feathers retained a fear of humans because of this heritage, even with the people she loved and trusted. Feathers was definitely the wild child with high intelligence and a very agile body. For these reasons, I realized she would be the hardest to find and then grab.

The following days, just before dawn after the breakout, Cheryl and I crawled through many different yards looking for Feathers. On our adventures, I kept alluding to the possibility that some surprised and irate neighbor might shoot us, thinking we were burglars. Even better, we would be arrested for trespassing, assuming we were demented peeping toms!

Proceeding with our mission of sleuthing, I then panicked at the thought of the possibility of having to call a particular husband at his place of employment and ask for help in bailing us out of city jail. My biggest fear was explaining why we were snooping around yards of unknown homeowners without their permission. Fortunately, these misgivings never became real since we were never seen by anyone.

Cheryl and I searched everywhere for Feathers, except Feathers was nowhere to be found. However, in a short time, Feathers periodically was spotted crossing the street by Cheryl's side yard at dusk. We were positive she was hiding someplace close. Over the following days, Cheryl put dry food on her back porch. Then we patiently waited and hoped for the best.

It wasn't too long before Feathers came back on her own accord. Feathers was hungry and scared, but not frightened enough to allow either Cheryl or me to grab hold of her. That meant we had to trick her into capture.

For the first effort, the door to the kitchen was left wide open. I set smelly cat food on the floor to lure Feathers inside, and Cheryl stood ready to close the door. Feathers gradually stepped in, but she flew back out the second there was movement.

Cheryl tried catching Feathers by playing birdie with her in the backyard. Feathers was wise to this approach and kept out of reach. I wasn't sure it ever would have been possible to hold on to a six-pound cat fighting for dear life to get away, even if Cheryl could put a hand on her. I had a feeling it might have sent my best friend to the hospital with severe cat bites and scratches if she succeeded. I was positive if spooked, Feather's adrenaline would have given her the strength of a bobcat in a desperate attempt to escape.

I convinced Cheryl the best possible means of catching Feathers was by means of a humane trap. The next day, Cheryl borrowed one from a friend and we set it up in the spot where Feathers ate moist food each day. Cheryl armed the trigger, and I put food inside it. Afterward, we retreated into Cheryl's house to secretly watch through the dining room window. As we stood peering through the glass, Feathers stepped inside the cage, walked over the trigger plate, ate the food, and then exited without setting off the trigger, which would close the door. Cheryl and I looked at each other with sheer wonder and total disbelief!

Over the following three days, the trap was set at mealtime and food was placed in it. Feathers entered, totally oblivious to what we were trying to accomplish. After finishing her delectable meal, she turned around and left without ever releasing the trigger. I was sure she viewed the whole thing as a delightful enclosure to dine in without getting disturbed.

The last approach was booby-trapping the cage itself. I came up with the idea of attaching a very long cord to the trigger. I could then pull the other end from a distance after Feathers started eating as usual. The trigger would release the door to finally close. At long last, Feathers would be captured! The slight problem was Feathers would never go near the enclosure if she saw me, no matter how hungry she was.

In order to accomplish the goal, I strung a cord with the one end attached to the trigger across the neighbor's driveway and behind Cheryl's wooden fence. That was where I sat and waited holding the other end. Cheryl went back into the house and stared through the dining room window. From her vantage point, she could watch for Feathers entering the trap. I couldn't see either Feathers or the cage from where I was hidden, only Cheryl. I waited for Cheryl's signal to pull the cord and never moved a muscle until Cheryl gave the go-ahead. At that precise moment, I yanked with all my might.

It worked!

The trigger released, and the door slammed shut. Feathers was finally captured!

The funny part of the whole adventure was that Feathers never noticed the door was closed since she had grown very accustomed to eating inside the trap. It wasn't until she finished and turned to leave that she realized she was snared. I never saw a cat go as crazy as Feathers did at that moment, desperately struggling to free herself.

I took the cage with Feathers secured within its walls to the veterinary clinic. This tiny fugitive required a health check before she could go back with the other cats. In the safety of an exam room, I opened the trap and gently reached for her. She let me lift and hold her without a struggle. Because a part of Feather's could never be tamed, I decided she would live behind closed doors and definitely behind locked windows in the safety of my home with my feline crew.

In time, the remaining apartment cats who could not be placed joined my thundering herd inside the main arena (the back section of the house), with a few joining Cheryl's crew in her home; and the garage apartment for cats was closed.

Cheryl was positive we were never in any real danger on our mission to find Feathers as we crawled through many yards while inadvertently looking into a few windows without the occupants' knowledge. I being the worrywart was not as confident and was very relieved neither one of us managed to get into any trouble with the sleuthing. I was even more thankful I never found it necessary to call my husband from jail because of the escapade.

Tender Cat

I define a tender cat as a very special kitty possessing exceptional gentle and loving traits. These attributes were given to a very wonderful kitty by the name of Tail Chaser. As I watched Tail Chaser over the years, his gentle and loving nature taught me that this world can be a wonderful place to live in if these compassionate traits are shared with others.

When Tail Chaser was born, I wasn't sure if his birth mom was Annie or Annie's sister, Mini Mouse. I suspected it was Annie because she was unquestionably an extraordinary tender cat, and Tail Chaser positively inherited this trait. In contrast, Mini Mouse was very practical and accepting in her personality. Because of this ability, she rolled with the punches that life threw her way much better without feelings easily getting hurt.

Both Annie and Mini were beautiful calicos. Annie's coat contained vibrant patches of color, and Mini's fur featured stripes of different shades of colors. Of the two, Mini Mouse certainly was the devoted mom. She raised Tail Chaser as her own kitten. Annie didn't know what to do with a kitten. She "purrferred" to play with Tail Chaser rather than be a mother with the do's and don'ts that came with the job. For this lucky little boy, he actually acquired two moms who loved him.

Annie passed on to her son his deep red-striped coat and copper eyes. This made Tail Chaser quite good looking. Even though he sported such fine beauty, it never went to his head. He certainly was not obnoxious or hard headed. Tail Chaser always kept a tender and gentle side.

As a kitten, Tail Chaser was rambunctious and adventurous. He loved Mini and obeyed her without question. Tail Chaser also loved Annie and followed her every chance he found. This habit at times got him into trouble, but having nine lives helped Tail Chaser avoid a few disasters.

Tail Chaser was given his name when he was a small youngster for obvious reasons. He found enormous pleasure in chasing his tail. Little by little, Tail Chaser's name was shortened to TC as he grew from a cute baby into a handsome adult.

In adulthood, this striking tom was a challenge seeing as TC took everything to heart. TC's feelings were easily hurt. The few times TC managed to do something wrong, he never was scolded since one stern look made him crumble. Then it was imperative that he was consoled until he recovered.

TC liked his feline buddies and the humans he knew. He made strong bonds with a few special friends; and fortunately, I was one of them. When he gave his trust, he did it totally. As a result, the attachments were long lasting and never once wavered.

Sometimes the gift of tenderness Annie bestowed upon her son was a burden for TC. Because he retained such deep gentleness, he was sometimes anxious of the unknown. However, if held and cuddled, TC soon realized there wasn't anything to fear.

As TC matured into his middle years, I explained that TC actually stood for Tender Cat. He was quite pleased at long last that I recognized how special he was. He acknowledged the enlightenment with loud purrs and his head held high with catly pride. He was delighted I finally understood the true nature of his very gentle and loving traits.

This Old Man

Roten Kotzen was a very elderly Persian cat with flaming red hair and copper eyes. He came to live with my thundering herd in the last year of his life.

When he entered his super senior years, this kitty developed health problems his human mom could not handle. Betty loved him and wanted his final days to be as good as possible. As a result, Betty decided it was in his best interest he reside with me to receive the care. Even though Betty could not keep Kotzen, she often came over so they could spend time together.

Kotzen lived his entire life as a solitary cat until he met my crew. For the first time, Kotzen formed strong feline friendships, discovered girls, enjoyed daily catnip, and savored fresh baked chicken. I watched this grumpy old man go from a lonely senior then blossom into a very content and happy gentleman of elder years.

This old man, this old man,
He came wobbling up my path.
With a knick-knack paddy-whack,
I gave the cat a hug.

This old man went purring home.
This old man, this old man,
He came scratching at my door.
With a knick-knack paddy-whack,
I gave the cat some nip.
This old man went rolling home.

This old man, this old man,
He noticed my female cats.
With a knick-knack paddy-whack,
Guess who discovered delightful sex?
This old man went strutting home.

On the day Kotzen became a heavenly angel, I added the following final lines.

This old man, this old man,
He died on the first of May.
With a knick-knack paddy-whack,
I gave this cat some wings.
This old man went flying home.

This old man, this old man,
He's as happy as can be.
With a knick-knack paddy-whack,
I say a prayer for him.
This old man is now at peace.

Dinnertime

At a family gathering, a wonderful meal was served. After enjoying the last delectable item, a very dear friend proclaimed,

"Abundant in scope
And splendid in succulence!"

I thought to myself what a perfect description of the way a cat feels after he finishes his meal. First, he savors every last tidbit. He then wraps up by licking the plate clean. Upon completion, the cat sits quite content, washing his paws and face.

In point of fact, I think these were the words spoken by a cat and overheard by a human. Then the human decided to acknowledge them as his! Now when I see a cat enjoying a meal, I listen carefully and hear him proclaim very softly,

"Abundant in scope
And splendid in succulence!"

I See Fairies

A friend once told me I saw fairies behind every bush. Initially, I thought she was teasing but soon realized she was serious. Betty explained how I witnessed things no one else did, especially when I looked at my cats and watched the antics they "purrformed."

I was surprised and taken off guard by the statement. I never before gave any serious thought either to my observations of my cats or the manner in which I perceived life as far as that was concerned. These views just came naturally to me.

After Betty's comment, I kept passing through my mind the idea of seeing fairies behind every bush. Chuckling under my breath, I came to the conclusion that she was most definitely right!

Well, almost . . .

It is not that I necessarily see fairies everywhere. I see potential beyond normal reality for the foremost reason that I view many things in life with my heart. Because of this, I share in my cats' hopes, dreams, and, too often, sorrows that are very real. I also witness life from a perspective I lived as a child. As a matter of fact, I never allowed that special ability to ever change and stop participating in many kinds of wonders others cannot even begin to imagine.

It just might be that I do see fairies behind every bush; perhaps it is purely an overactive imagination playing tricks on me. Deep down inside, what I really perceive is a reality full of wonderful and magical possibilities when I look at my cats.

I was born with the gift of imagination. My dad showed me how to use it. He had a way of finding magic in many things around him, especially in the wonder of animals. I continue to hear the wisdom Dad taught me, and I still envision life exactly the way he wanted me to see it—with fairies behind every bush!

Limitations

My very good friend lost her leg in a tragic accident a number of years ago. It was hard for Betty adapting to life without it. As a rule, she maintained a positive attitude about the handicap, but there were moments the reality of it did get her down.

One of those times, Betty admitted to me, "I will always be a cripple!" When she made this comment, I was taken off guard. Then I thought that she was right with her assessment, even as difficult as it was for me to admit.

Later, I was looking at Joseph. He was my handsome Maine Coon kitty who was partially paralyzed in his back end. As I observed him walk across the room, I wondered if he too felt the same as Betty since he also lived with a disability.

I realized Joseph watched the other cats climb to places he could never reach. Surely, he must have experienced the same emotions as Betty did. However, if Joseph retained any longings of "purrforming" just like any other cat without a handicap, he kept those feelings to himself.

Joseph recognized he could never reach places beyond his capabilities. He fully understood he would never fly through the room without stumbling. He accepted the drawbacks his legs imposed on him and never let it hinder the manner in which he lived life.

Deep down within me, I believe Joseph viewed himself as never having any restrictions. He was happy and content with his world in spite of the handicap. Nonetheless, I admit I have had moments when I wondered if Joseph also missed being so-called normal and wished he didn't have to deal with the limitations imposed upon him because he was crippled very much like Betty.

Shadow Dancer

I consider myself quite privileged to be allowed to share in the cats' wisdom that the challenges of some very exceptional cats are met with an inner strength and then conquered. I have come to realize this is a true gift from heaven.

Shadow Dancer, a proud Maine Coon cat, was determined on living his life to the fullest. Even when he recognized his health was declining in the battle with cancer, he adapted to the progressing changes and learned to compensate for them. Throughout Shadow's illness, he never let his physical problems put a damper on his love of life and the devotion for the people he adored. When his body could no longer remain on this earth, Shadow left with dignity.

> *I awaken in the light,*
> *Slowly moving through time.*
>
> *I grow in the warmth of the sun,*
> *Merely fading into the darkness.*
>
> *I am noticed by everyone,*
> *Ever changing,*
> *And still remaining the same.*
>
> *I speak with such loud expression,*
> *While quietly whispering into thoughts.*
>
> *I dance to the song of a gentle rain*
> *With great joy singing within my soul.*

I am here for just a moment,
Yet staying for a lifetime.

I am born "The Shadow Dancer,"
Seen touching very special hearts.

Page's Kittens

While working closely with deaf cats, I discovered how these marvelous creatures deal with the loss of one of their five senses. It seems humans frequently take hearing for granted. Felines apparently do the same. If a cat never acquires hearing or loses the capability, the cat compensates quite well without it. Actually, there's never an issue or a problem for the feline lacking this gift; at least, most of the time it's not an issue. In contrast, a human sometimes treats the situation as a definite handicap that must be endured.

Page was my white Maine Coon cat who was deaf. Page was born with hearing, but it diminished and left her totally deaf shortly after birth. This trait happens in white cats if they have an autosomal dominant white gene that suppresses pigment formation. It may produce partial or complete deafness. As for Page, she was totally deaf.

I eventually taught Page some sign language to communicate with this pretty kitty. Page was smart and knew when to disregard any signs in the same manner as a typical cat with hearing ignores me. If it was not significant to acknowledge me, Page turned her head and didn't see the signs. This allowed her the "purrfect" opportunity to completely overlook whatever I was saying.

Shortly after Page gave birth to a litter of kittens, my best friend and I agreed it was in Page's best interest to have her move into my home. Page had come down with an upper respiratory infection. The doctors did not want her nursing or in contact with the newborn babies, thereby preventing the infection from transmitting to them.

Through a series of unfortunate circumstances, each of the babies died, except for two. One kitten passed when Page was still with the babies. Page accidentally rolled on top of him and couldn't hear his distress cry. Three others were taken by the deadly upper respiratory infection after Page was no longer in contact with them. The two who did not succumb were two white boys with bicolored eyes. One boy maintained the ability to hear, and the other one lost his hearing soon after birth in the same manner as his mom did.

Unfortunately, the kittens acquired this very deadly virus through the milk they received before they were pulled away from Page. Showing no mercy, the infection took the lives of the three babies in a matter of days. Grammy, the deaf one, was unaffected by the infection; but John Henry, the one with hearing, wasn't as lucky. In spite of the best medical care and home nursing, it was touch and go if John Henry would live or succumb to the illness. Without question, I spent most of my time at Cheryl's home, helping with John Henry.

It was late Thursday evening after the onset of the infection. I went home to take care of my thundering herd and catch a few hours of sleep before returning the next morning. When I entered Cheryl's bedroom, which had been turned into an intensive care unit for the kittens, Cheryl was holding John Henry and crying. I thought at first he died. But thank heavens, it wasn't the case; although he was having great difficulty breathing. Cheryl was exhausted and scared. Unable to think straight, she turned to me for help.

I took John Henry in my hands and, ever so gently, massaged his back to give comfort. Then I focused my attention on what this baby required. He was put on a little oxygen to catch his breath. Temperature was maintained by wrapping warm hand towels around his tiny body. Some drops of kitten milk were fed every few minutes for nourishment from a bottle. Liquid medications were easily administered with a syringe. Between times, John Henry slept on a blanket on my lap as the nebulizer's mist was aimed in his direction, which helped his breathing. At the same time, I told this precious kitten I wasn't about to let him die, too. In my mind, I was very determined he was going to pull through and get better.

Maybe it was John Henry's strong will to survive, or possibly the Lord Father's intervention, or my stubbornness of not giving up, or a combination of all three that allowed John Henry to improve and finally recover. It didn't matter how it happened. I was grateful beyond words for the miracle.

For some unknown reason, Grammy never did come down with the upper respiratory that took his siblings' lives with the exception of John Henry. Obviously, I was most appreciative.

These two kittens grew into very handsome Maine Cooners. John Henry stayed with Cheryl, Grammy was adopted by Cheryl's father and his wife, and Page remained with me.

During those long days I worked with Page's kittens, I learned life can be ever so fragile and unpredictable as in the unforeseen outcome of some of Page's newborn babies. I also witnessed that sometimes miracles do take place.

How Do You Get a Snoodle?

How do you get a Snoodle?
Fairly easy . . .
Just mix a Shadow with a Noodle and a wonderful Snoodle is brought forth!

Rosie was a cute, blue-silver Maine Coon cat. She was quite dainty, except for the manner in which she walked. Then it was as if she wore clodhoppers on her paws. She also developed the habit of turning into a limp wet noodle when held in anyone's arms. Accordingly, her nickname became Noodle because of it.

Shadow was a very handsome blue Maine Cooner. He was stocky and quite loving. He enjoyed giving head butts that were extremely hard, often bringing stars to the recipient's eyes.

Once old enough, Rosie was bred to Shadow. The union between Rosie and Shadow produced one very big kitten. When born, the kitten weighed nine ounces. Also, a very large curl was centered on the top of her head.

Gently holding this baby for the first time, I looked at the kitten and thought of different names. Not using my imagination initially, the name Curly came to mind; but then it dawned on me . . .

What must a kitten who has a curl on the top of her head be called?
It seems so obvious.
Call the baby Curly, of course!
No, this pretty little girl shouldn't be burdened throughout her life with such a name.
How then shall the kitten be addressed?
Her name ought to be Snoodle, most definitely!
Why bequeath such a name?
Think for a moment.
What else is created if a Shadow and a Noodle are united?
The answer to the question is reasonably straightforward.
Without a doubt, from the union between a Shadow and a Noodle, a Snoodle is born!

What's in a Name?

I am of the firm opinion the cat has three names. The first one he receives at birth from his mother. It is shared by the two of them and, possibly, the cat's littermates. The second name is given by the human caregiver. It can be most formal or something quite silly. The third name is one the cat decides he will answer to—only when he so chooses.

Sometimes I selected names for my cats. Other times I was informed by some what their names happened to be. I have picked names fitting the personalities. I occasionally decided on names honoring someone. In a few situations, I kept the names the cats were given. Then there were specific times I renamed several who required a more appropriate one. Quite often I used traditional names but changed the spelling to make them unique.

The following is a mere sampling of some of my cats' names.

Noir

It was late afternoon, and not much was going on at the Humane Society in West Texas where I volunteered during my spare time. Actually, I was the only one present with the animals. Since nothing needed attention, I sat at the reception desk, daydreaming. Before long, a gentleman in his thirties entered with a large wicker basket under his arm.

The man placed the basket on the counter and opened the lid. He reached inside and pulled out a very terrified black cat with long hair. As he plopped her down in front of me, he began sharing some details.

He said the cat was seven years old and was never allowed outdoors. He then handed me some medication and informed me she developed cystitis. Finally, he said he was moving and could no longer keep her. Consequently, he came to surrender her so we would find a new home for her.

Astonished, I looked at the man and asked if it was possible to keep the cat at least long enough until she was over the cystitis. Lacking any emotion, he replied, "No." Just no. He filled out the necessary papers and left without any further word.

As I stood by the desk, I held the seven-year-old cat. She was trembling. The kitty was quite scared that she didn't want to let go when I gently put her into a cage behind me. I kept looking at the kitty when she glued herself at the back corner. I realized she would never be put up for adoption with age and color not in her favor. Plus, having cystitis, she would not survive the stress of staying inside a shelter.

I don't know if it was the bewilderment I felt toward the man for doing this to someone I assumed he cared about, or because I felt distressed realizing the cat's fate. Whatever it was that made my resolve disappear into the wind, I decided the black cat was going home with me.

After a few minutes, I called my husband and explained the situation. The one request he made was to have the cat checked out by our cats' veterinarian. For me, that was a no-brainer. I agreed.

When my shift was over at four, the foremost stop was the veterinary clinic where I was a technician. There the cat would be examined before coming home with me. The last thing I wanted was to introduce a feline with something contagious into the household.

In a few minutes, I arrived at the clinic and found Peter, a young high school student, working at the front desk. He inquired about the cat's name. Looking at him, I didn't say anything for a few minutes. I thought to myself the cat was called Tar Baby, but I couldn't address her with such an uncomplimentary name. This kitty deserved one she could be proud of and something that would reflect her beauty. After mulling it over in my mind, I decided on the name. At long last, I grinned at Peter and said, "The cat's name is Noir."

Peter seemed puzzled and inquired why that particular name was picked. Smiling, I replied, "I chose it because the cat is jet-black, and noir means black in French."

Noir came home with me and became one of Pat's favorite cats. She lived a long and happy life with her new family and her distinguished name.

MeMe

Meee—Oh my!

Oh my,
Oh my,
Oh Me.

Meee—It's mine!

Oh my,
Oh my,
Oh Me!

Me was a very young white Maine Coon cat with bright yellow eyes. Me came to me since she developed a very bad case of ringworm and was infested with fleas. The fleas were easily eradicated by means of a flea bath. The ringworm was another matter. Therefore, she was required to stay in isolation. She remained sequestered until she was over the fungal infection, thereby preventing my resident colony of felines from getting infected. She had to spend over two months in the guest bedroom because of it.

The day this kitty arrived at my home, I let her out of the carrier in the bedroom. The kitty's eyes sparkled in the light as she sat on the floor in front of me. With a pouting chin and big ears, she gazed at me.

Looking down at this young feline, I addressed the cat by her given name. I cocked my head and said, "Vuela," meaning flight in Spanish. The young cat sat stiffly at my feet. She looked at me and then turned her head away, ignoring what I said.

With the bright idea that this young cat answered to her second name, I simply said, "Blanca," which means white in English. No further luck was attained.

This time, the very frustrated young feline not only turned her head in the other direction but also stiffened up at full attention. She quickly let out a sigh of irritation as if to say I was nowhere close at guessing her real name. Seeing the reaction, I tried one more time and softly said, "Vuela Blanca."

By then, the young Cooner was thoroughly disgusted with my feeble attempts at speculating the name. She let out several big huffs, relating her feelings quite clearly. Finally, at wit's end, I asked this young cat, "Well, what is your name?"

With catly pride, the young cat put her two front legs together and stared directly into my eyes. Then she took a deep breath before half-closing her eyes. Without any further delay and at the top of her lungs, she burst out, "Me!" Laughing, I again asked what her name was. Once more, she replied, even louder, "Me!"

There was no doubt this kitty knew her name. From that day forward, this young Maine Coon was called MeMe; and that was the one name she answered to without a question.

DECOUPAGE

Page, my Page,
You are a pretty white cat.

I look at you're beautiful coat,
And what color appears?

White is not a color. True white contains absolutely no color. To see white, it must have some color within it.

Decoupage is an artistic technique in which layers of different colored papers are assembled on top of each other to create a final work of art. What is seen on top is not always what is presented underneath.

In the cat kingdom, a cat's white coat masks a color or colors. It can almost be thought of as layering of colors, with white added last, thus covering and hiding the color or colors beneath it.

When my best friend acquired a young female Maine Coon cat for her breeding program, Cheryl was at a loss as to what she should name the cat. Given that decoupage is much like the masking effect in white cats, I suggested the name Decoupage since the kitty was white. I thought it suited the cat because white was undeniably masking her color. Eventually, Decoupage was shortened into Page.

Page gave birth to one litter of kittens before she came to live with me. Most of her kittens were white except for two little calico females. The father of the kittens was cream. I am still not sure if Page's white was masking the color blue, possibility red, or both.

As Page matured, her coat grew long and lush. When she walked, it almost touched the floor. Since the fur was thick and silky, it provided an air of royalty. Still, the true color could never be seen by just looking at the coat. The secret was in Page's genes, although it was always fun to think about.

SAM ROOFUS

Sam, Sam was once a roof-squatting cat.
He climbed up high and couldn't get down.
I grabbed a ladder and climbed up, too.
There we sat—both Sam and I.
Reaching on over, I grabbed this cat and carried him off.
Sam, Sam was no longer a roof-squatting cat.

In 2000, Pat and I added a garden room at the back of the house. During the framing, a young, red-striped cat managed to find himself on top of the roof. I am not sure if he climbed there or one of the subcontractors conceivably put him on it, knowing we liked cats and would possibly give him a home.

This young tom stayed on the roof for days and never attempted to leave. I tried enticing him with food but found little luck at persuading him to come within reach. He only ate if the food was left on the roof's edge without anyone around. Then out of frustration and concern, I borrowed a ladder to retrieve the kitty—myself!

When I reached the roof, I calmly sat on the shingles, staring at the young tom. He, in turn, watched me, only inches away. I slowly reached over and grabbed him by the back of his neck in the same manner a mother cat carries her kittens. I held the tom tightly and didn't let go until we were both back on the ground, where I secured him safely inside a carrier.

On that day, this young tom received two names. In honor of our contractor, Sam was chosen. Roofus was then presented since the name was derived from the place where this cat was found. Thus, Sam Roofus received his name.

TINKER BELL

At a distance, what do I see?
It appears to be a cat on top of a roof.
Is this unusual?

No, I don't think it is.
It is in a cat's nature to seek out high places, although this is different.
Why?
The cat is a young kitten, soaring from rooftop to rooftop.
She flies with the grace and ease of a small fairy.
Could it be she is a fairy-cat?

Tinker Bell was unquestionably a fairy-cat dressed in a shaded, black-and-white coat. This kitty was a beautiful Domestic Longhair with copper eyes who was abandoned on the streets without any means of shelter. Since she found it necessary to stay away from many dangers she faced in her travels, this kitty learned the art of flying high into the sky. She possessed the nimbleness of ascending from rooftop to rooftop, tree branch to tree branch, and fence ledge to fence ledge in a blink of an eye.

Even when this fairy-cat retired from the streets and was added to my thundering herd, Tinker Bell never lost the high-flying ability. The difference, she then soared from cabinet top to cabinet top, cat tree to cat tree, and windowsill to windowsill in a blink of an eye.

WILLOW BEND

As the young willow becomes strong,
Its tender branches bend ever so gently toward the river below.

With the years quickly passing,
The tall willow grows sturdy while climbing higher into the heavens.

Even in maturity,
The willow's branches remain tender, softly stretching for the river below.

Willow Bend was a tiny three-month-old kitten who had been beaten and left on my back porch inside a box in early spring of 2002. Holding the baby for the first time, I could not help but fall in love with this forlorn and helpless kitten. He possessed deep blue eyes, which were definitely crossed, and wore very scruffy fur. He was all legs with very little body attached. What body he wore showed the bruises from being abused. The way he melted in my arms definitely captured my attention. However, it was this kitty's purr that stole my heart.

Willow overcame his beginnings. He grew into a very handsome and mischievous cat who loved giving kisses to anyone who asked and some who didn't. He never met a stranger, and he turned into a very good therapy cat with quite a bit of patience on my part.

CHERISH

My Siamese cats were highly intelligent and displayed a fierce loyalty to one person—me. They were also quite talkative. They could carry a conversation on any and every subject deemed worth regarding. What's more, they would get into mischief faster than a blink of an eye.

I acquired my first Siamese cat, a beautiful blue point, with the assistance of my dad. Cackie stayed by me for a little under twenty years. Shortly before Cackie went to the heavenly home, Twinkle blessed my life. Twinkle was a seal point Siamese kitten. She became the kitten Cackie always wanted. Cackie loved her, and Twinkle treasured Cackie. They were always close by each other.

Cackie's health failed, and she returned to the heavens. Then Twinkle helped me find my way. She carried on in Cackie's paw prints, even though they were awfully big for her at the time. As she matured, Twinkle made her own paw prints alongside Cackie's inside my heart.

Twinkle was with me for seventeen years when the heavens called her home. It was the first time since my teenage years I was without a Siamese cat, and I felt a deep sadness because of it. At the same time, I was ready to close that chapter of my life until this little homeless kitten appeared on the doorstep.

The kitten was part Siamese. I didn't want to let her get close because I was still hurting over the loss of Twinkle. Pat stepped in and said, "Let this kitten into your life. No, she isn't a full-blooded Siamese cat, but she contains enough that will allow you to still cherish the memories of Twinkle and Cackie by loving her." I have to say, my resolve rapidly faded and I adopted the kitten instead of placing her. I christened the kitten Cherish. It was soon shortened to Cherry.

Cherry was never really a Siamese cat, although she received enough Siamese to remind me of two cats I loved and always will. Sometimes I think the Lord Father was sneaky in his ways. He saw my sorrow and helped heal it with a tiny life who needed a home. He also found a little help accomplishing the act through a caring husband.

The Last Santa Muffin

Back in the early nineties, my cats' doctor was telling me about one of her patients. He was a diabetic cat and wasn't doing well in his current situation. Ever since his caregiver died, the granddaughter was looking for someone to adopt him. He required a special person who could handle his health problems if he was going to have a chance at living.

I intently listened to the details about this cat, but I resisted volunteering any help. I had recently lost a kitty and felt I wasn't ready to take on another one, especially a cat with special needs. Afterward, I went home and continued with everyday activities, trying not to think of the cat who required a skilled caregiver; but it wasn't working.

A day later, I was on the tennis court, playing a game of doubles. I couldn't concentrate on the game because my focus was centered upon the diabetic kitty I didn't know but kept creeping into my thoughts. Later that evening, I told my husband about the cat. Knowing me so well after being married for many years, he grinned and finally asked, "When are you getting him?"

The next day, I called Kathy and said I would take on the diabetic kitty, except there was one stipulation: the kitty had to pass a health check. Kathy was delighted. She agreed to contact the granddaughter and tell her the good news.

A couple of days passed without a word. At that point, I was wondering if the granddaughter really had any intention on placing the cat. Then the phone rang. It was Kathy. She asked me to come later in the afternoon to the clinic and meet the kitty.

In the meantime, Kathy went over the feline with a fine tooth comb and checked him out for both the feline immunodeficiency virus (FIV) and the feline leukemia virus (FeLV). He was negative on everything . . . except fleas. Obviously, he received a flea bath and definitely protested, quite loudly, over the insult.

Somewhere around 4:00 p.m., I went to meet my new kitty and take him home. Kathy brought him into the exam room and gently set him on the floor. He was probably one of the biggest cats I had ever seen and quite handsome. His fur was long and lush, which made him look so much like a Maine Coon cat. He wore a perfect black-and-white tuxedo coat with a goatee on his chin. This kitty also sported a very pink nose that set off his good looks. Even though he was a slight bit overweight, he appeared to be in somewhat good shape. The one thing I noticed was that his fur was dull, probably from the shampooing or the poor diabetic management, possibly the two. It required a little help, which I was able to correct rather quickly with a conditioning shampoo.

Truthfully, I didn't care if this cat was the ugliest one ever born. Even before meeting him, I decided in my mind he was mine. As I gently stroked his head, he never moved a muscle, but he kept his green eyes completely focused on me.

I inquired what name the cat was given. With a large smile, Kathy replied, "Muffin." The name was not exactly a boy's name. Naturally, I added a little extra and called him the Muffin Man. I felt every cat should have a name to be addressed with pride. The handsome Muffin Man then gained one.

I then asked about the Muffin Man's glucose numbers and the insulin he was taking. With Muffin Man's sugar remaining high and his current insulin soon to be discontinued, Kathy and I decided to begin another one. Armed with the supplies to last until I could stop at a pharmacy and purchase a vial of insulin plus more syringes, Muffin Man and I left the clinic.

The first thing on the agenda after arriving home was giving the newest addition another bath. This time, it was with a special conditioning shampoo to remove dander, dullness, and dry brittleness from a cat's fur. The shampoo worked miracles. After the second insult to his feline sensibilities in one day, Muffin Man's coat became soft with a beautiful shine.

For the next couple of weeks during quarantine, Muffin Man stayed in the master bedroom. I was quite surprised when I watched him walk for the first time. His leg muscles were quite weak that he could barely walk. The neuropathy was probably caused by the poor glucose control he previously received.

When Muffin Man did take some steps, he just crept under the bed; but I was determined he was not about to live his life beneath it. Then every time he headed for the sanctuary, I went after this kitty and pulled him out. I placed the grumpy cat either on the cat tree or the top of the bed. I wore out the knees to a pair of jeans by this game of hide and seek. In the end, I won. Muffin Man started to enjoy his new world and never again hid.

In addition to getting Muffin Man acclimated in his new home, I also took him to the entrance hall staircase and coaxed him upstairs to further strengthen his muscles. Initially, he couldn't take more than two steps at a time before sitting down to rest. I was patient, and it paid off. When Muffin Man's strength fully returned, he flew up the entire set of steps at full speed, with me running after him in pursuit.

I quickly discovered Muffin Man possessed quite a sense of humor. Anytime he wanted a reaction out of Pat, he headed over and parked himself in front of him. He sat motionless with his mouth slightly opened, baring his teeth. Not sure what Muffin Man wanted made Pat uneasy. He couldn't help but speculate if he was Muffin Man's next meal. In a short time, I would hear Pat's call of distress to get the Muffin Man. As I approached, Muffin Man took a slight jump in the air, quickly ran off, and climbed the nearest cat tree with a grin as he chuckled with victory.

It was definitely evident Muffin Man loved the girls. He gradually acquired a choice few. It didn't matter if they were two-legged or four-legged. He admired them equally. He showed his fondness for me by circling his front legs around my neck, wrapping his back legs tightly around my waist, and resting his chin on my shoulder. I could then carry Muffin Man without having to use my arms to support him.

If this handsome cat thought a little feline was cute, he followed her and chirped sweet nothings, apparently only a cat possess the ability of comprehending. He would throw himself on the floor right in front of the pretty female and roll from side to side while expressing loving secrets in hopes she'd respond. Even though these advances were totally ignored, the Muffin Man was never deterred. He tried to win the female's affection anyway.

I was well aware Muffin Man's diabetes was a challenge to control. He constantly kept me on tiptoes because of it. To at least keep on the same page with him, I used a glucometer for humans to track his blood glucose levels and made many clinic trips for health checks. I tried to remain at least one paw ahead of his condition. I succeeded—most of the time. Still, there were a few occasions he crashed without warning. With the possibility of this happening again, I always maintained a close eye on him.

There were times when I had to be away from home. During those outings, I was uncomfortable leaving Muffin Man behind due to the unpredictable glucose swings. Consequently, he became a man about town with me. He traveled inside a special carrier, which looked more like a knapsack. He loved accompanying me everywhere in it. Muffin Man definitely took great pleasure in being the "purrfect" companion. Since he behaved so well, he visited places that didn't allow pets, except no one realized he was with me.

Inside the car, Muffin Man rode on the backseat on a special cushion specifically made for him. The cushion allowed Muffin Man to see out the window. Since he was not secure in a carrier, he wore a harness that made him appear as if he was a professional motorcycle rider. It was then fastened to the seatbelt for safety.

The Muffin Man always looked forward to visiting at my best friend's house, and it remained as one of his "purrferred" outings. Countless times, if he wasn't ready to leave, he figured the best way to stay longer was to crawl under Cheryl's dining room hutch or glue his body beneath her bed.

One time, Cheryl and I had no alternative other than take apart her entire bed so we could retrieve him. After completing the task, Muffin Man merely laughed at the whole ordeal. I swear he recognized, "purrcisely," what he did; and it pleased him to no end.

On a hot summer day, I was in the midst of errands. One of the stops was at the local US Postal Service. The temperature was too warm for Muffin Man to stay in the car. I carried him, secured inside his carrier, over my shoulder into the building. The line was long and moved very slowly with just two windows available. I waited for almost half an hour and there still remained a number of people ahead of me. Muffin Man was growing impatient. Promptly, he expressed his irritation. He let out a loud meow, which grew louder as it amplified off the walls. Even with the room filled with people, it echoed in every direction. Everyone looked around, including me, to see where it came from. No one volunteered any credit for it, especially me! People laughed at how real it sounded. I then peeked at Muffin Man and recognized the mischievous twinkle in his eye. There was no question he enjoyed the commotion. I definitely realized he acted out on purpose.

The Muffin Man was given an eye for colors, red in particular. Not just red but the flaming red color found in fire engine-red lipstick. Whenever Muffin Man received a kiss on his nose from Cheryl that left some red lipstick on it, he carried his head high, proudly displaying the gift. To this day, I am not sure if he liked having a painted nose or, possibly, the fragrance pleased his sense of smell. Perhaps he savored the taste as he licked it off. Whatever went through his mind, he never let it be known.

Music is known to soothe the savage beast. For Muffin Man, it helped demonstrate his singing talent. He possessed quite a melodious voice. He loved crooning along with his favorite theme tune from *The Country Reporter* and could carry a song a cappella, too. If I whistled, he came from wherever and listened. Shortly, he joined in, singing since he couldn't whistle. Granted, Muffin Man lacked the ability; but it never stopped him from trying.

Funny, how the years passed before my eyes. As the first Christmas approached after the Muffin Man was a heavenly angel for almost five months, I still greatly missed his companionship. Nevertheless, those I care about the most have a way of communicating they are watching over me; and Muffin Man was no exception.

On Christmas Eve, the doorbell rang. I answered it. It was FedEx with a package addressed to me. I was quite surprised because I wasn't expecting another delivery. Wondering what it was, I eagerly opened the box. Placed inside was a very special Santa Muffin that had been made by the designer of stuffed animals I dealt with for several years.

Santa Muffins were a tradition Muffin Man and I began seven years earlier. A designer who lived in California made wonderful Christmas characters in cloth. She also assembled felines dressed as Santa cats both Muffin Man and I created together. When finished, they looked just like the Muffin Man.

Each year, the designer sent new samples of materials along with pictures of novel accessories, which could be included with the Santa cats. I carefully laid everything out on the floor and let Muffin Man walk around the different pieces. The items he showed interest in or sat on were the ones chosen. The two of us put together a delightful assortment of Santa cats. These cats were then Christmas gifts for his "purrferred" two-legged girls, Cheryl and Kathy. Of course, there was also one for me!

In early October, about two months after I lost the Muffin Man, the last order of Santa Muffins arrived. Together, Muffin Man and I had worked on them a few weeks before he died. With everything that happened, I forgot about them until they appeared.

Long ago, I told the designer the story behind these Santa cats and how special they were. I wanted to give my thank-you for the Santa Muffins she just sent. This time, I sadly explained they would be the last ones I'd ever have her make since Muffin Man was no longer with me. I said it was time to retire the series of Santa Muffin cats.

The designer was quite touched by the news. Without saying a word, she designed and made one last Santa Muffin as a special remembrance. In a way, it also was Muffin Man's gift from heaven.

That special surprise was in the FedEx package. The moment I opened the box, I realized what the designer did. Looking at the Santa cat, I started crying.

The Santa Muffin was magnificent. Not only was it the grandest one the designer ever made, but there was something special included—a crystal angel had been pinned on the suit collar. Later that afternoon, I proudly placed the Santa Muffin on the living room couch to celebrate Christmas with me.

To this day, the Santa Muffin remains in the living room, sitting on a tiny wingback chair acquired specifically for it. I am positive Muffin Man returns from heaven and grins with pleasure each time I glance at the last Santa Muffin that was created in honor of his memory.

It seems whenever I look at the special Santa Muffin, I think of the Muffin Man. I remember him as a complete ham since he found ways of getting smiles, giggles, and outright laughs in almost every situation he faced.

Muffin Man formed great attachments to his "purrferred" people and let everyone aware of it. He overcame tremendous physical challenges due to the diabetes. Beyond a doubt, he turned each day from a struggle into a reward. He was and always will be my Muffin Man.

Hunting Gloves and a Fishing Net

There have been particular occasions in which very special people helped me with my love of animals. Because they went the extra mile and gave of themselves so generously, I will always be in their debt.

Jim is a very dear friend and one of these people. Without his very brave help, I never would have rescued Whisper. I also have to give much thanks to his very patient wife, Carla, for putting up with both of us in the pursuit.

Quietly, I sang into the breeze:
Whisper, Whisper, Whisper my cat.
Hear my voice, Whisper my cat.
Now come, come from wherever you're at!

During the early spring of 1994, nights continued to be cold and there was still a brisk chill felt into the late morning. However, nature was awakening and coming alive once more. I could smell the sweet scent of blooming flowers filling the crisp air with their delightful fragrances. Since this season is the beginning of life, springtime has definitely remained one of my preferred times of the year.

I was out feeding the next door neighbors' cat, Tammy, seeing that she had taken up residence in my backyard. She decided years earlier it was much more fun having two homes than just one. As time went on, she returned to her original caregivers, Jim and Carla, less and less, especially during bad weather. To make life comfortable for this kitty, my husband and I built a high-rise condo on the back porch, which could be heated in the cold weather if needed. It certainly didn't take very long before Tammy accepted these arrangements as if she was the queen of England who had a castle built for her pleasure and comfort.

It was early morning, with the tail end of night lingering, scarcely light enough to see very well. At a distance, I could barely distinguish a black-and-brown tabby cat sporting more ticking in his coat than stripes. When he stepped a little closer in my direction, I noticed his large eyes and was almost certain they were green. I was positive he was a young male by the body features. He was also thin. Otherwise, he appeared to be in good shape.

I tried getting close with the offering of food, but the tom ran off. This was not unusual. Frequently, a traveling cat stopped and then was gone in a blink of an eye, never again spotted.

The area where my home is located turned into a popular place for dropping off cats. I guess the people who did it assumed someone would care for them. Sadly, not every cat was successful at finding a home. The ones who never got adopted and survived turned wild. They ended up having kittens who became totally feral.

Without saying, it wasn't a surprise the new face I was catching a glimpse of was either a wild or an abandoned feline, although something about this cat was special. Maybe it was the manner in which he longed for human contact but remained aloof. He was curious, except he was reserved and cautious. He certainly was unable to let his guard down and trust a human.

Each morning, the adolescent appeared on time, looking for breakfast. I started setting food out with the intentions of taming him. I wanted this tom to understand I was not going to hurt him. I just wanted to befriend him; yet I couldn't get closer than ten feet. If I spoke, he'd run off. Then again, if I whispered, he remained and ate. Thus, this feline was named.

Eventually, Whisper came for the evening meal, too. After eating, he retreated into the hedges and watched my every move. I purposely spent time playing with Tammy. I teased her with catnip and the birdie toy, hoping Whisper would come join the game. I had no such luck. He definitely sensed any plans of domesticating him and always maintained a distance.

On the occasions I did not see Whisper when I stepped outside to take care of Tammy, I softly called for him. In no time at all, he would approach with a smile covering his face, talking a storm up as he drew near. Nonetheless, he never came any closer than ten feet.

In the fall, I made this cat a heated house hidden deep behind the bushes in the back flower bed. The accommodations pleased him. He used the retreat in both rainy and cold weather after making sure there wasn't a two-legged person anywhere around the proximity of it.

I quickly concluded it was not going to be easy winning over the wild tom. The deed would take time and heck of a lot of patience. I also realized if this approach didn't work, I then needed to try other means.

Each day, Whisper wanted to stay; but I quickly realized he wore itchy feet. He heard the call tomcats throughout the ages have heard and heeded its voice. Soon he left to pursue its longing, too. He traveled for miles, often with others of his kind. Sometimes he was seen crossing the street by the country club. There wasn't a doubt he was searching for a tasty morsel from their kitchen's trash since eating was his great passion. Other times he was spotted running through the open fields in the company of other young toms.

In the weeks that passed, Whisper grew up and put on some weight. He was perhaps the only wild tom who was as round as he was tall. The one thing that could be said for sure: he never missed a meal!

Out on the streets, in the cat population, there are diseases spread from one cat to another that are eventually fatal. Both the feline leukemia virus (FeLV) and the feline immunodeficiency virus (FIV) are two of them. They affect male and female cats alike, although these conditions seem to strike male cats more than the females, especially the ones still intact. Male cats are territorial. They fight to protect their area and to be the top cat so they can romance a pretty female. Since they act in such a manner, diseases are easily spread among the males. This is still true today as in past years.

I was getting concerned Whisper, a whole tomcat, would become infected with a life-threatening disease if he stayed on the streets much longer. It definitely was in his best interest to be caught, neutered, and then retired from his wonderings as rapidly as possible. I was determined to make him an indoor cat for the main reason that I did not want to keep worrying about the many things that could hurt him in the outside world.

Over the following months, I tried every trick in the book attempting to get my hands on Whisper. I set the best cat food out as I softly spoke while he ate. Nevertheless, he never allowed me to come close. I was positive he was a mind reader and realized what I was seeking to achieve. Thus far, ten feet remained his safe zone.

Next, I tried using a humane trap. Well, I caught the next door neighbors' cats, both Tammy and Shasta, more than once; though I never caught Whisper. He just sat beside it with a satisfied grin on his face. Then he looked at me as if to say, "Do you think I am that stupid?"

After that failure, I attempted another approach. I put food in the corner of the garage with the far door set to close once Whisper entered to chow down a delectable feast. Quietly sitting behind the entry door of the house and armed with a remote garage door opener in my hand, I waited while intently listening. When I heard a cat eating, I pushed the button and closed the overhead door, not quite a foot off the floor, in order to allow a certain cat to enter. This too never worked. Here again, I caught Tammy a number of times and sometimes Shasta. Once more, Whisper smiled at my ineptitude.

It was laughable if I wasn't so concerned. I was worried Whisper already contracted something that could be his demise. Still, I was betting he beat the odds and was in good health. Obviously, I remained steadfast in the efforts to catch him.

On February 8, 1995, at 1:00 in the morning, the phone rang. I rolled over in my sleep and ignored it, assuming it was a wrong number. Pat grabbed the receiver and answered it. After a short conversation with the person on the other end, Pat handed the phone to me. It was Jim. Very calmly, Jim explained he just caught a wild tom in the garage. With the next breath, Jim said he was positive it was Whisper.

Sitting upright, I told Jim I'd be right over. I jumped out of bed and threw on some clothes. Pat looked at me as if I was out my head, though he did ask where I was headed at such an hour. Almost breathless, I responded, "I am going over to Jim's . . . he just caught Whisper!"

I ran out of the house and cautiously walked up Jim's driveway. Moving closer toward the open doors of the garage, I tentatively peeked inside of it. I stood motionless for a moment in total awe. It appeared as if a bomb exploded within the room! Things were all over the place. Plants were turned over. Some had broken pots with dirt thrown in every direction. There were many fallen books from the bookcases Jim kept along the walls. Many different kinds and sizes of tools were also scattered everywhere.

The kitchen door abruptly opened, and Jim came out. He was holding his thumb high in the air to show me where Whisper had nailed him. Proud as punch, he beamed a smile from ear to ear. He also flashed a twinkle in his eye because of his success. Triumphantly, he took me over to the spot where he placed Whisper.

I followed Jim into the storeroom at the far side of the garage. To my total amazement, Jim ushered Whisper inside the smallest pet carrier ever made. Bending over to get a better look, I gazed at the cat, making sure he was really Whisper. To my great joy, the kitty was most definitely Whisper! I then stared at Jim and asked, "How in the world did you accomplish this feat?" With pride of a victorious warrior and quite a bit of satisfaction in his voice, Jim related the means used to capture Whisper.

Standing there while listening to the tale, I kept looking at Whisper, almost nose to nose for the first time. I could not imagine what was going through the cat's mind. His eyes were dilated with total fear and complete mistrust, but the only thing I could think of was the fact that he was finally caught. I was relieved, realizing he would finally be safe.

With much enthusiasm in his voice, Jim explained how he went out to the garage on his last round for the evening. He was having a problem with stray cats spraying the inside walls and wanted to make sure none entered through the pet door. To his amazement, he saw a cat he thought was Whisper.

Jim knew I had been trying to catch Whisper without much luck. Suddenly, he saw a chance to achieve it for me. In a split second he moved between Whisper and the pet door. He quickly secured the opening before Whisper could escape through it.

Thus, a battle between the two began!

It was man against beast!

Jim donned his hands with hunting gloves in preparation. He figured it would help avoid getting scratched or bitten by his opponent. Next, Jim armed himself with a weapon—the fishing net. On seeing what was transpiring, Whisper desperately tried to get out. He scrambled in every direction, frantically and wildly looking for a possible exit.

Whisper soared up walls and over the cars. He tore through plants, knocking them over at the same time. He flew over workbenches, scattering tools both high and low. He kicked all types of books from the shelves. Brooms and mops tumbled like toothpicks from the wall rack. Whisper raced in every direction with Jim, gloves, and fishing net hot on his tail in pursuit.

At one point, Whisper climbed into the wheel well of Jim's truck. Jim reached inside with an extended gloved hand and tried grabbing him, which was definitely a mistake. Whisper rapidly retaliated. He bit Jim's thumb through the glove. Sure enough, many choice words were said by both as Jim quickly let go of his grip on this fierce warrior. Terrified, Whisper dashed across the cars, leaving not a scratch.

Adrenaline flowed inside man and beast, though each was tiring and nearing the end of their ropes. Still, neither was willing to surrender.

Abruptly, Whisper climbed straight up a wall. Jim lunged with the net, caught Whisper, and tried pinning him to the floor. With the strength of ten lions pumping through his veins, Whisper wiggled his way out of Jim's grasp. This time, Whisper darted into Jim's storeroom. Picking himself up and straightening the net out, Jim quickly followed. Jim cornered Whisper at the far corner and gave this wild tom a choice of either the net again or the small carrier sitting on the floor. With very little alternative, Whisper chose the carrier. After scrambling to get inside, Jim closed the door and latched it quicker than lighting. Both were extremely exhausted. While one was pleased, the other was terrified.

Even at such early hour, Jim told Carla he had to call me and did so without delay. Amid lingering adrenaline still pumping in his veins and happy with the outcome, Jim quickly placed the number.

This was the point at which I walked in on the scene.

After listening to Jim's story and looking at the poor garage, I smiled down at the cat inside the carrier who was very much Whisper. I gently took Jim's hand in mine and examined his thumb. I wrapped a bandage over the wound. Then I asked Jim if his tetanus vaccination was current. Carla smiled and said, "Yes, it is!"

I stared straight into Jim's eyes. Very seriously, I explained that anyone who goes against a wild tomcat the way he did was either very brave or very stupid. Carla laughed. It didn't matter; I was thankful for what Jim did that night. I was also appreciative both he and Whisper were still in one piece. As for the garage, that was another story.

I took Whisper, secured within the tiny carrier, home with me. I put both in the guest bathroom and closed the door until the veterinary clinic opened in a few hours.

I arrived through the clinic's threshold with Whisper in tow. The veterinarians knew me well. They understood my passion for animals would mean I called upon them whenever I required their help. Sometimes it was without an appointment. I already advised them about Whisper. Consequently, they maintained no doubt I would be there without advance notice when I caught him.

The veterinarian, the husband of my cats' doctor, cautiously dumped Whisper into a wire cage. Then he skillfully threw a lasso around Whisper and pulled him to one side while Kathy, my cats' veterinarian, administered sedation through an injection. I sat on the floor with my feet on the top of the cage to prevent Whisper from escaping as the medication took hold. A little more than five minutes passed. Whisper was down, up, and out of the anesthesia. Since his adrenaline was so high, the sedation had little effect on him. Therefore, the entire procedure was repeated.

Everyone was curious about the cat. Naturally, while sitting there, I repeated the tale of the capture from the night before. Both laughter and cheers, along with some shaking of heads, filled the air.

When Whisper finally went under the anesthesia, he was tested for the different viral diseases that could have been his downfall. In addition, he was thoroughly checked for anything else that would need to be treated. Amazingly, he was free of everything, including fleas. Whisper was then neutered and vaccinated.

Kathy rapidly worked on completing the necessary procedures before Whisper awoke as I petted him for the first time in his life. I recognized I was only able to accomplish it since he was unconscious at the moment. Needless to say, it was heartwarming to finally touch him.

Work was finished in record time. There wasn't a choice because Whisper wasn't going to stay under the sedation much longer. He was placed back into the carrier and awoke with a roar. Shortly afterward, I took him home.

It was then my work began. I had no idea how long it would take to tame a wild cat. I also wasn't even sure I would succeed at such a challenge, but I was determined to achieve the goal. It was man against beast, and then it was my turn.

It was woman against beast!

Well, maybe?

I placed the carrier containing Whisper inside a large cage in the spacious front entrance hall. The room was bright from the big windows that allowed plenty of daylight inside each day. The enclosure I chose was more like a kitty playhouse than a cage and contained multilevels. I also made sure Whisper had access to a litter box, food, and water before placing Whisper in it.

The reason I put Whisper inside a cage instead of letting him loose in a guest bedroom or the study was simple. I felt there was a good chance he might tear apart the room, attempting to find a way outside. Without a doubt, I really didn't want to deal with replacing, repairing, or performing major cleanup work. I also wanted Whisper near the main arena (the back section of the house) where I could give him extra attention.

I rapidly finished the preparations. Then I opened the carrier's door and hastily pulled my hand away. Lastly, I secured the playhouse latch. I quickly discovered if I put my hand inside for any reason, Whisper shared ideas of tearing it to pieces, except I still required some way of keeping him from hurting me while cleaning his home and feeding him. What I found out was that he feared the central vacuum. When I used it to catch the dust and fallen litter inside the playhouse, Whisper rapidly retreated into the carrier and stayed there until I finished the chores.

Over the following six months, I spent my spare time sitting outside of Whisper's playhouse and talking to him. Regularly, I read to this former street cat. There were moments I closed my eyes as I took a short nap within inches of Whisper. I often gave him special treats. I was patient. I never tried to make Whisper feel uncomfortable. Therefore, I didn't force the situation. I very much wanted Whisper to understand I would never hurt him.

Slowly, I gained Whisper's trust, though progress came by inches. The first victory happened when I could clean his house without the vacuum.

Whisper's great love of food helped the next breakthrough. He allowed me to put his food dish inside without removing my hand afterward. I could rest it beside him as he ate. The biggest thrill came when I was permitted to put a finger on his nose. After that, new steps came swiftly.

To my absolute delight, Whisper accepted me more and more with each new day. I will never forget the first time he let me pet him. His coat was rough, except the more I touched him, the softer it became.

My heart was racing with excitement when Whisper walked out of the playhouse and sat on my lap. At long last, it was time for the final health check and the introduction into the main arena to meet the other cats. It wasn't any surprise his health check was "purrfect." Allowing Whisper the opportunity of total freedom among the other cats was the easy part. In the wild, Whisper was social with cats so he was curious about his new family. He immediately fit in without a problem.

Years passed and Whisper's feral side faded into a memory. His days of traveling many miles were long over. Whisper turned into an ambassador. He genuinely loved people that it wasn't a surprise to watch him be the first one in line to greet anyone who entered my home to get his fair share of chin tickles and head rubs. In fact, he was actually making up for the missed ones when he was on the streets.

Eventually, Whisper forgave Jim for capturing him. Still, he maintained a keen eye out to make sure Jim didn't have his fishing net anywhere in sight whenever Jim visited.

Whisper never made any effort to go near an open door once he settled into his accommodations. I think there was a part of him that remembered what it was like on the other side, and he much "purrferred" the indoor life.

There were occasions I watched Whisper running in his sleep as he dreamed. I believe he was going through the fields of long ago. He was once again dancing in the sunshine with the feral toms of his youth. When Whisper awoke, he looked over at me and we smiled at each other. He then purred as he laid his head back down to enjoy more napping. He felt content, knowing it was better to dream of the fields than to be in them. Whisper was a gentle wild cat who whispered his way into my heart and the hearts of so many others.

During the last couple of months of Whisper's life, he faced his greatest challenge—cancer. It was one battle he could not win. Even in the final moments, it never conquered Whisper's spirit.

On October 9, 2001, I said good-bye to my very dear friend who started out as an orphan but worked his way up to be an ambassador. The manner this once fierce warrior employed his diplomacy demonstrated the skill of a master emissary I will always remember. He unquestionably possessed a heart of gold with the ability to bring smiles to everyone he came in contact with throughout his short life. I was truly blessed to have been part of his world.

> *Whisper, Whisper, Whisper my cat.*
> *Softly, I speak your name.*
> *Whisper, Whisper, Whisper my cat.*
> *Now and forever remain within my heart.*

February 1, 1993–October 9, 2001

CHAPTER 6

ALL THINGS POSSIBLE

*Everything deemed relevant
is conceivable
in the mind of the cat.*

I opened my mind and thoughts to many ideas. As a result, I observed the impossible turn into reality.

A number of events that I observed should be referred to as dreams. Perhaps these episodes could be called flights of the imagination or wishful thinking. Nevertheless, for me, they indeed took place. I cannot explain them in any other manner.

Many times I witnessed dreams come true if merely for a brief moment and then disappear, leaving behind memories. I saw gifts freely given because of love and devotion. I watched friendships formed, never to be broken. I soared toward the heavens whenever great joy was shared. Other times I stood in silence and cried when deep sadness could not be avoided. From all these moments, a magical way of viewing life awoke within me.

In the following tales, I have shared some of the revelations I participated in since I have been part of lives so different from my own.

The Prettiest Cat

Every creature here on earth is given a beginning and an end. Each one is made of an assortment of parts. When these parts are assembled into a whole, a soul is endowed by the Lord Father. Even though the living being is an individual, he also mirrors others of his kind. More importantly, the living being is a continuation of the one before and the next one to come. So too is the cat, unique unto his own "purrson," a reflection of every other cat, and a link between generations of his kind. The Lord Father put this into motion at the creation of time, and this cycle has persisted throughout the ages.

Many years ago at the end of a long day of assembling cats, the Lord realized there were some leftover parts. He decided to join them together, and they formed the funniest-looking little feline ever made. The other kittens and cats who were watching laughed. The Lord ignored them while he slowly bent over the little female and gave the breath of life, her soul.

Looking around for the first time, the small feline noticed many beautiful cats. She thought to herself, how lucky she was to be just like them! What a wonderful life she would have!

Before very long, the young feline became aware she was quite different from the other cats. She received front legs that were bowed and much too short. Her rear legs were quite long, making her back end stick high into the air. Instead of lush soft coat, she wore fur that was short and coarse to the touch. Plus, a goatee on her chin was most evident. Although very young, the young feline recognized she was quite pudgy. The worst part of all, she didn't have a tail, but a stump!

No!

How could this be possible?

The little feline looked up to the Lord. Tears fell from her eyes as she cried, "Why did you do this to me? Why can't I be as pretty as the other cats?"

In a soft and gentle voice, the Lord Father told the young one she was much more beautiful than all of the other cats ever made. The Lord explained, "When anyone looks into your big green eyes, they will see through them and feel the love contained within your heart. When you smile, others will smile with you. When you purr, it will be a song of joy for everyone to listen to, marvel at, and appreciate. With these gifts, you will always be the prettiest cat since the creation of time!"

The young feline was pleased with the Lord's words. She turned toward the other cats and smiled. They too smiled with her because they understood the Lord Father was right. She was most definitely much more beautiful than they could ever be with the special gifts the Lord had given to her on that day.

And so in an area just outside of New Orleans, this little feline was born. It was an early fall day right before the cold of winter set in for the season. She was given the name of Corkie.

Corkie's mother found refuge in a vacant lot filled with debris. It contained many places for a new mom to hide her litter of kittens and keep them safe.

Diligently, Corkie's mother taught her she needed to always be on the lookout for danger. This troubled Corkie because she longed to be a carefree kitten. Instead, her mother insisted she must learn the ways of a stray cat's life.

It was a struggle for Corkie in the first four months of life, except there were occasions when Corkie disregarded everything her mother instructed for survival. During brief moments, Corkie forgot the words of caution. She delighted in dancing under the sunshine and chasing butterflies through the wind. She loved to play and think about nothing but catching the next bug. Corkie found it fun to run and be free.

Suddenly, it happened!

Tires squealed, and Corkie flew to the curb!

It was late in the day with the temperature dropping. As a result, Corkie felt a chill that ran down to her bones. Given that Corkie hurt greatly, there wasn't any conceivable way she could ever stand on her feet. No matter how hard she tried, it was impossible to move very much. The only thing Corkie could manage was raising her head a few inches off the ground. It was at that very moment a car pulled over and stopped.

Then Corkie heard two voices. For the first time, she wasn't afraid. These humans gently lifted her off the road and carefully wrapped a soft blanket around her cold body. She felt safe and warm in the arms of the man who held her.

The man slowly sat on the passenger side of the car and cautiously cradled Corkie as not to cause any further injuries. The little ball of fur relaxed and purred with her entire heart. The woman drove them, directly, to the emergency veterinary clinic.

Corkie was required to stay in the hospital while the doctor treated the injuries. In a few days, she sufficiently recovered and was discharged. Then Corkie went home with the two humans who rescued her. These humans nursed the wounds and, best of all, loved her. With the tender nurturing given, Corkie grew strong and healthy.

On that cold December day, Corkie lost one of her nine lives. Nevertheless, she found a new life that gave her security and contentment. She lived with these humans for almost twenty years, sharing the gifts of love, smiles, and joyous purrs the Lord Father had bestowed upon her years earlier. Corkie was thoroughly satisfied, knowing she was the prettiest cat the Lord created.

I never ran across anyone before I met Corkie who always looked at life with a smile. I recognize there were occasions when some of Corkie's parts were not working very well. During those times, she had every right to be grumpy; but she never felt that way. Corkie was happy, and it definitely showed in her attitude.

There was never a moment I did not feel Corkie's love when I gazed into her large green eyes. I could not help but smile with Corkie whenever I noticed her smiling. What's more, Corkie possessed the ability to purr quite loud I could hear it in the next room. It was, beyond a doubt, a heartwarming song of great joy.

The only time I saw Corkie upset was the moment she left to return to the Lord Father. When Corkie closed her eyes for the last time, she cried. As the tears rolled down Corkie's cheeks, I realized how deeply saddened she was since she could no longer stay on this earth with the humans she dearly loved.

It has been years since Corkie returned to the Lord Father. Nonetheless, if I quietly listen, I continue to hear Corkie purring a song of joy from the heavens above.

Circle of Life

I once thought the phrase "a circle of life" was a cute cliché or, better yet, a good catch phrase in a song. However, there came a day when I found out the meaning behind those words.

Joseph was my Maine Coon cat who had a birth defect. He received a spinal cord injury that left him partially paralyzed in his back end. I basically taught him how to walk and eventually trained him to use the litter box on command. While cats are fanatical with their grooming, Joseph believed his back end was my responsibility. Therefore, I was the one who kept it clean. I can absolutely say this kitty grew rather accustomed to receiving bottom washes in the laundry room sink.

This handsome Cooner was born with a heart as big as he was in stature, and he loved everyone. Joseph's greatest ability was in nurturing sick kitties. Because of it, I called him my kitty nurse. He also had an uncanny aptitude to sense if anyone needed some extra attention for one reason or another. Joseph then placed that particular one under his wing. He became the protector and advocate of the special individual.

Kotzen, a tiny red Persian cat, came to live with my thundering herd due to health issues that had to be addressed. When Joseph took one look at the old man, it was love at first sight. The feeling was definitely mutual for Kotzen. He too found a true friend.

The biggest common link Joseph and Kotzen shared was both recognized they dealt with similar back end problems. Joseph acquired paralysis from a birth defect, and Kotzen developed severe back leg stiffness from arthritis in his back. Both boys found it difficult to walk. I believe they were instantly drawn to each other because of these handicaps. It was the first time Joseph met someone else exactly like he was, and I bet Kotzen felt the same about Joseph.

My very large Maine Coon followed the little Persian everywhere. They talked together for what seemed like hours. They particularly enjoyed sharing their secret tales and special stories over and over again.

Joseph demonstrated his affection for Kotzen in many ways, especially by gently nuzzling Kotzen and washing the elder's ears. Upon receiving the tender attention, Kotzen closed his eyes and smiled, totally content.

Since Joseph and Kotzen hit it off so well, I thought they had known each other all their lives. The instant friendship developed into a strong bond of love that would never end, even with death. For this reason, I believe Kotzen came back at particular times as a guarding angel to help Joseph.

Mostly, Joseph recognized his limitations. He didn't push his luck by either climbing or jumping. However, Kotzen was another story. Kotzen "purrceived" himself as superman. With that kind of outlook, he climbed and jumped to places that should have been off limits due to his disability. If I caught sight of him scaling a cat tree, I ran at top speed and tried stopping him. Repeatedly, I did not move fast enough and catch him before he reached a top perch. It always terrified me. I was afraid he would fall and injure himself, thereby becoming totally paralyzed.

Joseph understood my concern; consequently, he sought my assistance the moment Kotzen took off on one of his tears through the house. Joseph unquestionably knew the old man needed protection from harm.

Since I insisted Kotzen remain safe, I installed what I called a "kitty corral." This kept Kotzen from leaping from one perch to another perch or scaling cat trees that could be definite hazards to his well-being. It also maintained my sanity. The corral was high enough to keep the old man from hopping over it, but it still allowed Kotzen free access to the back half of the family room and away from the dangers of tall cat trees. Nonetheless, this created a separation between Joseph and Kotzen. It frustrated both of them until Kotzen promptly figured out the means to overcome such an obstacle.

At the exact moment Kotzen decided on a game plan, the old man stood at the side of the corral and called to his best friend. Joseph, in kind, approached the other side and carefully listened to his best buddy. After the clever idea was revealed by Kotzen, both boys bobbed their heads in unison. I swear Kotzen gave Joseph explicit instructions on how to hop over the corral, and Joseph agreed to every word the old man just said.

Shortly thereafter, Joseph and Kotzen took a quick peek around, looking for me. If they couldn't find me, a big thud soon rang through the air. It came from my well-behaved Joseph.

Beyond a doubt, Joseph had a hard time placing his back feet; yet he somehow managed to jump three feet high and clear the corral top! Staring at Joseph's flawless leap, I couldn't believe my eyes. Joseph reached the other side and landed on all fours without one ounce of difficulty!

Having much pride in the accomplishment, Joseph checked out Kotzen's food and water. Kotzen sat directly behind Joseph and patiently waited. Satisfied, after eating delicious morsels Joseph was not allowed to have, Joseph turned around and nuzzled his friend, telling him, "Thank you!"

Afterward, Joseph leisurely climbed on the bottom bunk bed and bedded down. The old man waited until his young friend was settled before he stepped on to the bed to be with his best buddy. Kotzen nestled alongside Joseph. This very large Maine Coon categorically surrounded the little Persian. Then Joseph gently washed Kotzen's face and ears while the elder purred. Both slept for hours. The old man snored, loudly, while the young one purred, softly.

Kotzen was happy, and so was Joseph.

During this time, Joseph and Kotzen developed a ritual they enacted together. It was their secret. They shared it with no one else, not even with me. I made sure I was quiet and out of sight when it started. Otherwise, they would stop if they thought I was watching them. As I intently listened, I could hear their wonderful singing. If I wanted to see the recital, I peeked from a hidden spot and silently observed.

First, both boys faced each other. Next, Kotzen softly sang to Joseph. Joseph then returned the chorus to the old man. They repeated this back and forth while adding new musical notes into their refrains. Their song sounded incredibly sweet and tender. Unquestionably, it was a tune understood by them alone. Still, it was absolutely wonderful to witness such a magnificent recital! Finally, the duet finished when the boys gently touched their heads together and purred.

Time passed in a blink of an eye, and Kotzen's kidneys started to rapidly fail. Everything was done to try to stop the progression, but they were worn out from age and couldn't be fixed.

In Kotzen's final hours, Joseph stayed beside his best friend as the old man slept. Joseph took naps but never for very long. He remained alert and kept a watchful eye on his pal. Occasionally, Joseph ran circles around Kotzen, preventing any of the other cats from coming too close. Joseph also nuzzled Kotzen, seeking to wake him. Heartbreaking, it wasn't possible.

Kotzen was slipping away—quietly and peacefully.

Joseph did not understand what was happening. He begged me to do something. I felt totally helpless because there wasn't anything that could wake Kotzie from his final sleep. There wasn't anything on earth that would make him young and healthy. With tears burning my eyes, all I was able to give both boys were rubs on their heads and tickles behind their ears.

A little before 7:00 that evening, I held Kotzen in my arms as I sat on the floor, with Joseph hanging on to my lap. Joseph was carefully watching his old man, and nothing could divert Joseph's attention away from Kotzen. When Joseph sensed the moment Kotzen drew his last breath, Joseph stood upright and put his paw on the old man. I have seen a cat cry before and saw it again at that moment. Tears fell from Joseph's eyes while he nuzzled, chirped, and purred to his best friend for the last time.

I knew Kotzen was at peace, although losing him greatly saddened me. I never liked letting go of my cats for any reason. Because of their lifespan, it's something unavoidable. Even realizing the old man had lived a life much longer than expected, I was not ready to say good-bye. At the same time, I sensed that these same emotions of loss were also being experienced by a certain feline, my Joseph.

Early the next morning, I stopped at the veterinary clinic and informed my cats' doctor about Kotzen. While there, I explained how Kotzen slipped into a coma the afternoon of the previous day and traveled on his last journey. Peacefully, he went to heaven at 7:00 in the evening.

After relating the news about Kotzen, I returned home. I opened the door and stepped into the house with a heavy heart. In the hallway, I stood motionless for a second and listened. Coming from the background, Joseph's singing was ringing out loud and clear. It was the same melodious tune both Joseph and Kotzen formerly shared many times together.

I was definitely intrigued by the singing. Without a second thought, I promptly walked into the family room. Stepping inside, I noticed all the cats in the formation of a circle around Joseph. They were very silent with heads lowered. Each cat was stationary, except for Joseph. They were keenly watching Joseph's every move. Having my curiosity piqued, I stood behind the circle, frozen in wonder, and observed the proceedings.

Joseph was singing and bobbing his head in the same manner as he often did with Kotzen. I believe Kotzen's spirit was there, singing and bobbing his head along with Joseph. They were saying good-bye to each other. I also believe the other cats were aware of what was happening. Out of respect for both, they silently gave their blessings to the old man as well as to the young one.

In a few minutes, Joseph stopped. He briefly became stationary before he raised his head high and then lowered it. Very tired and with sadness in his heart, Joseph freed Kotzen's spirit to fly to the heavenly home. As quickly as it started, it was over. Gradually, Joseph then settled down on the same place where both he and Kotzen had been together the day before.

After the ceremony finished, some of the cats walked up to Joseph. They bent over him for an instant, nuzzled him, and quietly left. Others, with heads lowered, backed away and carried on with their different activities. In their individual ways, they said farewell to Joseph's best friend and gave their condolences to Joseph. When my turn came, I walked over and sat with my little boy. Tears trickled from my eyes as I petted Joseph's head. In my heart, I too said good-bye to his best friend while I gave sympathy to my little boy.

On the morning after Kotzen died, I witnessed "a circle of life" and came to understand the meaning behind those words. It unfolded when Joseph said good-bye to his best friend Kotzen.

Joseph opened the circle of life he and the other cats shared with Kotzen. In the midst of great sadness inside his heart, Joseph released Kotzen's spirit and allowed Kotzen to return to the heavenly home. For Joseph, the living circle was then noticeably smaller without his best pal in it any longer.

There was something more Joseph shared with me on the morning after losing Kotzen. He showed me that the strong bonds of love and devotion can never really be broken. Love definitely continues after death, and friendships carry over into heaven. And yes, sometimes the spirit of the one who left this world does come back to remind their special loved one of this great gift. Despite that, I wish with all my heart it didn't hurt quite as much for those remaining behind, especially as it did for Joseph.

A Special Hug

Weeks after losing Muffin Man, I still was not coping. The Muffin Man was a special cat who captured more than one piece of my heart, and I couldn't stop the pain from the loss. Mostly, I kept the grief inside and never shared any feelings on the matter with anyone. I really didn't want to talk about these emotions. I just wanted to work through everything on my own. I wasn't sure someone else would ever understand such a reaction. I particularly didn't want to be criticized or told to get over it.

On a Friday night, a few weeks after the Muffin Man died, I went to bed early. I wanted to sleep and not think about anything. It seemed easier than handling heartache during the waking hours. Strangely enough, I have used this method as a coping mechanism since childhood.

At about 1:00 in the morning, I stirred to what sounded like Muffin Man "purrforming" a melody in the hallway by the laundry room. It startled me at first, thinking it couldn't be feasible since Muffin Man was an angel in heaven. Surely, it was just another cats imitating Muffin Man!

Quietly, I tossed the covers back and slipped out of bed. I didn't want to disturb my husband. I was afraid if I told him what I heard, he might have me committed—and quickly! Keeping very quiet, I left the bedroom and tiptoed into the hallway. Joseph, a Maine Coon, with Twinkle, a Siamese, and Megan, a little Domestic Longhair, awakened. All three followed right behind me.

I was surprised the cats didn't hear Muffin Man. Then it dawned on me that they never paid much attention to Muffin Man whenever he crooned one of his songs. They always ignored his serenades, so why should this be different? I guess they accepted it was Muffin Man singing a tune as usual.

Not wanting to chance an ending to the sweet melody, I didn't turn on a light. Still quite groggy from sleep, I managed to peer into the hall's shadows and recognized Muffin Man. This time, I was positive I was sleepwalking. I kept muttering it was just a dream, although deep down inside my thoughts I didn't care because my Muffin Man was back.

Spotting me, Muffin Man stopped the recital and stood on his long legs. He was so handsome in his black-and-white coat. He wore the stature of a young and robust cat. He stared at me with his large green eyes and started purring. I sat down on the floor, and he trotted over to me.

Putting his front paws around my neck, I picked up Muffin Man. Then he wrapped his back legs around my waist while he nuzzled his nose on my neck, the same manner as he did many past times. He always loved gluing himself around me. That way, I could carry him without the use of my arms. Joseph and Twinkle nestled alongside me, and Megan snuggled on my lap.

I held on to Muffin Man ever so tightly. It felt good hugging him again. He purred and purred. Occasionally, he also chirped sweet nothings. I felt happy for the first time in weeks. The sorrow I had been living with disappeared. If it was a dream, I didn't want to wake to reality.

Gradually, I relaxed and leaned against the cabinet at my back. Muffin Man purred even louder when I tickled and petted him. Megan, Joseph, and Twinkle also joined in on the purring. Feeling content, I drifted off into sleep. Shortly, my head seemed heavy and bobbed. Then Muffin Man gently snuggled his head closer, giving support.

Morning rapidly approached, and I awoke. I glanced down somewhat disoriented. Megan was under my chin and sleeping on my chest. Both Twinkle and Joseph were curled together right next to my legs. They too were deep in sleep.

Thoroughly confused, I looked at Megan. Where was the Muffin Man? Did I just dream he had been with me the night before?

I straightened my back, causing Megan to wake. She gently touched the side of my face with her paw as I started crying. Purring her heart out, Megan licked my tears away. Then she cocked her head and stared directly into my eyes. With a very serious expression, she softly meowed. I believe she was telling me everything was all right. I held her tightly exactly as I did the night before with Muffin Man in my thoughts. I rested the side of my face on her fluffy, warm body and kissed her for the tender kindness.

Years have passed and the memory of that night still haunts me, though I no longer view it as a dream. There is a good chance it did happen since the bond Muffin Man and I shared was quite strong.

Muffin Man returned and gave me one of his special hugs at a time I desperately needed it. He realized it was the best way of easing my sorrow. With the Muffin Man's help, I was able to close away the sadness in a secret pocket in my heart.

I have come to the realization that the magic of seeing beyond reality is maybe just imagination, but it is also a marvelous way in which to perceive and deal with many things throughout life.

My Prince

Once there was a "purrson" whose providence was one of royalty. It happened when Jayme was born. Jayme received more than a destiny of nobility. He was given gifts of tenderness, devotion, and kindness, which he freely shared with everyone.

Jayme entered this world on a warm spring day in April of 1988. Since his mother was extremely poor, she sought a shelter for giving birth. Afterward, she went into foster care with her children. The young mother quickly became saddened, knowing she was without means of income and was way too immature to be a good mother. Because of this, she realized she would have to let her precious little ones be placed with suitable families. In that way, they could thrive and be provided with a better life she could never offer.

Deep down inside her heart, Jayme's mother believed her newborn son should receive everything required for a growing child. Reluctantly, she allowed a young and caring princess to adopt him into her home. Hence, Jayme's adopted mother, Princess Megan, fulfilled his needs. She lovingly raised him, and he became a very compassionate individual.

Jayme was a very happy child of common beginnings but quickly learned he was destined for much more. At first the idea of reigning as a prince never entered his mind. He enjoyed life as a happy-go-lucky youngster. Gradually, with maturity, Jayme recognized his destined path.

Thus, Jayme's journey unfolded.

When Prince Jayme entered his teenage years, he accepted the fact his life was changing since he would be the future leader of the kingdom. At first he never quite understood what it entailed. He only knew the subjects respectfully bowed in his honor when they greeted him as he walked about the homeland. This custom caused embarrassment for Prince Jayme each time it occurred. Little by little, he accepted the tradition with humility and humbly acknowledged the responsibility of the position.

The young prince definitely loved the life that was bestowed upon him and everyone in it, especially his mother, Princess Megan.

Princes Megan was very petite with long, flowing hair. Her eyes were green and danced with sunlight. She sang songs of happiness that were heard throughout the land. Princess Megan nurtured everyone; and like her son, she shared happiness with each "purrson" she met. This magical princess also possessed the ability to sense if she was needed. Quicker than the eye could see, she then flew through the air to be with the one in distress to console him.

Princess Megan raised her son well. She shared her wondrous gifts of nurturing and gentleness with him. She taught Jayme to respect others and listen to his inner voice of wisdom for guidance. By doing so, Prince Jayme could then make just and proper decisions as the prince of the kingdom. Watching her son grow, Princes Megan felt he was destined to be special. One day, when he was old enough, she believed he would lead with greatness.

Years passed and Prince Jayme acquired the skills to rule justly, especially from the inner wisdom. Jayme became the respected and loved leader to every subject in the kingdom. In no time at all, Prince Jayme's kingdom prospered under his wise leadership.

As a tender lad, Prince Jayme fell madly in love with a beautiful woman a few years older than his tender age. She descended from the Oriental civilization. Her large blue eyes twinkled with life. She wore dark and very short hair that was soft to the touch. It followed the lines of her face, giving a classic look. This exquisite woman was quite sleek in stature and walked with the elegance of the Oriental culture. She definitely was a beauty to behold. The romance between the two appeared to blossom; but it ended, leaving Prince Jayme heartbroken.

Seeking his mother's advice, Prince Jayme learned for the first time that things in life do not always turn out as expected. Princess Megan understood this was a hard lesson for her son to learn. She hoped, in time, true love could come his way. Princess Megan knew he would find happiness only then.

Princess Megan kissed her son and softly whispered she loved him.

As a grown man, Prince Jayme fell in love for the second time with a girl much younger in age than his years. She was a free spirit. Some called her a flower child. Long chestnut hair surrounded her face and flowed over her shoulders. Her eyes were round and carefree. She took great pleasure in living merely for the moment. She never stopped long enough to make a commitment to anything or anyone. This relationship also did not flourish and ended just like the one of Jayme's youth.

Heartbroken once more, Prince Jayme asked his mother for advice on what he did wrong. Megan wisely responded, "There's nothing you did that caused the relationship to fail." Princess Megan further explained, "Whenever you open up your heart, you must be ready to accept the fact that not everyone will respond in kind."

Princess Megan kissed her son and softly whispered she loved him.

Prince Jayme ruled the land with total benevolence, although the subjects were saddened watching their prince without anyone to love and be by his side. They wished as did his mother he could find someone who would treasure him.

One day, while walking through the hills of the kingdom, Prince Jayme met a pretty young woman. She too was out walking, enjoying the sunshine. The young woman was tall and slender. Her short chestnut hair captured the light and sparkled. She was beautiful in a simple way, catching Prince Jayme's eye.

Reserved, Prince Jayme greeted this pretty young woman. He asked what she was seeking on her journey. Shyly, she looked up at the handsome prince and responded, "Sir, I am looking for someone I can love and share my life with forever!"

Quite surprised and shocked by the young woman's honesty, Prince Jayme asked how she would recognize the one she was searching for during the quest. Tenderly, the young woman stared directly into Jayme's eyes and proclaimed, "I have found the special 'purrson' I am seeking!"

Surprised and shocked yet again, Prince Jayme gazed down at this pretty young woman with affection. Suddenly, he realized he too had found true love.

When the two touched, music of great joy rang throughout the kingdom. The subjects joyously cheered and danced to the wonderful news of their prince finding true love. They raised their voices high toward the heavens, singing the words, "Our beloved prince has found someone to love and who will share his life—her name is Lady Ginger!"

Princes Megan was thrilled beyond words. She joined the singing and was heard above all others. Megan then flew about the land with such tremendous happiness her heart almost burst. Young and old celebrated the union of Prince Jayme and Lady Ginger. Everything would be possible since their prince found true love.

The bond shared between Prince Jayme and Lady Ginger grew strong as the years passed. They became as one. Princess Megan was pleased for her son and her daughter, Lady Ginger.

Unexpectedly, Princess Megan became ill and would have to leave this world before long. Prince Jayme had never experienced death before that moment. Sadly, he was about to discover what it meant.

During Princess Megan's last hours, she shared one last gift with her son. This time, she gave him the gift of insight for looking into his heart. If he needed her guidance, Princess Megan's love would be there to nurture and help guide him.

For the last time, Princes Megan kissed her son and softly whispered she would always love him.

Princess Megan's body was tired, and her time here on earth had grown short. With a deep sadness never experienced before, the prince said good-bye to his mother. On a mild and warm winter day, Princess Megan left her children and joined the others who have gone on before her. Princess Megan's spirit soared to the heavens, and she was gone.

The skies darkened as the kingdom mourned the princess mother's passing. For the first time, the subjects did not hear Princess Megan's songs of happiness throughout the land.

Lady Ginger, like Princess Megan before her, nurtured her prince. She stayed close when he mourned for his mother. She too was saddened by Princess Megan's passing but was more dismayed by the prince's grief. Lady Ginger gently held Prince Jayme as she looked deep into his eyes. Tenderly, she reminded him of Princess Megan's last gift.

With Lady Ginger's help, Prince Jayme carried on with his duties. He found the insight for looking into his heart. True to her word, Princess Megan's love was there to nurture and guide him. With the aid of Lady Ginger and Princess Megan's last gift, Prince Jayme turned his eyes to the future.

In life, things happen for reasons that may never be understood. Regrettably, the prince would soon face this once more. Lady Ginger, his beloved, became ill. She began a journey that would also take her away from Prince Jayme. Way too quickly, Lady Ginger left her prince and joined Princess Megan in the heavens above.

Prince Jayme lost his mother and then his beautiful Lady Ginger. This time, Prince Jayme's heart was totally broken, and there wasn't anyone in the entire kingdom who possessed the power to mend it. Not having Lady

Ginger beside him, Prince Jayme could not find Princess Megan's gift of insight for looking into his heart. Without Megan's love to nurture and guide him, it was more than Prince Jayme could handle. Just a few months after Lady Ginger's passing, Prince Jayme left the kingdom and joined his beloved and mother in the heavens.

To this day, the subjects throughout the kingdom still mourn for the great losses of Prince Jayme, Lady Ginger, and Princess Megan. Even though life always moves forward with one existence passing into the next, a little sadness remains when someone dies who is cherished and respected—as it was in the prince's kingdom.

I met Prince Jayme at the moment of his birth on April 14, 1988. It was 4:00 in the afternoon when I held him for the first time. I assisted Princess Megan with the adoption of Jayme and was privileged to have been a subject in Prince Jayme's kingdom. I watched my prince grow into a handsome gentleman whose wise leadership flourished, never be forgotten throughout the land.

During Prince Jayme's life, I too shared in the great joys that blessed him. I also grieved alongside my prince during the overwhelming losses. In my prince's final moments, I held him close and cried when he left to join the ones he greatly treasured. Then it was my turn. I was the one heartbroken.

Ever since Prince Jayme united with Lady Ginger and Princess Megan in the heavens, I no longer have my prince to reign over the kingdom. For this, I will always feel saddened.

The Shark Frenzy

Alfalfa was a handsome cat with long, flowing, vibrant red hair and green eyes. His twin brother, Spanky, received a softer red coat and golden eyes. Together, both were rescued from the streets when they were juveniles. During the first four months, the two young cats lived as wild kittens since they were born to feral cats. They were eventually captured in humane traps and brought to the local shelter in West Texas.

That was where we met.

The confinement in the shelter was difficult for these two cats. They were terrified of everything, from noises and people to other cats. Subsequently, they spent most of their time huddled together behind the litter box in the back of the cage.

The first time I saw these toms, I knew their stay would not be long given that they were classified as not adoptable. I tried hard not letting my guard down when I volunteered for the reason that many sad stories came in every day. The regrettable part of the job was realizing that most of the animals would never leave to new homes. However, something about these two redheads caught my eye. Whatever made me slip and really look at them, I wasn't sure. I just found that with my defenses weak, I melted and decided to help them since they stole my heart.

I talked to the director. I wanted him to give me the chance to work with these two wild cats. It took a heck of a lot of convincing to get him to relent on keeping them, although such persistence paid off. He finally gave in just so I would stop pestering him and allowed me the opportunity to socialize these toms. If I succeeded, they would be put up for adoption. I recognized it was a difficult challenge, perhaps an impossible one since they were not baby kittens but juveniles and had never been touched by humans.

After I related the background of these two cats to my husband, Pat suggested some names from an old television show, *Our Gang*. I decided the larger of the two should be called Spanky. He was outgoing and won over much easier with soft words, gentle touches, and smelly cat food. I named the other one Alfalfa. He was smaller in stature, wiry in personality, and definitely skittish.

Unlike Spanky's breakthrough of allowing me to pet him, Alfalfa was another story. He expressed little to no trust in humans. He stayed behind Spanky and was not willing to be won over as his brother had been. He jumped, hissed, and growled at the least little movement made in his direction. He would lash out with claws without a second thought. Gradually, with determination or plain stubbornness on my part, I penetrated his resolve and got him to accept me. It took weeks of perseverance, but I accomplished the goal.

There was a small glitch I ran into with these endeavors. It was a problem I did not foresee and something that still made these cats not adoptable. As time went on, I faced the realization that Spanky and Alfalfa trusted no one else except me. Because of this complication, I adopted them. Right before heading home, the important stop was at the veterinary clinic where I worked. They required a complete health check, vaccinations, and most importantly, neutering!

Then it was home.

After a period of isolation and a final health check, I slowly began to introduce them to my resident cats. This turned out to be quite a challenge, and I started questioning my good sense. I often wondered if it was the right thing for these feral cats.

These brothers were still so wild. I had to teach Spanky and Alfalfa how to interact with the feline crew and Pat. It was definitely a challenge. It took every trick I learned on feline behavior to break through their defenses.

Spanky's love of food was my best ally. Basically, it allowed him to partake in many kinds of delectable leftover tidbits in the other cats' dishes. As a result, he soon found the rewards in becoming one of the crew.

Alfalfa could not be tricked in the same manner. He found it harder to adjust as one of the thundering herd due to his nervous disposition. An even more frustrating thing occurred each time Pat raised his voice an octave or two—poor Alfalfa would wet his pants!

Luckily, Alfalfa developed one weakness; and fortunately, I stumbled on it. He loved chasing small toys across the floor. Very quickly, I took full advantage of this knowledge and played for what seemed hours at a time with him. Little by little, he relaxed when the other cats joined in on the fun. The best part was that as Alfalfa's comfort level rose with the surroundings, he stopped having accidents whenever Pat's voice raised a notch or two. He finally understood he did not have to fear either the felines or a particular husband.

More and more, I noticed Alfalfa chose one special toy. It was a small gray-and-white shark made out of a plush material, measuring about three inches in length. It quickly turned into Alfalfa's choice plaything, and he developed a love affair with this shark that continued throughout his lifetime.

Sharky was Alfalfa's security toy. Alfalfa played with the shark and carried it everywhere. Given the slightest opening, he brought the shark to me. We could then play a game of chase. I threw it. Next, Alfalfa brought it back for me to throw again. Most times, I tired way before Alfalfa did.

Alfalfa always kept a close eye on Sharky and slept with it under his head. He must have thought it enjoyed swimming inside the water dish since it was often found there. Soon after it was scooped out, the other cats regained access to the water. Other times it must have been hungry because it was found inside the dry food bowl. There again, it had to be retrieved; otherwise, the other cats refused to eat the kibble. Unknown to Alfalfa and for sanitary reasons, Sharky briefly disappeared and took a spin in the washing machine.

Over time, Sharky showed wear. The fins fell off, and the material wore thin with holes appearing. I stepped in at that point and diligently sewed it. When stitches had stitches sewn into them, I thought it might be in Sharky's best interest to retire. Before proceeding, I began a search for a new one. I figured the hunt would be an easy task. I ridiculously thought any shark, or perhaps a whale, would fit the bill.

Ha!

Foolish me!

That was my idea and not Alfalfa's. Alfalfa definitely retained his own thoughts on the matter. Initially, I sought any type of small shark or whale. Steadily, I fine-tuned the quest and looked for an exact duplicate of Sharky.

I searched for toy fish in every conceivable retail place. I hunted inside toy stores, pet shops, gift boutiques, discount retailers, and so on. I even checked out newsstands at airports. I tried every imaginable place and then some, including exploring through catalogs. Each time I acquired a new one, I joyously presented the possible replacement, only to have Alfalfa tell me in no uncertain terms it was a poor substitute. Still, I never gave up with the search.

Typically, Alfalfa would stare at the newest acquisition for a few minutes.

Politely, he then took it and carried it over to his playhouse where he kept Sharky. He wanted to show Sharky what I had given him. There it would stay, soon ignored with the other rejected fish.

Possibly, I was persistent, or more likely, just plain crazed with my search. I am not quite sure which it was—probably both! From the growing obsession, I looked everywhere. I found sharks in all colors and sizes. Each time I ran over in my mind the new one must be gray, not big or too plush! If I found one that somewhat fit the description and one Alfalfa did not have, I tried to convince myself that well, maybe, *just maybe*, it might be the right one! Upon returning home, I presented it to Alfalfa with great expectations it was the perfect replacement.

How ridiculous I was to think such a thought!

Like so many times before, Alfalfa and I went through the same ritual. In a few minutes, the new shark wound up with the other poor imitations inside his playhouse. At that point, I believed both Alfalfa and Sharky were having a good laugh at my stupidity; but they were too kind to tell me.

I realized I was not going to win trying to find a perfect duplicate. Gaining some sense, I bent to Alfalfa's wishes and accepted the fact that Sharky was here to stay, permanently. I did explain if Sharky wanted to live into old age, he required some repair. Alfalfa understood and agreed.

For Sharky's survival, he desperately required a new skin. After learning the lesson of the shark's significance to Alfalfa, I figured the type of material stood high on the priority list. Much to my relief, after checking out just three fabric stores, I located the right shade of a gray cotton blend and the perfect white material. Both were plush, but not too plush! I quickly bought the two and took them home.

With Alfalfa sitting beside me, closely watching, I carefully sewed Sharky's new skin over the old one. I then gave the fairly restored fish back to Alfalfa. He smelled Sharky, chewed it, and threw it high into the air! Alfalfa was delighted while I was thrilled and relieved at the same time.

Dancing across the room, Alfalfa chased the shark back and forth. He whispered secrets to this special fish while they played together. When he tired, Alfalfa gently carried Sharky to the other sharks inside the playhouse. Alfalfa sported a smile on his face as he presented Sharky. He wanted the wannabe alpha sharks to admire Sharky's new attire.

Alfalfa kept his entire shark collection together and occasionally batted one around other than Sharky. Sometimes I sensed he took pleasure in counting these poor substitutes, making sure none was missing. Even though they were never his first preference, he still never allowed any of the other cats to play with them, not even his twin brother, Spanky, or his sweetheart, Miss Pansy, a beautiful Maine Coon cat.

Sharky always remained the top shark, except it no longer resembled one of its species. Rather, it looked more like a three-inch gray cigar with a white stomach and two small black eyes. It didn't matter to Alfalfa. Sharky was still a majestic gray shark swimming in the depths of the ocean to be "purrsued" and captured!

Whenever I watched Alfalfa with his sharks, I envisioned Alfalfa as the captain of a magnificent ship hunting the great ones. With wind tossing his red hair and the spray from the ocean's waves splashing his face, Alfalfa sought only the largest in the sea. He approached each new challenge of the chase with adrenaline rapidly pumping throughout his body, and he never gave up in each quest. He definitely succeeded in every thrilling sporting adventure!

As for me, I maintained the mission of seeking the perfect shark. Throughout the years, I eagerly presented new ones, thinking one of the latest finds might possibly be the perfect fish. Once again, Alfalfa "purrsisted" to indulge me by adding another pitiful imitation to his collection.

Around the age of fourteen, Alfalfa's back vertebrae started fusing, which put pressure on the nerves that controlled his rear legs. Over the following months, Alfalfa gradually lost most of the feeling in them. Before long, he was no longer able to walk with them.

Actually, Alfalfa adapted quite well to this situation because surgery was out of the question due to other health issues. Alfalfa learned to use a kitty wheelchair and enjoyed getting around in it. He mastered the art of walking, running, drinking, eating, and sleeping with it attached to his body. What's more, he took delight in traveling at full throttle over his brothers and sisters with these new wheels. For a once fearful cat, Alfalfa adjusted to the unfortunate condition beyond expectation.

Alfalfa fought many battles with his health over the years and never let the difficult times slow him down. It was amazing to observe this once feral cat accept so much adversity and overcome it.

On Friday night, January 10, 2003, Alfalfa could not win his final battle with hepatitis. Courageously, he lived with the liver disease for fifteen years.

This time, he could not send it back into remission. He left this life to become a heavenly angel. I believe Alfalfa is once again the master fisherman, sailing on the heavenly sea in search of the perfect shark!

I have not purchased another shark after losing Alfalfa, but it seems I find myself looking at them whenever I run across any, remembering a proud captain and his attachment to a magnificent great shark, Sharky.

A Love Story

Love has no boundaries. It doesn't make a bit of difference whether love is shared by people or cats. This joyous emotion can be experienced by anyone who opens his heart to this wonder, nurtures it, and then cherishes the gift for all of time.

A prime example of a love story is "Romeo and Juliet." It is a tale in which two individuals meet through destiny, fall in love, and lose each other in the course of death. Then these lovers ultimately reunite in the heavens. This also applies to the love story of Alfalfa and Miss Pansy.

On February 22, 1992, a litter of kittens was born to a Maine Coon mother. In this litter, there was a small solid-blue female. She was very plain and nondescript. The sole distinctive mark she acquired was a tiny pink spot on her paw. At the age of three months, each of the kittens, including this little girl, was ready for prospective forever homes. However, no one even took a second look at the little girl. Therefore, she remained in the home of her birth.

It is strange how nature can play tricks. This ugly little kitten who nobody wanted except the initial caregivers grew to be the most beautiful Maine Coon cat ever imagined. She turned into a showstopper and a Supreme Grand Champion in The International Cat Association. Then she was demanded by everyone who took notice of her. Needless to say, it was too late! She stayed where she was really loved—with her original caregivers.

Pansy, as she was known, delighted in the accolades she received on the show circuit. She was very proud of her beauty and accomplishments. She absolutely relished the attention she received and acknowledged it, too. Occasionally, Pansy was headstrong, although she maintained a gentle and loving side for a very special redhead by the name of Alfalfa, Alfie.

When Alfie and Pansy laid eyes on each other, it was love at first sight. Their relationship blossomed and matured over the years. It also remained very tender as in the beginning. On the day Alfie and Pansy met, a romance began that was quite strong it never ceased and was destined to continue as long as there is a heavenly home.

Alfie was of common ancestors, and Pansy came from an aristocratic background. Alfie was an alpha cat who ruled his home well. He seemed worldly and wise next to Pansy's young age. Pansy brought to Alfie her innocence and zest for life. She also touched a part of Alfie's wild side and calmed it.

Alfie was always sleek of body and agile in movement. With youth, Pansy had more legs and big feet than body, making her clumsy quite often. In no time, Pansy's stature grew much larger than Alfie's, but Alfie stayed the dominant of the two.

Pansy was constantly outgoing, and Alfie was always shy. Both were of equal intelligence, and each maintained definite stubborn streaks. They would argue and fight one minute. Then they could be found caressing each other with total fondness the following one.

Not one of the differences or similarities in these cats' personalities mattered to either of them. They really respected and cared about each other. Possibly, it was the combination of their different traits that made them inseparable.

Alfie and Pansy shared a playhouse together and slept close to each other when they spent their nighttime hours inside of it. Alfie adored Pansy and loved every bit of Pansy's devotion. Pansy often held Alfie with her long legs surrounding him whenever she gently groomed Alfie. Then Alfie would relax and fall into a deep, restful sleep while sporting a smile across his face.

Sometimes Pansy lost her temper with Alfie for whatever reason known only to them. When it occurred, Pansy took pleasure in cleaning house and pitched Alfie's collection of sharks in every direction, which definitely got Alfie's attention!

If this heartthrob Cooner spoke one word or flicked a paw, Alfie ran to Pansy without a moment's delay. He was positive she wanted some romancing, but it wasn't always the case. There were times Pansy developed a headache and had no desire for a romp in the hay. Alfie always craved more, even though he lost the family jewels at a young age. As quickly as he mounted his true love, Pansy flipped Alfie over her head and across the floor. Pansy categorically was in charge in that particular department, and Alfie bowed to her wishes on the subject. Reluctantly, Alfie relented until Pansy came into the mood and said yes. Then they sang their special love song, making music throughout the subsequent days and nights.

The romancing part of their relationship helped Alfie keep his health problems in check. Nonetheless, I bet the experts would have questioned such an idea by stating there must be a medical explanation for it to occur instead!

Any time these two cats were away from each other, the one left behind remained glued at the door until their reunion. Because of health problems, Alfie made numerous trips to the veterinary clinic. Alfie quickly caught on that Pansy would nurse him until his strength returned if he pretended he was totally injured upon arriving home. For this reason, Alfie never missed a chance to play the wounded soldier. Most of the time, both Pansy and Alfie "purrferred" traveling together. In that way, Alfie had Pansy to watch out and care for him.

Pansy protected Alfie. She often came to his defense when Aflie deemed it necessary. Alfie enjoyed this knowledge and took full advantage of it. He learned how to be a great manipulator since he realized Pansy was his defender. The moment Alfie felt he received the raw end of a deal on anything, Alfie yelled for Pansy. With head lowered, Pansy grumbled words that required *zip* on any translation and ran to Alfie's assistance. Then Pansy quickly backed the strongest opponent away from Alfie by the expression on her face. Not a soul questioned Pansy's intentions, especially me! Everyone yielded to Pansy's demands. As for Alfie, he simply rolled on his side and laughed amid total pleasure.

Life was perfect. There seemed to be no end, though things do not always stay that way. Alfie's health started to fail. Pansy realized it and remained close beside Alfie. On the day Alfie was dying, Pansy desperately nuzzled Alfie, hoping to make him better. For the first time in their relationship, Pansy could not help Alfie. Still, Alfie tried so hard to respond. With a paw, Alfie stroked Pansy's head while she begged him not to leave. Alfie purred one last time, attempting to soothe Pansy. Heartbreakingly, Alfie then closed his eyes and quietly left.

Pansy panicked!

It was more than Pansy was able to handle. She couldn't let Alfie leave. Pansy fell on the floor and panted. She tried with all her might to join Alfie, except she didn't succeed.

Alfie went to heaven, and Pansy remained on earth. Distraught, Pansy spent most of the time in Alfie's bed where he slept during his final hours. As Pansy dreamed of Alfie, a tear was seen falling from her eye. Then she called out for Alfie, but there was no answer.

Pansy's heart was completely broken without Alfie. Years passed, and the time finally came for Pansy to leave this earth. On that day, Pansy's spirit joyously soared to the heavens and she joined her handsome Alfie. At long last, with Alfie's and Pansy's souls bonded together, the heavens can now be heard rock-n-rolling to their love song—if Pansy consents!

Many laughed at the relationship between a common boy and a purebred girl. It was predicted it would never work out. Obviously, very few understood the depth of the attachment formed between Alfie and Pansy. Their relationship lasted for a lifetime on earth. It was then renewed in the heavenly home, as it was in Shakespeare's "Romeo and Juliet," when the two lovers also eternally joined each other in the heavens.

CHAPTER 7

Never say "grow up"
to a cat
since adulthood
is merely an extension
of living life
as a kitten.

BALANCE

I was never quite sure what would make me an adult. After a great deal of soul-searching, I came to the conclusion that it meant a balance between childhood beliefs and adulthood thoughts. In many ways, I have kept the ideas from my youth since I still dream the dreams of childhood, see the wonderful magic emanating from my cats' antics, and keep the special memories of loved ones alive through my numerous tales by means of the childhood imagination I never lost. At the same time, I live inside the boundaries of adulthood.

More Than One Cat

There's a danger, I suspect, in living with a cat.
If I start with one, then the craving begins to grow.
Without a doubt, they become extremely addictive.
Wherein lies the hazard, existing with a number.
Soon I will grow poorer and downright stranger!

One cat is not any trouble.
The second is a breeze.
The third is easy.
The fourth is a given.
The fifth is a pleasure,
While the sixth just appears.
Suddenly, I find I'm surrounded by a houseful!

Oh my!
Here comes another.
Should I dare?
It is really not hard . . . but heavens, so much hair!

Cats stretched out on the sofa and chairs.
Ten-ton weights curled up and asleep in my bed.
I've swiftly learned the art of squeezing into extremely tight places!

Litter boxes now stacked around the kitchen area.
No bother, I say.
No trouble either.
One box here, one box there.
Oh my, there seems to be fifteen and still growing in number!

Feeding time is a snap.
Learning the art of a feline short-order cooking is, absolutely, a plus.
Line up!
Dish out!
Pick up!
Thank heavens for a heavy-duty dishwasher!

Laundry is done round the clock.
Each load is sorted and pretreated.
When I look for volunteers to help fold,
How amusing, not a cat can be found.
Oh well, the chore beats exercise class any old day!

Cleaning time's a breeze.
The vacuum scatters the group of fur shedders in a blink of an eye.
With the entire crew hidden from sight, the house now looks totally unused.
Finally finished, the dragon disappears into its lair.
Then fur bunnies begin to mysteriously emerge once more!

My language has downright changed.
New words and phrases are most acceptable to my cats.
Funny, how my sentences make sense to only my thundering herd.
No wonder my husband wants me committed!

Now I reckon a cat in my past life I must have been.
Surely, this must be true,
Since my behavior categorically appears "purrfectly" normal to me!

Attachments

I made attachments with many cats who had very little time left here on earth. In the course of each meeting, I totally opened my heart up, only to have it broken when I had to let go and say good-bye. It was not by choice. Mainly, it was because I could not change the way life had been presented to them. If I choose to love, I must accept that I will face sadness and grief with each farewell.

Somewhere, somehow,
It should be possible to touch someone and never let go.

Somewhere, somehow,
It should be feasible to hold a loved one close,
Not for a moment but for eternity.

Quiet Angels

Quiet angels are the cats who came to me for what seemed a brief second, and then they were gone. They became heavenly angels before I was ever given a chance to know them. For the brief time they were with me, I cared and loved these angels.

Buster Brown was a young brown tabby who was abandoned in the area around my home. When I caught him, he was in ill health and died because of feline leukemia, the feline leukemia virus (FeLV).

Red Man was a handsome, three-year-old longhair cat. He was rescued from the streets by my best friend and me, only to lose his life to complications from feline aids, the feline immunodeficiency virus (FIV).

Black Kitty was another stray six-month-old little girl who had been hit by a car in the middle of the road. She died just minutes after I rushed her to the veterinary clinic for treatment.

These three kitties possessed a bright outlook on life. Unfortunately, because of neglect from unknown humans, they were abandoned until they crossed my path. They didn't receive very much in this life and left before they could be given a fresh beginning. They were very young and innocent to die so regrettably, which can also be said for many cats in similar circumstances. I hold on to the belief that at least they recognized I tried making their momentary life here a little better.

Even though their short lives were difficult on earth, they are now at peace in heaven. The joy that was taken from them here on earth will at last be theirs for eternity.

It greatly saddened me seeing these young kitties die. I cared about each one of them. Their lives meant something to me. At least, these quiet angels will find contentment, realizing they shall always keep a place in my heart.

Who Is Superior?

I thought how wonderful to watch dogs act submissive before their human owners. Then I realized how marvelous to observe mankind learn obedience toward their dominant felines!

I have always believed man is not the superior one here on earth. In my opinion, it is the majestic feline, the domestic cat!

Think about it.

Who is delegated to clean the litter box on a regular basis as the other closely watches, making sure it is done correctly?

Who proceeds to the grocery store, again and again, in every kind of weather, seeking the most mouth-watering tidbit for mealtime while the other waits in the comforts of home?

Who prepares a delectable feast for dinner with high expectations it is the right choice, then quickly realizes it is considered litter box material with the demand something else be offered instead?

Who buys a very expensive toy and presents it to his esteemed master, merely to have it completely ignored and then discovers the container it came with is much more interesting?

Who will not move the slightest in bed throughout the long night so as not to disturb his bedmate's precious sleep, even though sleep is deprived and shoved aside on a nightly basis?

Who gets utterly frustrated when the other refuses to come when called for the fiftieth time and finally goes to locate a certain one who declined to "purrsent" himself?

Who gives love freely and then learns his companion gives love with conditions, sometimes with a notarized written contract containing two sets of witnesses' paw prints on it?

Ah, by now, the answer should be easy!

The human is categorically not the one in charge in this relationship. As far as the feline is concerned, the human never will attain such an esteemed position either. In the feline's mind, all things are carried out for the exclusive satisfaction of the honorable cat, and the wise feline maintains complete pleasure in knowing this simple fact. For me, it is a no-brainer since I easily bow to the fact: the cat is superior of the two for the ability to train his human counterpart so completely!

A Cat's Promise

Star was my spider monkey. Actually, she was a little Abyssinian kitty.

This precious cat tried hard to be the best in every endeavor she undertook. In addition to her zest in life, Star always brought a loving heart to her caregivers.

I wanted to give Star the world but could just offer a short period of time. In Star's tender way, she gave her gratitude for my help.

My last breath never did say "good-bye,"
For my love for you is completely timeless.
I bestow my purrs, my wishes, and my dreams,
With you whom I have treasured,
More than fresh catnip and Fancy Feast dinners.

I give what no thief can steal,
The memories of the times together,
The tender and love-filled moments,
The countless smiles shared,
The trials that brought us closer,
And the many paths we traveled, side by side, upon.

I present a solemn promise.
Even though I am home in heaven,
I will always be close at hand.
Whenever and wherever you beckon me,
My spirit will be drawn to you,
By the never-ending bond of our love.

I will come to you,
Anytime you are in need.
Call me and I will appear,
With soft meows, full of hope and comfort,
To lighten your worries,
To lessen every trouble,
And to be your strength to proceed on your course.

I take from you,
The love and the millions of memories,
We have shared through the years.
Beyond doubt, I enter my new life,
As a million-dollar cat.

Grieve not by my departure,
My soul mate for whom I love so much.
Our lives will forever be joined as one.

Sometimes It Takes Ten Years

Some things in life are worth the wait, and this definitely was one of them. Periodically, it can take many long years to go by before it occurs, as in the case with Kody Bear (Kody). Even now I find it incredible whenever I think about how much time elapsed before Kody was at the point I could trust him with total freedom among my feline crew. About ten years passed before Kody would socialize with the other cats and stop his mission of trying to beat the living daylights out of them. When he finally realized how sweet it was to be a part and not apart from the group, it was probably one of the biggest thrills I ever experienced.

I have always explained to others when the introduction of a new cat to a resident cat, or cats, is done correctly, the process should definitely progress in the cat's timeframe. Still, I never thought it could take as long as ten years to accomplish, but it most certainly can.

Kody Bear was a very handsome Burmese cat. He was stocky in stature with a plush and soft coat. His fur was colored like rich chocolate, and he flaunted deep golden eyes. Yet there was a time he wasn't very handsome.

A little more than eleven years earlier, the phone rang. It was a girl I was slightly acquainted with from the local cat club I had joined. She was seeking my help. I talked with her at length. It seemed her cat was very ill, and she could not continue to afford the high veterinarian bills she had stacked up after each visit at her current veterinary clinic. I then suggested she make an appointment at my cats' clinic and explain her financial situation. Possibly, they might work something out on keeping the costs at a minimum and allow her to pay a certain amount each payday. I said she could use me as a reference, and I would help her with any nursing care at no expense on her part.

Sue called and took the cat for an evaluation. Afterward, with Sue's permission, I talked to my cats' doctor and asked how it went. Kathy explained how ill the cat really was and how much treatment was needed. She also thought the cat didn't have a very good chance to survive. At that point, I asked if I could provide the nursing care and promised to cover the expenses on the medical supplies. Kathy grinned. She knew if a cat required special help, I would step in when asked. She set me up with the medications and other necessary supplies for Kody.

I called Sue as soon as I arrived home and explained the game plan. She was very much relieved and welcomed the assistance. A little bit later, I went over to Sue's apartment to begin the fluids, the force feedings, and the medications for her kitty.

When I first arrived, I noticed a very tiny cat inside a cage on the middle of the living room floor. There wasn't much else in it, except a dirty litter box and old food. It did have a water dish, which required changing. The room was dark, so it was difficult to tell very much about the cat until I bent over and touched the kitty. The cat was very thin, and most of his hair was missing. Actually, he was quite pitiful. I bit my tongue to hold back tears since I never saw one in such bad shape as Kody was in and still be alive. I gently spoke while carefully lifting Kody into my arms. I was afraid he would break into two if I held him too tightly. One thing for sure, his eyes spoke everything I needed to know—Kody wanted to live! It was then in my hands to figure out if things could be repaired, and he could have the wish.

As soon as I started giving Kody the meds and fluids, I told Sue how necessary it was to clean out the cage and put something soft for Kody to lay upon to prevent sores. I gave Sue special food for Kody to eliminate malnutrition and bring the cystitis under control.

Before leaving, I made arrangements to come and administer Kody's treatments over the following days. After the second day, I realized Kody required more help than the once-a-day visits afforded. I then asked if I could take him home with me to provide the crucial nursing care.

Thankful, Sue agreed. Honestly, she was relieved.

After arriving home, I was obliged to give Kody a flea bath because he was infested with fleas. I felt they were a contributing factor to his anemia. At that moment, I had no idea if Kody would even survive a bath. If he was going to get better, it was necessary to free him of these awful parasites. Besides, I could not allow fleas inside the house. I unquestionably didn't want my resident cats also coming down with them.

I made sure none of the cats were anywhere around the laundry room before going inside with Kody in tow and closing the door. Everything was prepared ahead of taking Kody out of the carrier. When ready, I gently set him in the sink. Carefully, I poured warm water over his body and covered him with flea shampoo. I then wrapped him with a towel and held him close for a good ten minutes before rinsing him off, giving the shampoo time to kill the nasty critters. While rinsing Kody, I was amazed by how many came off his almost hairless skin. Finally finished, Kody was once again wrapped in a warm towel and held until he was dry.

I couldn't believe my eyes—Kody survived the ordeal!

A little bit later, I arranged a large playhouse in the study. I sometimes used that particular room as an isolation area for new cats upon entering my home. By doing so, it allowed the necessary time for adjusting to the different surroundings, getting tested for medical issues, and receiving treatment for anything that turned up during the initial exam. After passing the medical tests, I then introduced the new arrivals to my thundering herd.

In the interim, Kody was made comfortable inside a very large playhouse with fresh food, water, and a number of warm towels. The next chore was to throw my clothing and the towels into the wash. I finished by sanitizing the carrier and spraying the room with a flea spray before letting my thundering herd have access to it again.

Even though Kody was quite sick and possibly wouldn't live, I hauled him into the clinic the following day and had him checked out for the feline immunodeficiency virus (FIV) and the feline leukemia virus (FeLV). Here again, there was no choice. If he was to stay with me, he couldn't have these deadly diseases. I explained to Sue that if he tested positive on either of them, she should let Kody go peacefully to heaven. Sue consented and gave authorization to the clinic, permitting them to do whatever was required. She also allowed me control over Kody's future medical care.

Kathy drew the blood and tested it. To my relief, the analysis was negative on FIV and FeLV. However, Kathy had reservations about Kody's recovery given that he was badly malnourished, weighing around four pounds when he should be closer to ten. He also was quite anemic, suffered with a serious bladder infection, showed signs of kidney failure, struggled with an upper respiratory infection, and wore very little fur over his tender skin from sleeping on his own urine.

Kody was only four years old to be that close to death, but he was hovering on it. The amazing part, he wanted to live. For the simple fact that he was a fighter, I promised I too would fight with him.

Over the many coming days, I force-fed Kody because he refused to eat on his own. Fluids and other meds were administered. Kody's sleeping towels were changed about six times a day since he still leaked urine from the bladder infection. The skin on his neck required protection. It had become quite raw from the scratching he did when he was battling the fleas. This time, I thought about using a soft collar to cover it. The collar was fashioned from some of my husband's old tube socks and loosely wrapped the skin while shielding the area, allowing the skin time to heal. Kody also made daily clinic visits for nebulizing because of the respiratory infection.

Slowly, as each day passed, improvement started. First, it was inches and then followed by leaps. Kody overcame both the respiratory and bladder infections. Since his bladder had been blocked from a previous infection, his kidneys were damaged. I diligently worked at stabilizing them. Needless to say, the fluids continued to cleanse them. Little by little, the efforts worked. Kody's health returned. I was elated to actually notice Kody turning into a real cat once more. Not wanting to incur more problems, everything was kept in place to make sure he would keep his newfound health.

Given that Kody was prone to bladder infections, he needed an acidifying diet to prevent future ones. He hated it, saying it mildly. It took about six months and some chicken liver mixed with it to persuade Kody to eat on his own. Finally, Kody decided the food wasn't that bad. It was wonderful to observe this kitty beg for food at last, especially the prescription diet!

Kody put weight on his once skin-and-bones body. He soon topped the scales at ten pounds plus. The missing fur grew back, and the kidneys stabilized. Feeling in good health, he turned into a very active cat and discovered he loved playing with toys. Pat then took Kody out of the playhouse in the study for one-on-one attention and the exercise he lacked when inside of it.

As time passed, Sue stopped coming to visit with Kody. She also stopped calling to check on him. I sensed she realized she could not care for Kody. I think she appreciated he was in the best home possible, where his needs were completely met and, the greatest part, Kody was loved! I believe she just didn't want to say the words she couldn't keep him with the unending expenses from his ongoing medical issues.

After Kody's health returned, I moved Kody's playhouse in the main arena (the back section of the house) with the other cats. I wanted to begin the process of introducing him to the feline crew.

I found only one slight obstacle.

Kody had never been neutered. Up until that moment, he was too sick to even think about it. At long last, Kody was in good health and began feeling his tomcat oats. True to form, he did what any other whole male cat would do in this situation—*spray!* I decided at that point it was time for a talk with Kathy about fixing the problem.

Kathy and I quickly agreed on the solution. If Kody was well enough to spray, Kody was well enough to undergo anesthesia. Not long after, Kody Bear lost the family jewels. One more time, he defied the odds and made it through the procedure.

Periodically, Kody was faced with other health issues but none that couldn't be conquered. He beat many odds, and I am positive it was because of his strong and determined will to live. He eventually required an operation to enlarge his urethra. The procedure prevented him from blocking, ever again, when urinating. For a cat bordering on death at one time, he made it through the surgery and quickly recovered.

During the coming years, I tried every trick I learned on feline behavior to stop Kody's feline aggression. I hoped to conquer his tomcat hostility and allow him among the other cats. This was one area where Kody was incredibly stubborn with his opinions and did things his way. He was the most gentle and loving cat until he was loose with the other felines. He then had only one thing on his mind: he was determined to tear them into shreds!

I wanted to keep Kody close by the cats. I thought if he could watch how they mixed with each other, he might calm down enough to appropriately interact with them. In that case, I could let him out without any restraint.

In the meantime, I recognized Kody required plenty of exercise space to stay healthy, except his current playhouse did not offer this luxury. Shortly, I found a solution I stumbled across in a cat magazine and purchased a jumbo enclosure. It contained Dutch doors for easy access and cleaning. On the outside door, a sign that read "Kody's Place" was hung.

Kody's new home was positioned in the middle of the cat trees inside the sunroom area. This gave Kody a "purrfect" advantage to observe his surroundings while allowing everyone else the opportunity to see him.

The playhouse was quite large. I could actually walk inside with ease. It was the size of a small room, containing multilevel perches and catwalks. A cat tree, bed, covered litter box, food and water, and toy basket along with scratch pads were also available in it for Kody.

Kody moved into his new home, which had been placed in front of a window. This gave Kody the chance to bask under sunshine and view outdoor activities. Very quickly, I realized Kody never looked out a window before since it scared him. Gradually, he accepted the benefits it offered and enjoyed the accommodations.

The other cats climbed all over the outside of Kody's enclosure, delighting him when they did. He realized how fun it was to extend his paws out toward them. They too thought it was entertaining to stick theirs inside and tease Kody. Friendships were made, even though Kody still could not run free among the crew. Some of Kody's favorite felines became Tigger, a Domestic Longhair, and MeMe, a Maine Coon.

MeMe found enormous pleasure in sleeping on top of Kody's playhouse. Stretching out, she periodically dangled her tail inside the enclosure, keeping it just far enough away from Kody's grasp. This drove Kody crazy as he tried to grab and then miss it, but he prized the game anyway. Tigger's trick was playing paddy paws with Kody. Each took their turn seeking to catch the others' paws. Both of these games, with the three cats, were daily rituals.

Pat taught Kody to wander about the main arena with a harness on his body and a lead clasped on the back of it. Pat walked Kody among the cats and let them socialize together. Kody was fine as long as he was in tow but became a missile if he escaped. Then Kody strategically headed for the nearest unsuspecting and innocent victim in order to thrash! I had a hard time figuring out how Kody could be an angel one minute and a complete terror the following one. By showing this response, Pat and I were always kept on our toes whenever he was with the crew.

At nighttime, Pat watched television upstairs. Kody accompanied him, giving this kitty free time. The other cats didn't have access to the front part of the house or upstairs. As it turned out, it was an ideal opportunity for Kody to run without any restraint for as long as he wanted. It was also fun to watch Kody sprint up the staircase at full speed with his tail upright in the air! He did this to get there and search for tissues to eat before he was stopped. I am positive Kody knew where every tissue box, toilet paper roll, and paper towel was located. Silk flower arrangements were Kody's next mouth-watering prize to seek, munch on, and then throw up! Finally worn out from the adventures, Kody curled on top of Pat for a nap. Often I found both sleeping very comfortably together.

One day, when I was cleaning Kody's playhouse, Page, a Maine Coon cat, jumped over my back into Kody's Place. I was stunned because Kody did not attempt to either chase or hurt her. Instead, he ran to Page and licked her face. I froze in total shock and disbelief. Then the thought passed through my mind. Could it be that Kody is finally ready to interact with the cats without any restraint?

Over the following two weeks, I let Kody roam about without a harness and lead. Whenever he escalated, showing indications of aggression, I escorted him back into his special house. These outings became longer and longer until the moment arrived when Kody protested bloody murder about spending anytime inside the enclosure.

I finally won!

No, it was Kody who won.

Kody no longer required a division to separate him from the rest of the feline crew. At long last, Kody chose not to be a bully. The attitude change was totally Kody's decision. I had nothing to do with it. He was the one who decided about doing away with the aggressive behavior. Maybe there was something in this togetherness thing he had been watching for so many years that amended his thoughts. I will never know for sure what exactly altered his thinking. The reason really didn't matter because for the first time, Kody could be in direct contact with his feline buddies without any confrontations. He really loved the close bonds he then formed with them.

Thereafter, when I looked around for Kody, I found it very interesting to observe him sleeping inside the big basket on the floor. Frequently, he was curled in a ball with Twinkle, a seal point Siamese. Occasionally, I would notice Kody on top of his former playhouse in another basket, where he was passing the time of day with Sam Roofus, a young, red-and-white tabby. Never in my wildest dreams did I ever consider these interactions would someday occur! Without a single doubt, I was undeniably pleased to see it happen.

Having no expectations and a great deal of patience on my part did pay off because Kody finally learned the social skills for running free among the resident thundering herd. Kody made strong friendships that would never be broken. The only regret I had was that it took about ten of those years to conquer Kody's male aggression and get him to be as sociable with cats as he was with people.

In life, there are things that can change and there are so many that cannot.

Death can be fooled for a moment but not forever. Sadly, time ultimately did catch up with Kody. Kody's health deteriorated. He finally exhausted his nine lives and not even his strong will to live could help him win his last round with health issues. Kody's kidneys were failing, and this time the progression could not be stopped.

I was in the laundry room, conquering my ironing for the week. Kody came in and rested by my feet. After finishing, I sat on the floor with Kody. I wanted to give him some tickles. Cautiously, he stepped on my lap and stretched out. This time, Kody looked at me with sadness in his golden eyes. I understood what he was telling me.

Kody was saying *good-bye*.

It was 3:46 in the afternoon on July 1, 2002, and Kody went into cardiac arrest. He was gone before I could say a word. Thankfully, it was quick and he never suffered. Still sitting on the floor, I gently held Kody as he went home.

My precious Burmese left this world to join his other brothers and sisters in the heavens. I was happy for Kody, but I couldn't help feeling brokenhearted because he was no longer on this earth with me. I was also greatly saddened for Pat since both Kody and Pat were the best of friends for the many years Kody shared with us.

I firmly believe patience does pay off; although admittedly, it can take quite a bit of time to accomplish the goal, as it did in Kody's case. Kody Bear was a remarkable cat who defied death for over eleven of his fifteen years. He lived with chronic kidney disease and a few other health issues, starting before our first meeting. Kody possessed a will to live that defied everything imaginable. He absolutely was beautiful of spirit as he was handsome in stature.

KODY'S BEAR

I gave Kody a pillow bed shaped like a brown bear and was positive that Kody would use it. I think Pat considered I was out of my mind with the idea. Deep down inside, I had a hunch Kody would like it because it possessed two of his choice things in life: the bear was soft and definitely cozy.

When I put the bear inside Kody's playhouse, Kody didn't have a clue what to make out of the thing. However, not much time passed before Kody fell in love with it. He agreed the bear was an ideal bed. Then I'd notice

Kody with his chin resting on the bear's head right between its ears while he stretched out upon its body. Other times Kody curled in a ball on its back.

Presently, I can see Kody enjoying the pillow whenever I look at it, even though Kody is a heavenly angel. I can't help but believe Kody occasionally sneaks back to sleep on the bear. I only have to close my eyes and picture it.

Kody rode his bear on home, alleluia!

Three Girls from Next Door

In the early nineties, new neighbors moved into the house right next door to mine. They came with their two cats. Both cats were shaded silver in their coats. One was a Domestic Longhair and the other a Domestic Shorthair.

Tammy Fae was the cat dressed in the long and lush coat. She wore black eyeliner around her beautiful yellow eyes and flirted with them whenever she wanted anyone to notice her. She always maintained a slender physique and was very proud of it, too! Tammy was very outgoing and took satisfaction from being the center of attention. Tammy could also be a tomboy and a princess at the same time. It didn't matter which it was because she enjoyed both positions.

Shasta was the shorthaired cat and sported a stocky, round body. She was very cute and quite cuddly. Shasta was the worrywart of the two kitties and took life quite seriously. She found pleasure in simple things and never forgot to show her gratitude for them. As a kitten, Shasta believed her duty was looking after Tammy Fae and did so into adulthood. I have to say that the one thing Shasta especially enjoyed more than anything was the company of her humans.

Both cats were independent and feisty. I think that is why I fell in love with them since they definitely recognized what they wanted and didn't waste a second going after it.

Jim and Carla moved into their home in early spring and went on an extended vacation during the following summer. Seeing as I did not know them very well at the time, they asked a friend of theirs to come each day and look after the pool and take care of the cats. On each visit, the friend was accompanied by her grandchildren. Both Tammy and Shasta did not like either the kids or the friend for that matter. Thereafter, they decided to run away from home and assume residence on my back porch.

Watching them through the window, I felt sorry for these cats. They acted so forlorn. I knew who they were, and I was also well aware they had a good home with food and water supplied to them. Yet they refused to return to their residence as long as a particular woman was enlisted for tending to their necessities. Soft hearted me, I began feeding and taking care of them in my yard.

Every time I was outside, Tammy and Shasta followed me wherever I ventured. They also never wasted a moment telling me tales about how they were abandoned. These two storytellers further embellished their pitiful tales by describing that wicked lady and those boisterous, mean children who came just to throw old bread crumbs into their food bowls. They swore the worst part: they were never given any fresh water to drink and had to find some from the puddles made by the sprinkler system. And sadly, what they missed most was someone who could give them a little TLC and love since that terrible woman and those two little hellions hated cats. Worst part: they enjoyed terrorizing Tammy and Shasta whenever possible!

I listened to the tales and smiled. I knew better than believe a single word these two cats were telling me. Still, I looked after them because they had me wrapped around their paws.

When Jim and Carla returned from the holiday, Tammy and Shasta refused to go back to them. Their feelings were hurt. Consequently, these two headstrong cats thought Jim and Carla should be sufficiently punished. These kitties were also mad as sin, feeling they had been abandoned and left in the hands of such a horrible person, the friend. They believed the conditions under her watchful eye were so dreadful they were obliged to find someone else who would treat them properly, and that person was me.

Jim and Carla became good friends with my husband and me because of these two cats. As a result, during future vacations, I took care of Tammy and Shasta. I looked after them next door since I wanted Tammy and Shasta to realize their place was with Jim and Carla and not with me. I did everything to make these kitties recognize this but failed.

For the duration of their human parents' absence, I went next door and put out fresh water and food in the garage for these cats. Tammy and Shasta ate their banquets and then supervised everything I did. After cleaning the pool, I sat on a lounge chair with both cats beside me. When I was sure they were enjoying the warm sun, gentle breeze, and catnaps, I'd quietly return home. Before putting one step into my yard, the two cats were back on my porch, waiting.

Eventually, Tammy and Shasta returned to their original home less and less. They still visited with Jim and Carla whenever Jim and Carla were outside. Afterward, these cats returned to their chosen residence—my home.

First, Tammy made her way into the main arena (the back section of the house) and joined my thundering herd. Soon after, Shasta followed. Jim and Carla then came over to my house and visited with their cats.

These cats adored Jim and Carla, although they decided they "purrferred" to reside with me. They especially desired to be indoor cats. Because of Jim's allergy problems, Jim and Carla realized the cats could never be inside with them. They were comfortable with their cats' preferences. They allowed them to remain and live in their selected home.

Right before Jim and Carla moved to a nearby city, which was closer to their grandkids, an abandoned brown tabby made her way into their yard. This young female tried convincing Jim and Carla to take her in, except she was unsuccessful. Amazingly, not really, she too found her way over to me; and I ended up adopting her.

I was always a little suspicious that Jim somehow managed to put the brown tabby inside my garden room in order for me to rescue her. I have a sneaky feeling Jim figured I would give her a home since he could not take her to the new residence.

Carla named the cat Cuddles. As for me, I would have named the kitty after Jim's mother who was spirited, talkative, and headstrong—just like Jim! Obviously, the young cat definitely demonstrated the traits.

Needless to say, I hated when Jim and Carla left. I appreciated they permitted Tammy and Shasta to stay with me. By doing so, it was as if a part of Jim and Carla remained behind. Also, since Cuddles appeared at the midnight hour with a twinkle in her eye, I never forgot the twinkle in Jim's eye either!

I was grateful to Tammy and Shasta for helping develop the friendship between their first caregivers and their second ones, my husband and me. Beyond a doubt, I came to be as fond of Jim and Carla as I was of their cats.

Totally Misunderstood

Some cats are totally misunderstood. At least that is what they try to convince me of immediately after I catch them up to mischief. I have two suspects who match this description quite well: Timmy, a three-legged tabby, and Garfield, a headstrong cream boy.

By totally misunderstood, I mean these cats can be hellions one moment and wonderful cuddle bugs the following minute. They have the ability to get me madder than sin, almost at the point I want to string them up for their behavior. Then on the flipside, they can be so sweet I can't help but adore them. Without any reservations in my mind, they view themselves as "purrfect" and well-behaved felines with the rest of the world a little wacky, especially me!

If I look at these two cats, I see two charming earth angels wearing slightly crooked halos and sprouting a pair of devil's horns at the same time. They can either be very good or very good at it.

When Timmy was born, his back leg on the left side became entangled in his umbilical cord. Because of this unfortunate mishap, he lost the foot along with the lower part of the leg. The people who found this baby dropped him off at my cats' veterinary clinic, where he was raised by the staff. Even though Timmy was well cared for, he never received particular social skills necessary for him to develop into a well-behaved adult. By lacking either littermates or a mom to teach correct feline etiquette, Timmy developed some attitude problems. As a result, my cats' doctor asked if I would give Timmy a good home; and I agreed.

Timmy fit in my household resident felines without much fanfare. It helped having a kitten to play with him since Timmy was two years old going on the age of six weeks. He needed to learn how to properly interact with both cats and humans. Kitten play definitely helped Timmy acquire some good feline manners. He improved greatly, but he still found trouble keeping his temper. Even now, each time he loses it, there is no reasoning with him. The ideal way of calming this kitty is sending him to his room to chill out. The other personality of Timmy has never stopped turning him into a "mushmallow"—giving kisses while being held and cuddled.

Garfield was a headstrong and mischievous kitten. He never lost this attitude as he grew older. The word *no* to Garfield just meant how fast the act could get accomplished before being stopped or doing it, knowing punishment for the deed will shortly follow. This approach carries on to this day.

It never fazes Garfield in the least bit to take a bite out of the human who is petting him and then purr his head off while obtaining the pound of flesh. Recognizing when to back off before Garfield escalates definitely helps his temper remain in check, except don't ask Garfield's veterinarians how loving he can be! They have seen his temper and his don't-touch-me side on too many occasions.

Timmy and Garfield are now full-grown adults. Both have improved greatly over the years, but they retain moments that are questionable. Currently, when solicited about this matter, either one doesn't miss the slightest chance to inform me they are always sweet and would never think of doing anything wrong in a million years. If I have a weak moment and think differently, these kitties rapidly put me in my place by informing me I am having a flight of fantasy and they are totally misunderstood!

CHAPTER 8

COUNSEL

⌣ᴧᴧ⌣

*To give advice
is judged not "purrtinent"
for the all-knowing cat.*

⌢ᴧᴧ⌢

Quite frequently, I am solicited for kitty advice. For the most part, it's about how to deal with a particular behavioral predicament. I generally address the problem in a short note or with a brief conversation.

Occasionally, I am asked for guidance on making the right choice, as a kitty is coming to the end of his life. This is hard for me because what I do may not be what someone else can carry out. I try hard to direct the person without making any of the decisions. It is only when I see the kitty requires help that I step in and firmly guide the caregiver with selecting the necessary options.

I also write notes and letters of condolences to friends following the loss of their cat. Often I find that it affects me, deeply, especially if I had been close to the kitty. For a few, I give gifts of remembrances along with letters of explanations of these gifts.

I Wish You Enough

Over the years, I have listened to many versions of this saying. When I first heard these wishes, they were spoken to me by a teacher who taught me math in high school. She said if there was one thing she could share with me, she would give me some thoughts to remember her by in the coming years. I have never forgotten the wishes, nor have I forgotten that exceptional mentor.

Since then I have presented my adaptation of the verse to some of my cats' doctors in appreciation for the expert and compassionate medical treatment of my little ones when it was dearly required.

I wish you enough heavenly sunlight,
To constantly maintain a bright attitude.

I wish you enough cool rainfall,
To definitely appreciate life a great deal more.

I wish you enough warm happiness,
To forever keep the tender spirit alive.

I wish you enough painful sorrow,
To allow even the smallest joy appear much bigger.

I wish you enough earthly gain,
To completely satisfy any desires for wanting.

I wish you enough regrettable loss,
To always be grateful for all blessings.

I wish you enough bountiful hellos,
To help face the one lasting good-bye.

A Letter of Advice

This was a letter I sent a dear friend when she asked me for help. Pam was worried her daughter might be too attached to her super senior cat, thereby clouding good judgment when making necessary decisions for Sophie. Pam wanted my thoughts on how to assist her daughter. She sought to shield Anne from hurt, but she realized she must accept the fact that it is not always possible to achieve.

> Pam,
>
> As for Sophie . . .
>
> I have a strong belief in life, all life. It is given to every living creature here on earth by a greater power . . . the Lord Father. Since man is theoretically the caregiver of this world, it puts a tremendous responsibility on every one of us. As a human, I cannot create life or take it; but there are times I have the power to ease the suffering of the special creatures under my care and allow death to come quickly. It is a decision made when the one dying has said enough, disengages from this world, and walks the path each one of us will someday walk. It is then time to release my charge; and I do, although I will walk with my little one as long as there remains a desire to live. When there is no more fight or the only thing left is unrelenting pain and suffering to come, I will say good-bye.
>
> Sometimes I chose "the gift of peace" if my cat cannot live any longer without agony. With the compassionate aid of a veterinarian, I helped my kitty leave this life because there was no other alternative. I did it out of love for my cat and not for me.
>
> I stood by my little one's side on other occasions, cradled him in my arms, and allowed the Lord Father to take over.

There was no distress as my cat slipped quietly away. I did not have to opt for a quick release through euthanasia as a higher power stepped in and helped.

Whatever I opt for, it is not easy. My heart always questions me. Even so, I cannot make the decision for my cat. I allow the cat to inform me.

There is no easy answer, dear friend. I cannot tell someone else that a decision must be made. It is something that should be done individually. Money is not an issue. Therefore, Anne can give the best quality of health care available to Sophie, allowing some more precious moments together before the final good-bye. Anne loves Sophie, and she will recognize the time when they must part. Until then, both can be with each other, enjoying life.

I can help Anne understand the questions she should ask. The following examples might help Anne find guidance with the next step . . .

Does Sophie keep food down? Is she in pain that cannot be eased? Is she able to get to the bathroom (litter box)? Does Sophie want to just hide? Can she still enjoy small things in life? Does she respond to me? Is there quality of life for Sophie? Is Sophie asking me to let go, so she can?

Sophie needed a great number of teeth removed. Such a procedure sounds horrible, but it happens to many kitties. A number of mine had some drastic dental work done, too. They are fine today.

Old age, for any creature, demands special adjustments. Physical ailments are part of it. These problems can be treated. No veterinarian would put Sophie through any procedure if there is not already quality of life or if it is not possible to have a better quality after it is done.

It is difficult watching Anne and Sophie go through their trials. I know your heart is breaking for both. You are wise to listen and not tell Anne what to do. It might not be your option; it's Anne's choice. One day Anne will call with tears, recognizing it's time for Sophie to leave. Until then . . .

Be strong and listen.

I will also contact Anne and listen.

Something to Think About

I wish the energy of duplicating a life, even a cat's life, could be aimed at finding cures for diseases, especially cancer. Sadly, I have said good-bye to many loved ones because there wasn't a viable medical treatment available that could alleviate their problem. Surely, it would benefit everyone if the money spent for cloning would be used in eradicating diseases.

I also wish cloning wasn't done for the sole purpose of wanting to keep the original alive in an exact carbon copy. Truthfully, it cannot be accomplished.

A while back, someone asked me, "What do you think about cloning—cloning cats in particular?"

At that moment, I didn't have a clue on how to respond. I just shrugged my shoulders, admitting I didn't know.

The acquaintance further inquired, "How does man think he can create a life, specifically a cat's life?"

Here again, I didn't have a reply. I wanted to find the right answer about what I believed before expressing my thoughts on the subject. This time, I shook my head and remained silent, acknowledging just uncertainty.

I maintained many mixed emotions about the procedure. I thought about future cats born into this world and never getting adopted since a potential home for a stray might be taken away by a clone. Consequently, I wasn't sure I could ever answer the question appropriately.

The middle of the night has always been the time I do most of my serious thinking. So it was not an unusual hour to question myself on what I believed, chiefly on the whole idea of cloning a living being. As the hours trickled away, I found an answer.

I do not agree with cloning another living being for many practical reasons. My main objection is that I think it is wrong to try to duplicate another living creature. I believe each living being is a unique individual. Man is able to jumpstart the process of growth inside a cell. This cell then divides and develops into a living form, but the Lord Father gives this creation its real life. He imparts a soul, thus making these cells more than a combination of living parts; and only the Lord will ever have the capability of giving this incredible gift.

Nature has always been able to initiate the process of a life. With modern technical skills, man acquired the knowledge to replicate the procedure. Through this process, a cell is capable of thriving and growing into a living form. Neither man nor nature has ever been capable of giving true life—the soul—making these cells a living being. In reality, it is done by the Lord Father.

Presently, when I am asked about cloning, I respond:

"Man can engineer a cell to expand into a living form, except the Lord Father makes it a living creature by providing the soul. Genetically, the clone is an identical to the one it came from, although it will never be an exact carbon copy. I do not think humans should be quite so egotistical to believe they are the ones who created this living being. It saddens me to think mankind presumes it can be accomplished and continues for reasons that absolutely don't make much sense."

I guess I have found an answer since I can truthfully say, "I don't believe in cloning another living being, particularly a cat, for the purpose of keeping the original alive because it cannot be done. From original DNA, a new life is created, having the genetic makeup of the one it was derived from and nothing more. The new life stands apart and is distinctive from the original for the clear-cut reason that it has its own soul given by the Lord Father."

A Letter of Condolence

Every time I lose a kitty belonging to someone else, especially one I have been close with, it hurts as much as if I lost one of mine. I doubt that part of me will ever change either.

I helped raise Chutney, a very handsome Maine Coon cat. After he was adopted, I lent a hand in his care over the years. Needless to say, when Susan and Geoff lost him, I too felt their sorrow.

This was the note I sent them.

> Susan and Geoff,
>
> I am truly sorry for your loss . . .
>
> Sadly, I have walked the path you just traveled, and I am afraid I'm destined to do it again in the future. I have said good-bye more times than I wish to count or remember, and it never gets easier. For this reason, I truly understand it is difficult letting go of someone you love, but time helps put things in perspective, and life continues, even though it has changed. Chutney will always be in your thoughts, and his love will remain within your hearts.
>
> The following is a quote from an essay, "The Once Again Prince," I was given years ago written by Irving Townsend. I often read these words and have taken comfort from them. I hope you can, too. I also added my version to his words at the end of it.
>
> "We who choose to surround ourselves with lives even more temporary than our own live within a fragile circle, easily and often breached. Unable to accept its awful gaps, we still would live no other way. We cherish memory as the only certain immortality, never fully understanding the necessary plan."

The life of a cat, often a mere fraction of our own, seems never-ending until one day. This moment has come and gone for the both of you, Susan and Geoff. You now find yourselves in a somewhat smaller circle, unable to believe you will not catch Chutney stretched upon his much treasured blanket with his lion under his head as each day passes. Think of him enjoying these simple pleasures and dreaming of things only a cat daydreams about with his half-closed eyes and bushy tail gently moving with contentment.

Chutney is a majestic cat, strutting quite proudly in heaven. His purrs will not go unheard. Now close your eyes and gently listen. Take comfort knowing he is with your first kitty, Pretzel, and someday, they will joyfully greet you again.

The Prayer of St. Francis

This is my interpretation of the traditional prayer of St. Francis. I believe since St. Francis is the patron saint of animals, it belongs to each and every creature here on earth.

Oh Father,
Grant that I may never request to be consoled as to console.
Watch that I may never seek to be understood as to understand.
And see that I may never ask to be loved as to love with my whole heart.

Oh Father,
Permit me to bring peace where there is hatred.
Let me present healing where there is pain.
And allow me to offer confidence where there is doubt.

Oh Father,
Bestow upon me the gift of sharing hope if despair abounds.
Provide me the ability of leaving light should there be darkness.
And furnish me the capacity of departing joy when there is sadness.

Oh Father,
By forgiving others, I will be pardoned.
In giving of myself, I will receive.
And through passing, I will again be born.

Things Broken

There was a time when I dropped a glass dish but caught it in midair. As a result, I prevented it from breaking. I confess being quite pleased with diverting the dish from disaster and, definitely, the garbage. Afterward, I did other chores and never gave a second thought on what almost happened.

Later, somewhere around 4:00 in the afternoon, I served my cats their tasty dinner. When every cat finished, I began washing and drying the dishes. Suddenly, the same dish, which was almost lost earlier, flew out of my hands. It hit the tile floor and shattered into many pieces before I could stop it. There was nothing left aside from cleaning up the mess.

I was angry and annoyed for such carelessness and kept muttering under my breath that I should have paid better attention to what I was doing. Thinking it was totally my fault, I blamed myself and felt irresponsible for allowing the dish to fall and break.

Sometimes seemingly stupid things can really bother me. This was, undeniably, one of them. It was a small dish, and it could easily be replaced. Even knowing this, I still kept thinking I should have been more attentive and prevented it from slipping out of my grasp.

After completing the feline responsibilities for the moment, I started preparing the evening meal. As the frustration within me subsided, I gradually recognized that what was upsetting me wasn't that I broke the dish. I was distressed because I recently lost my beautiful Abyssinian cat, Star, and felt I failed her. I realized, many times, I did save her life, although eventually the day when there was nothing more that could be done to alter her destiny came. It didn't matter how much I tried. There was nothing on this earth that could stop the progression of the kidney disease that took her life, but a part of me found a difficult time accepting the situation.

I smiled, thinking perhaps it was the same with this dish broken earlier. Even though the dish was once redirected from disaster, it too had a destiny to meet. In the end, nothing could change its final outcome.

Little by little, I put into perspective the loss of Star and made peace with myself. I came to terms with the fact that the ultimate outcome couldn't be avoided, and it didn't matter how hard I tried because that was completely beyond my ability. The progression of the disease was slowed toward the final conclusion, even though the ending didn't change. For that reason, I shouldn't take on the burden of guilt, believing I failed.

In life, I recognize some things are out of reach and cannot be conquered. The means of attaining this feat is found in the Lord Father's hands, not in mine. Time may stop for a moment as I help extend life, except it can't be done forever. In the end, I must let go and move on with living. Nevertheless, it doesn't mean the special one just lost should be forgotten.

Paw Prints in Our Hearts

A very good friend of mine lost her kitty and said, "I never thought it would upset me as much as it did to lose my cat since she wasn't one of my favorites, but it did."

I responded by explaining my feelings about it. From a familiar saying, I shared my thoughts and said, "Each one of our cats leaves paw prints inside our hearts. It turns out some leave bigger ones than others. All the same, it really doesn't matter if these paw prints are big or small. We still care and love every cat exactly the same. Needless to say, it upsets us when we lose any of them."

Never Give Up Hope

Not long ago, a friend was presented with a very poor prognosis of her cat's health. She was scared and cried because she didn't want to lose her kitty. Noni turned to me and asked, "Should I give up hope?"

My heart also cried when I heard the details of the kitty's condition. I understood the situation was serious. It was very likely Callie might not live through the weekend. She was ever so fragile and gravely ill from kidney failure.

Medical support and some very good nursing were certainly required. It was one area in which I could definitely help on account of my nursing skills. The most important part I recognized was that Callie demonstrated a will to live. I had a hunch she would fight to stay on earth a little longer because of it. If it was meant to be, Callie would survive and have some quality of life. Time would tell if it was possible after some intensive medical intervention and a great deal of TLC.

First, I made clear the doom and gloom Callie faced. I explained to Noni she must understand what to expect of Callie's condition and the stiff odds Callie faced. I then related it was imperative to have hope and never forsake it. With it, mountains could be moved and miracles made. Still, I cautioned Noni not to forget the reality of the situation, to keep in mind the time was coming when both she and Callie would have to let go of each other.

With Callie nestled upon my lap, I looked at Noni and smiled. With a belief coming from deep inside my soul, I shared with her, "Hold on to hope and greet each day you have together as a gift. Don't think about what will come in the future for the reason that tomorrow will take care of itself. Be like a cat, like Callie, and just enjoy the present moment!"

Don't Keep Me In

What the cat does not realize is that I have the ability to translate his language. By accomplishing this, I can pass what the feline is saying to his caregiver. I perform this task so the caregiver will not be fooled and then cater to the cat's orders.

Now keep in mind if the caregiver's steadfastness weakens, with his nerves on the verge of exploding from a protesting and screeching feline, I know of a means to cope with the situation. I highly suggest the caregiver downs a jar of chamomile, uses industrial-strength earplugs, and sips from a tall glass of any kind of wine while stretching out on the couch with the TV's volume on high until the cat relents in his demands.

When an outdoor cat is made an indoor feline, he will adapt and settle in without any desire to set one whisker in the exterior sanctuary any more. At least, this happens most of the time. On the other paw, a cat may protest greatly and insist he should be "purrmitted" to leave his home with the purpose of venturing in the great never-land of the outdoors.

This is a song a cat teaches other felines to use for this particular situation. The feline sings it over and over again, seeking to break his caregiver's resolve.

I will go where I want to go and do what I want to do.
Don't keep me in!
I will run through an open door and flee to the far-off fields.

Don't keep me in!
I will cry a screeching howl and shred every nerve.

Don't keep me in!
I will sing this song to you and demand I get my way.

Don't keep me in!
And I repeat: I will go . . .

An Irish Cat Blessing

I had fun on a St. Patrick's Day by giving a card I made with my version of an Irish blessing to someone I worked with for a short time. It undeniably drew a few giggles.

> *May the road rise up to meet your paws.*
> *May the wind be always tickling the fur on your back.*
> *May the sunshine be ever warm upon your whiskers.*
> *And may there constantly be fresh catnip in your home.*

A Cradle in the Clouds

My best friend's sister was faced with the fact that her kitty had entered end-stage renal failure. Reluctantly, Gretchen accepted the reality of the situation. She never before administered medications to her cat, let alone give an injection or force-feed the kitty. With the guidance of her cat's veterinarian and the support both her sister and I provided, she met each challenge in the kitty's care. Gretchen turned into Mesa's nurse.

Mesa's final days quickly passed. Then the day came when Gretchen held Mesa as this kitty went home.

Close your eyes and see me,
Chasing a butterfly with heartfelt delight under the warm rays of the sun.

Stand quietly and hear me,
Singing a melody with loud purrs through the changing song of the wind.

Look to the sky and smile at me,
"Purrsuing" a workout with youthful energy in the unending limits of the horizon.

Gaze at the stars on a clear night and spot me,
Living a life with great happiness inside the eternal home of the heavens.

Think of the special times of my youth and realize I am once again young,
Dancing ballet with boundless joy within the mellow glow of the sunset.

Say good-bye and feel peace in me,
Sneaking a catnap with total contentment in a soft cradle of the clouds.

CHAPTER 9

*A cat's "purrceptive" sixth sense
gives the cat the ability
to reach a human's inner soul.*

THERAPY CATS

The utilization of animals, especially cats, for therapy is a somewhat new concept in the human medical field. It has not been until recently it became more and more accepted. What doctors, staff, and families have come to realize is that these highly trained animals reach out to patients when humans are unsuccessful, helping break down barriers so treatment can begin. By accomplishing this, these devoted creatures bring hope, compassion, and comfort to us humans.

My Therapy Cats

For the longest time, I resisted the idea of allowing any of my cats to participate in a particular animal-assisted therapy program. I wasn't sure I wanted them to join a group that was mainly a dog's organization. I was positive some of my cats were more than capable of meeting the requirements to be therapy cats. I just wasn't certain about enlisting them in a program geared for their canine counterparts.

A good friend, my cats' veterinarian, convinced me that a few of my cats would make excellent therapy volunteers and that I should at least give it a shot. After much soul-searching on my part, I permitted my special felines to partake in the program, and the main reason these particular cats were chosen was straightforward. They enjoyed interacting with people.

Undeniably, the training was a challenge for me. My cats were required to measure up to the same standards as the dogs had to meet, and they needed to "purrform"—outstandingly.

Why?

Fundamentally . . .

I felt that since there weren't any other cats in the program but mine, my cats would be under the microscope so to speak. Anything and everything they did in service would surely be under much scrutiny. To my delight, my cats lived up to every demand I asked of them and so much more than I ever thought possible.

I quickly realized my therapy cats possessed a way of helping us humans when no other person could achieve this goal. Plus, they accomplished it since they enjoyed what they did. Because of their abilities to touch a human's inner soul, I observed the small steps taken by so many when the cats reached out to help. I saw smiles appear and pain forgotten, even if it was momentarily. I also witnessed hope begin when despair became overwhelming.

I feel each one of my therapy cats brought different positive attributes to the program. For this reason, they excelled beyond my expectations.

By accomplishing this goal, they developed into true pros whenever they participated in therapy service.

Mini Mouse was my first therapy cat. She was a petite Domestic Shorthair painted in calico colors with a roaring purr that was easily heard across a very noisy room. She walked into the therapy program with flying colors and set the standards for upcoming cats in the organization. Mini was the first and only cat to receive the honor of Therapy Animal of the Year. After Mini retired, she continued to make occasional appearances at special events.

Miss Pansy, a Maine Coon, was my second cat to be certified. Previously, she acquired the title of Supreme Grand Champion in The International Cat Association. Pansy was a showgirl who loved the limelight and cameras. Because of it, she was outgoing and thrived in the attention she received in the therapy program. Pansy also retired when she entered her senior years.

At present, I have three therapy cats: Traveling Thomas, Willow Bend, and Daisy Mae. In the future there will be others to follow in their paw prints.

Traveling Thomas is the first boy I enlisted in the program. Thomas is a red-and-white Domestic Shorthair who is quite serious when in service. He craves tickles and brushes from patients. As it turns out, he is undeniably attentive and loving with anyone coming for a visit or to work with him.

Willow Bend, a Siamese mix with definite blue crossed eyes, was a challenge to train. Initially, he was rambunctious. He wanted to investigate every nook and cranny. Beyond question, his concentration span was limited because of curiosity. With plenty of patience, Willow settled down. Nonetheless, Willow still remains inquisitive and demands total attention. Otherwise, he is off to find some. To the patients' enjoyment, he has never stopped giving a kiss whenever asked for one. Quite often he gives them too freely before I can stop him.

Daisy Mae, a Domestic Shorthair, is Miss Prissy. She is dressed in a thick black-and-white coat. She loves to be told she is pretty, especially how lush and silky her fur is to the touch. She "purrfers" traveling inside a buggy than staying in one spot. Hospital visitation is one of her choice activities as well as having a rehab patient chauffeur her around with a wheelchair.

Over the years, some very special events occurred. As a result of these moments, I firmly believe my therapy cats are special angels sent from heaven to guide us humans by creating miracles every time they reach out to help.

The following accounts are prime examples of these experiences.

Mini Mouse had just entered the therapy program and was in service for the first time at a local rehab hospital. There was a patient not responding to anyone. She wasn't reacting to the therapists, the doctors, or her relatives. Essentially, she was comatose and had virtually given up on life.

The therapist in charge of her case questioned the woman's family if she liked cats. They related how much she adored them. The therapist asked if it was all right if Mini Mouse visited with the woman, and they agreed. The therapist then wheeled the woman over to Mini and set her hand on Mini's back.

Mini started purring. It was quite loud even the people across the gym could hear her song of joy. Shortly afterward, the woman moved two of her fingers ever so slightly on Mini's soft, warm coat. Suddenly, a faint smile brightened the woman's face.

One of the members of the woman's family was thrilled beyond belief and began to cry. She said it was the first time her loved one showed she was still inside her body.

These were the initial steps in the patient's journey of coming back into this world. It then took weeks of intensive therapy before she was well enough to leave the rehab hospital and return home, but she did. Thanks to Mini who helped initiate the way, the woman accomplished it.

Years later, I was at the same rehab hospital. A patient came over to the therapy table while Thomas was stretched out in his soft-sided bed. The woman asked, "Where is the other cat?"

I glanced at the woman and pointed to the other carriers where both Willow Bend and Daisy Mae were waiting for their turns to be with the patients. I explained I was just able to have one cat out at a time. She looked over at the other cats and said, "No! The one I'm looking for isn't there!"

Taken off guard, I stared at the patient and thought for a moment she must be confused because Thomas, Daisy, and Willow were the current ones in the program; and all three were here.

Once again, the woman asked, "Where is the cat who purrs?"

This time, I was definitely puzzled and thought for a moment. Mini Mouse was the cat with the thundering purr heard across the room. However, I retired Mini two years before this woman was a patient. I kept wondering if it was possible the kitty she referred to was Mini Mouse, but how could it be feasible she knew my Mini?

Politely, I responded Mini Mouse was my cat with the great purr and she was at home. I explained Mini entered her senior years, so I decided to retire her from the program.

The patient reached over to pet Thomas, although she seemed greatly saddened by not having the chance to visit with Mini. Shortly, she shared some details about herself. Apparently, she had been very ill from a stroke and was here for rehab many years earlier. She saw Mini during the previous stay and always remembered her. She greatly enjoyed hearing Mini purr and was looking forward to seeing her again.

I still was unable to recall the patient.

Throughout the afternoon, I kept staring at the woman, trying to identify her. She looked very familiar, but I couldn't put it together who she was. I had seen many patients come and go over the years; I just had a hard time placing her.

At last it dawned on me who she was. I finally recognized the woman. She was one of the first patients Mini helped when Mini joined the therapy group. The woman was the patient who did not respond to anyone until she met Mini. Since then the woman had gotten older and definitely appeared in better shape than the first time I saw her. Once more, she was here for treatment. The big difference was that she wasn't as debilitated. I was amazed and speechless. It happened long ago and the patient had been quite out of it. For me, the remarkable part, she remembered Mini Mouse!

Mini Mouse reached a part of the patient's soul on that day many years ago and brought her back. As a result, she never forgot Mini for accomplishing the wonderful deed. Since that afternoon, I have never forgotten the woman.

Miss Pansy was a showgirl during her youth. She thrived in the limelight, especially when the cameras appeared. Pansy was beautiful and unquestionably knew it. This outgoing attitude definitely spilled over into the therapy program.

I took Miss Pansy on a visitation to see a cancer patient at a local hospital. In the hospital, Pansy rode in a baby buggy seeing as it was somewhat difficult carrying a twenty-two-pound Maine Coon around for any length of time.

Miss Pansy loved being wheeled around in the special carriage. She believed she was a queen every time she rode in it. What's more, she was categorically delighted acknowledging her subjects while she strolled through the hallways.

The second we entered the elevator, Miss Pansy noticed the reflection in the mirror covering the back wall. She recognized that the likeness was her stunning image. She immediately perked up and cocked her head from one side to the other, admiring how striking she was in the buggy with her therapy cape. If anyone blocked her view, she "purrcisely" told them to move and do it quickly!

The elevator filled with passengers, different floor buttons were pushed, and then the doors closed. Pansy realized she obtained an audience to "purrform" in front of, to her great joy. Perking her ears up, she didn't waste a second by executing a grand show. She kept admiring herself in the mirror with extra vigor. People started laughing. The more everyone laughed, the more this Cooner flaunted her beauty in the mirror and didn't hesitate to state how gorgeous she looked in her cape. Some of the passengers laughed so hard they held their sides, some got red faced, and some just egged her on to continue such dramatics. I laughed so much my face started to blush.

With each new stop of the elevator, no passenger left. One man commented he wanted to stay and watch Miss Glamour Queen. He remarked he could always go back down to the particular floor later.

Each time the elevator doors opened at the different stops, the awaiting people stared at us very curiously. I think they thought we were having a party. Understandably, they stood motionless and simply watched with quizzical looks on their faces. The doors then closed and left them behind, remaining to wonder what in the world was going on to cause that much laughter.

Finally, the sixth floor arrived. Miss Pansy and I departed with our escort, the charge nurse. A gentleman also exited at the same time. I was about to push Miss Pansy's stroller down the hallway when the gentleman put his hand on my arm and stopped me. He bent over and stroked Pansy's head. Then he straightened his posture and smiled with gratitude.

The gentleman simply said, "Thank you!"

As soon as he saw the puzzled expression on my face, he explained that it had been quite a long time since he laughed and briefly forgot his troubles. He said he was headed to see his wife inside a room down the first wing. Unfortunately, she was quite ill and he didn't expect her to live much longer.

The gentleman's smile disappeared as he left, and it was the first time I saw his pain. With my heart aching for him, I watched while he walked toward his wife's room. His steps were slow and deliberate when he entered. He was also slightly bent over, not from age but from the burden he was carrying.

The gentleman disappeared behind the door, and I never saw him again. I didn't know who he was or what happened to him. I mainly remember Pansy made him laugh and forget his troubles for a few minutes inside a very packed elevator.

Traveling Thomas is my first boy who joined the group of kitty volunteers. He is a handsome Domestic Shorthair and is undeniably quite serious when in therapy service. I have to say Thomas mastered the required routines and had them down pat in record time. He is the charmer with his half-closed eyes and smile. Thomas craves tickles and brushes from patients or any other available pair of hands.

Thomas definitely adores getting petted and makes serious "bread" (also referred to as making "biscuits") that shows great appreciation for the attention. Of all my therapy cats, Thomas is certainly the lover. He can be very flirtatious and doesn't miss a chance at expressing it either.

One afternoon, Thomas gently climbed upon a patient's chest at the rehab hospital and intensely made "bread" with his front paws. The patient giggled and then broke into full laughter. The harder she laughed, the more Thomas kneaded in earnest. Of course, her enthusiasm caused Thomas to bounce into the air. Each time he landed, he again initiated the routine, creating smiles and chuckles from everyone who took notice.

The second he was through, Thomas gave the patient a gentle butt on her chin with his head. Then he returned to his bed on the therapy table and curled inside it, patiently waiting for some tickles, which the patient generously showered upon him.

Later, the patient said she hadn't enjoyed herself quite so much in ages and it felt good. She suffered from severe pain that was not alleviated by any treatment she received. While stroking Thomas, she told him how grateful she was for his help to forget about the physical discomfort—the tremendous pain—she lived with every day.

Willow Bend is my clown. His active and inquisitive Siamese nature has always been a challenge to keep in check. He hates sitting still for any length of time.

When Willow visited a patient at a hospice, I wasn't quite sure what to expect. Even though we were there privately and not through the organization, I wanted Willow to "purrform" as a good therapy cat.

The patient was someone I wasn't acquainted with for very long, but I felt as if I knew her forever. She was definitely a person I greatly admired. Birdie had been a missionary for most of her life. Through Wycliffe Bible Translators, Birdie, along with her coworker and best friend of forty-five years, translated the New Testament into the native language of the Tucano natives in Columbia. They were working on the Old Testament when Birdie went home to heaven.

Birdie was sitting in a chair reading as Willow and I entered the room. She was thrilled when she realized I brought a kitty to visit with her.

I opened Willow's carrier, and he proudly strutted out to greet Birdie. I placed him in his soft-sided bed right beside Birdie. Willow looked at her as he lazily stretched his entire body length inside of it and out of it. Happily, he nuzzled her hand while she petted him. In a few minutes, Willow's curiosity got the better of him. He couldn't stand it any longer and wanted to investigate the room. With Birdie's permission, I allowed Willow to go exploring.

Willow slowly walked around and checked out every nook and cranny. He discovered the window and chattered to the birds singing on the other side of it. He noticed flowers placed upon a table, but I did not give him the chance to get in them. With each step, he turned toward Birdie and made a comment in his tiny voice. She laughed and continued the conversation with Willow.

Finding out there was nothing else to inspect, Willow jumped back on his bed. He again stretched out and purred as Birdie petted him. When she stopped, Willow sat upright and looked directly at her. Purring nonstop, he reached over and kissed Birdie's forehead. He turned around and jumped down. Then he nonchalantly walked over to his carrier and crawled in it. In typical feline manner, Willow made a circle before settling down, lowering his head, and finally closing his eyes.

Birdie explained Willow was tired and should go home so he could rest. I stared at Birdie and smiled. I recognized it was Birdie who was tired, not Willow. Willow had sensed it, too. With catly intuition, he understood it was time to leave and let Birdie have some rest.

I closed Willow's carrier. I then bent over and gave Birdie a kiss on her cheek. I left with a heavy heart, carrying Willow and his bed. I walked down the long hall to the building's main entrance. There was a sad feeling inside me, thinking it was for the last time. Somehow I realized I was never going to see this special woman any more.

Birdie died early the following morning.

Later, Birdie's family thanked me for brightening her afternoon with

Willow Bend. Birdie related how Willow made her laugh with his long stories and comments. She told them the best part was Willow gave her a kiss! For me, knowing Willow brought joy to Birdie was all the thanks I ever expected.

Daisy Mae, in some ways, maintains some of Miss Pansy's traditions since Miss Pansy's retirement from the program. Daisy also loves strolling around in a carriage, and she is delighted whenever patients push their wheelchairs through the rehab hospital with her sitting on the seat as did Miss Pansy.

When a patient came to work with Daisy at the rehab hospital, the patient was resisting walking and strengthening her leg muscles. She was in quite a bit of discomfort from surgery and was scared she would fall if she attempted to walk. Nothing anyone said could persuade her differently—until she met Daisy.

The therapist suggested to the woman she could push Daisy around the hospital using the wheelchair. At first, the woman refused. After a great deal of convincing, she finally agreed because she loved cats. Tentatively, the patient stood behind the wheelchair and held on to the handles, with the therapist standing at her side. Daisy sat on her bed that was placed upon the chair's seat. Slowly, the patient put one foot in front of the other and started to walk. The woman was thrilled to observe how much fun Daisy was having; she walked around the entire hospital before ever realizing what she accomplished!

Daisy gave the patient enough confidence to put the fears aside. By accomplishing this, the patient began walking to a full recovery.

In the course of witnessing these small miracles, my cats have shown their great compassion and understanding of us humans. I can truthfully say that is the reason these special angels were chosen to be therapy cats, and it is the reason I will continue to volunteer my cats in a dog's organization.

We Who Lived Our Lives

In 2001, I joined the animal-assisted therapy group with Mini Mouse. At the time, I didn't have any idea how loved and cherished the animals were who participated in it. I have since come to admire the group for both their committed work and the devotion they have for their four-legged ones.

I wrote this when I went to the organization's first blessing of the animals.

> We have lived our lives here on earth to serve,
> Rather than to have been served.
>
> For this, you chose to honor us,
> Here in our final resting place.
>
> In demonstrating this great kindness,
> We are truly blessed.
>
> By sharing our memory with others,
> We will live forever.

Therapy Animal of the Year

A while back, I was asked what a therapy cat did. Below was my response. Later, I used this reply in the presentation I made on behalf of my cat, Mini Mouse, at the awards dinner for the animal-assisted therapy organization on May 8, 2003.

Mini was a little Domestic Shorthair calico who won the 2002 award for Therapy Animal of the Year. She beat out over seventy dogs to achieve this honor. It was the first time in the history of the organization a cat ever won this award.

Was I proud of her?

You bet!

Years passed quickly after I gave the speech, but I will never forget the honor Mini received. Here is an excerpt from the presentation:

> "You raise me up so I can stand on mountains . . . You raise me up to walk on stormy seas . . . I am strong when I am on your shoulders . . . You raise me up to more than I can be."
>
> These words sung by Josh Groban describe so well what Mini Mouse accomplishes as a therapy cat.
>
> Mini has a sixth sense that tells her if a human needs her gift of giving. She then offers it freely. With loud purrs, soft touches, and kitty winks, she has the ability to reach out and break through barriers no human can seem to penetrate.
>
> Mini brings smiles where tears are found. Mini brings hope when despair has taken over. Mini brings confidence if self-assurance has been lost. Mini brings acceptance whenever rejection appears present. And the best part is: Mini does it because she loves accomplishing it! As for me, I am the one who is blessed to be a part of Mini's life.

Mini was abandoned on the streets along with her siblings. Immediately upon the rescue of these kitties, Mini was blessed with a litter of kittens. She was a devoted mom and raised some beautiful little ones. From Mini's humble beginnings of motherhood, she was known for her purrs of joyful songs. It was apparent she never met a stranger and always sensed when someone could use her singing. It was because of this great ability that Mini became a therapy cat.

Throughout Mini's career in therapy service, she made attendance to the rehab hospital, hospitals, hospice, seminars, and the awards dinner. Mini's abilities set the standards for all future therapy cats. They were very large footprints she made for them to follow given that she was such a petite little girl.

In her retirement, I enlisted Mini's aid in helping me teach human parents of diabetic cats how to check the blood sugar of their cats. She sat patiently each time, purring and smiling while they practiced on her. Never once did it bother her.

As health issues slowly began taking a toll on Mini, her spirit and sensitivity remained steadfast in reaching out to others. She never failed assisting a human in need.

Mini is now a heavenly angel, although I will forever hold her within my heart. Even with the passing of time, I still hear Mini's loud purrs singing inside my thoughts as she keeps reaching out with great compassion.

A Lesson Taught

One day, I was at a rehab hospital with my cat Mini Mouse. Out of the blue, a therapist looked at Mini while Mini allowed a patient to tickle her tummy. She said, "Look, this cat is acting just like a dog!"

Her comment annoyed me since she seemed to be mocking Mini. I felt it was unfair because she had no idea how good my cats were as therapy cats, not that I was prejudiced.

I quickly made up this tale as a reply to the comment. Many patients and nearby therapists intently listened to the story. Even before I was finished, everyone who caught wind of the tale began to snicker and chuckle. By the look on the therapist's face, she wasn't quite sure if I was telling the truth or pulling her leg. It didn't matter. I made my point, and she never made another derogatory comment about my cats ever again.

Centuries ago, cats loved showing outward affection for their human caregivers by rolling over on their backs and allowing their tummies to get tickled. The cats did this with the grace and dignity only known to felines.

Dogs saw how much this act of tickling pleased the humans and wanted very much to participate in it. The moment they were alone with the cats, they asked the cats if they would show them what to do.

The cats huddled together to talk over, among themselves, the request. After much contemplation, they decided to teach the dogs this gesture that made humans so happy.

The very next day, the dogs rushed to the humans and threw themselves at their feet. They didn't waste a bit of time before rolling over to have their tummies tickled. The humans laughed as the dogs lost total grace and dignity. The dogs slobbered and drooled all over the place. When seeing such a performance, the cats became quite disgusted. They looked at each other and agreed they would never again allow a human to tickle their tummies in the company of a dog.

Now if by chance a cat is allowing his tummy tickled, it is always with "purrfect" decorum and never in the presence of a dog!

In Appreciation

Below is the "Romeo and Juliet" story I shared with three patients at a rehab hospital when one asked why I entered Miss Pansy, a stately Maine Coon, in the therapy program. They intently listened, as did Miss Pansy. Throughout the narrative, Miss Pansy cocked her head back and forth, agreeing with every word said.

Miss Pansy has always been the light of my life; but to a very special four-legged "purrson," she was much more.

When quite young, Miss Pansy met Alfalfa. At the time, Miss Pansy was rather tall and thin. She did make up for her awkwardness with a flirtatious and very outgoing "purrsonality." Alfalfa was strikingly handsome with his flaming red hair, and he definitely received the "purrsonality" to match it. Alfalfa was rather shy; and at the same time, he could be a hellion. Also, Alfalfa was much older than Miss Pansy and was quite set in his ways.

Even though Miss Pansy and Alfalfa were quite opposite to each other, such differences didn't matter to either of them. The moment they met, it was definitely love at first sight. Alfalfa doted on Miss Pansy's every wish, while Miss Pansy nurtured Alfalfa.

Miss Pansy grew into a striking showgirl. She acquired accolades, awards, and the title of Supreme Grand Champion in a cat association for such beauty. This was important for Miss Pansy because Alfalfa was there cheering her on with the quests. In time, Miss Pansy retired from the show circuit and settled down alongside Alfalfa in their cozy home.

The years passed and Alfalfa's health gradually failed. Miss Pansy never considered it a problem. She cared for

Alfalfa with great love and tenderness. For this reason, Alfalfa lived and thrived beyond anyone's expectations.

On January 10, 2003, Alfalfa started upon a journey that would take him away from Miss Pansy. Miss Pansy held Alfalfa close and gently nuzzled him. The tears flowed from Miss Pansy's eyes as she begged Alfalfa not to leave her. Alfalfa's body was dying, and nothing in this life could change what was about to happen. Alfalfa looked at Miss Pansy for the last time and spoke in a way words weren't needed. Shortly afterward, he closed his eyes and returned to the heavenly home.

With the loss of her Alfalfa, Miss Pansy no longer showed an interest in the world around her. She stayed in Alfalfa's bed for hours on end. Pansy cared about very little without Alfalfa by her side. The one thing she wanted was to go to her Alfalfa.

Hoping Miss Pansy would once again find joy in this life, I trained her to be a therapy cat. It was the first time since she lost Alfalfa she could find her way without him. Miss Pansy began to thrive. She again enjoyed every bit of the attention that was showered upon her. She reached out to others in need with an amazing sensitivity, and that is why Miss Pansy entered the therapy program.

After I finished, one of the patients gently put a hand on the side of Miss Pansy's face and said, "It's all right, honey. I know exactly how you feel. I too lost my spouse." Then with a very serious expression, Miss Pansy reached out with her paw and tapped the patient's arm and said, "Thank you!"

Everyone laughed.

Following retirement from the program, Miss Pansy sustained her flamboyant but nurturing ways. She definitely never missed a chance to express them either.

On Friday night on September 22, 2006, Miss Pansy gently consoled me. She wiped the tears from my face moments after Tammy Fae lost her battle to hypertrophic cardiomyopathy (HCM). Miss Pansy tried with all her might to mend my broken heart with tender purrs and gentle touches. Little did I realize that three nights later, Miss Pansy would not be able to wipe the tears away ever again. This time, she too would lose her battle to this heart disease.

Early in the evening of September 25, 2006, Miss Pansy joined her Alfalfa. With their souls now united as one, they soar in the heavens above while mine now grieves for the losses of both kitties.

My heartfelt thanks to the animal-assisted therapy organization for giving Miss Pansy the will that maintained her nurturing ways and allowed Miss Pansy one moment in time that, for me, will last forever.

CHAPTER 10

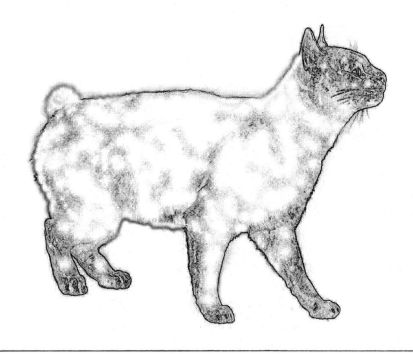

AS LIFE GOES ON

~M~

Living life to the fullest
is the only manner
in which
the majestic cat greets each day.

~M~

Little by little, with maturity, I recognized I was content within my world. I really loved what I chose to do with my life. I also continued to participate in the magic of my youth and still believed in mischievous fairies. What's more, I found the courage to finally reveal these wonders to others around me.

One Moment in Time

During my early childhood years, I never gave any thought that life could end. As I grew older, I learned quite differently. I came to understand life is rather fragile. Time quickly passes until the day arrives there is not another tomorrow left to come.

I have often wished I could fool time and keep a loved one with me. I guess this could be called bargaining or denial. I think what I really want is that life shouldn't have to maintain boundaries or include endings. Somehow I doubt these feelings could ever change.

> *When all tomorrows have come and gone,*
> *Just give me one incredible moment in time.*
> *Make it appear to last for a lifetime.*
> *Then allow it to continue throughout eternity.*

The Ability to Accept Change

There was a time I thought a cat was totally inflexible and intolerant of any change. Since then I have clearly come to another conclusion. The cat does accept change throughout his life. It is usually done very quietly and without much fanfare. Occasionally, the cat adapts to change because he finds he is in a situation and has no alternative but resign to it. Other times he welcomes change because it pleases him.

The capacity to deal with change was a trait belonging to a wonderful feline by the name of Alfalfa, and he definitely demonstrated the ability throughout the years. Many times he strived to accept new and difficult situations.

Slightly past the age of fourteen, Alfalfa's back vertebrae started to fuse causing pressure to be exerted on the nerves that controlled his back legs. Over the subsequent months, he gradually lost most of the feeling in these legs. Shortly thereafter, he was no longer able to walk on them. Surgery was out of the picture because of other health issues he had to deal with on a daily basis.

What amazed me most was that Alfalfa adapted rather well to this handicap. With great determination, he pulled himself with his front legs to places, including the litter box. After watching Alfalfa's resolve for independence, I decided to buy a wheelchair cart designed specifically for him. Still, I wasn't completely sure if he would accept it or totally reject it. Essentially, I wanted Alfalfa to have the chance of mobility again.

This unique cart arrived a few days after I ordered it. I assembled it on the floor in front of Alfalfa and showed him the different sections. He marked each piece with the side of his face. When I finished, I set the cart close to him. I wanted Alfalfa to understand it was not something to fear.

The next day, I put Alfalfa inside the cart for the first time. He wasn't sure about the whole thing, so I let him remain in it for a short period. By allowing brief sessions, he was becoming comfortable with a foreign concept. I could also make adjustments to the straps during the process. I had a much easier time with the corrections if Alfalfa was out of the cart than inside it, but that meant I was required to do it a number of times to accomplish the objective. Alfalfa was patient with the entire ordeal, even though he was in and out of the cart over and over again. As a result, I achieved two goals at once: permitting Alfalfa the chance to accept a strange object, and giving me the opportunity of modifying the fit before Alfalfa tried it out for the first time.

The following days, I helped Alfalfa into the cart and encouraged him to walk. Initially, it confused him; but he quickly caught on to the concept. He discovered how to back up, lie down, drink, eat, and fly everywhere with it attached to his body. The one frustrating problem happened whenever a wheel wedged on a chair leg or a wall corner, causing a complete stop. This astute cat quickly realized I would run to his rescue the second he became stuck. The other cats rapidly learned to keep tails, feet, legs, and bodies out of the way since Alfalfa had absolutely no hesitation about running over them with this new chariot. Because of these antics, Alfalfa soon was known as the holy terror on wheels.

Alfalfa fought many battles with his health over the years and never let the difficult times stop him. For this reason, it was natural for Alfalfa to adjust to the paralysis and the limitations the handicap threw his way. It was heartwarming to watch a once feral cat, afraid of everything at one time, accept a great deal of adversity and overcome it. Alfalfa was an exceptional cat, proving a feline does have the capacity to accept change, especially if the cat deems it is in his best interest, as did Alfalfa.

The Day My Heavenly Kitty Angels Came

I have always stayed with my cat as the little one left this life. Sometimes I would sit next to the departing cat in silence. As a result, I learned that some of my heavenly kitty angels appeared to help the kitty begin the crossing and then these angels would lead him home.

On the afternoon Spanky, a handsome cat with long red hair, walked on his final journey, the other cats were extremely subdued. I believe they were aware something was transpiring. I too felt this, although I wasn't sure if it was either the heartache for the coming good-bye or perhaps I sensed something more was occurring. When I sat beside Spanky, I reflected inwardly and soon understood what my cats "purrceived."

My heavenly kitty angels were among us.

These angels brought a feeling of tranquility. I could hear them purring inside my thoughts and see them through my imagination. They appeared ever so beautiful and healthy, precisely how I expected they would be.

It was apparent Spanky detected their presence and listened to them when they purred their songs of tremendous joy. Spanky too joined in and purred with the singing. While the heavenly kitty angels stayed close to Spanky, I noticed peacefulness come to him as he rested.

I gently stroked Spanky's head. It helped us both face the fact that we would shortly go our separate ways. The other cats watched Spanky with sadness in their eyes. Joseph, one of Spanky's much-loved kitties, curled adjacent to Spanky. Occasionally, Joseph softly nuzzled him while the tears rolled off my face, realizing these moments were rapidly disappearing.

Death is not easy to witness or accept. What helped me cope that afternoon was my sensing that Spanky's brothers and sisters from the heavens came to welcome him into his new life. At the same time, Spanky's earthly loved ones were giving consolation by quietly saying farewell to Spanky.

Many times I have wondered if I was out of my mind to think that these events actually transpired. Then a little voice inside me would tell me, "No, don't stop believing!" I have promised myself to never stop listening to the voice for the reason that I believe magical events of imagination do take place. It's only a matter of believing.

A Secret Pocket

Over the years, with every *hello* I have spoken, a time came when I had to say *good-bye*. Sad to say, there have been many final good-byes. With each one, I hurt deeply. I appreciated the fact that time helped to heal and lessen the pain. I was then able to put the sorrow into a secret pocket and keep it hidden in my heart.

Unfortunately, this pocket can unbutton. Sometimes it occurs without warning. Other times the pocket opens because an event brings back a memory. The moment the pocket unlocks, every past emotion comes pouring out as if the losses just happened.

Even knowing these emotions are right below the surface, I don't know if I can live any other way. Nevertheless, if there could be one wish I could have, it would be this pocket didn't have to ever again unbutton and those sad memories would remain safely tucked away.

Every Once in a While

Most undeniably, I am a cat person. As one, I have developed a unique language understood by others like me. This short tale is a prime example.

What is a nubby?
It is an itsy bitsy, teeny weeny, stubby tail, which my cat very proudly displays!

I was owned by the most handsome smoky blue Manx cat with a very tiny stump of a tail. I did not call it a stump. Rather, I preferred to say, "Smokey Bob has a nubby!"

Now let me share a little bit more about this cat who sported a nubby.

Smokey Bob, a beautiful Manx with a little nubbins of a tail, came to me and brought the gift of smiles. His stature was big and strong, but it bowed to his overwhelming gentleness. He left his existence as a wise street cat and turned into a loving homebound feline. He never was aggressive. On the other side of the nubby, he took great joy in being a vixen. He settled into a place he believed was true heaven on earth, the main arena in my home. Actually, it is the back half of the first floor of the house.

Life has many turns I could never expect nor predict. Sadly, it happened one particular Sunday morning, when I had to say good-bye to my little boy. Without a bit of warning, Smokey Bob was called to the heavenly home. He fought hard to stay, except it wasn't possible.

Smokey was about two years of age at the time. Sometime during a Saturday night in early May, he developed a high fever. I rushed over to the veterinary clinic in the morning at 7:00 with my boy and had him checked by one of the doctors. Meds were given by injection and orally. Instructions were also given on home care. I left carrying the required supplies and returned home with Smokey, having every expectation of a full recovery. Shortly after arriving, I nebulized, fed, and administered fluids. By 9:00 a.m. Smokey's fever was down, but he had a seizure. At first I thought it occurred because of the extremely high temperature he ran earlier since he seemed to improve afterward. However, at 9:30 a.m., Smokey had another seizure. I grabbed him and carried him in my arms. My husband, best friend, and I flew to the clinic as I cradled Smoky close by me, praying.

The moment we entered the clinic, Smokey stopped breathing. Cheryl and I immediately started CPR. Mike, one of the doctors, intubated and administered heart stimulants. The three of us continued the CPR for about fifteen minutes, although it was futile. My little boy's spirit could not stay.

It seems, like us humans, cats are also vulnerable to lethal infections and diseases. They can surrender to them as did Smokey Bob. They too can succumb without notice, even when expert medical treatment is given.

Occasionally, a free spirit blesses my world for a short time and then must leave. Smokey Bob's spirit now forever soars with great joy in the heavenly home.

October 26, 2001–May 11, 2003

This Time Innocent

I am a very light sleeper. Any sound or movement can awaken me. When I am disturbed, I find it extremely difficult to drift back into dreamland.

My husband has a habit of snoring at night, which can be quite annoying. Most of the time, I can give him a nudge; and he rolls over, quitting the serenade. This allows peace and quiet to return, giving me the opportunity of obtaining some rest.

One night I was extremely tired and retreated to bed hours before Pat. Later, when he followed, Pat fell into a deep slumber. With a routine that never changed, a few of our cats approached and snuggled in around us. Rosie, a little blue torbie Maine Coon, stretched out on her back between our pillows. She raised all four legs high in the air amid total comfort before folding them close to her body. Feathers, a petite blue Domestic Shorthair with large green eyes, nestled under my arm. Nana, a stately and slightly pudgy Maine Coon, bedded down close by my feet.

In the shadows of early morning, somewhere around 1:00 a.m., a low rumble began. I made every effort to ignore it, but the volume increased until it was a loud bellow. Even though my eyes were closed, I was positive the noise came from Pat. I gave him a gentle poke in his side, hoping to stop him from snoring. He turned over and faced another direction. To no avail, the roaring failed to cease. Not only did the level of sound significantly increase, but the length of each note also expanded.

I attempted to muffle the exploding thunder by stuffing the pillow over my head. This certainly didn't work. Consequently, I tossed and turned in a semisleep state. Feathers was growing impatient with my restlessness. Sleepily, she sat at full attention beside me and watched the proceedings, quite irritated. As the screeching roar carried on, I gave Pat a swift jab with my fingers this time. I was desperately wishing he would quit. Once more, he flipped over in his sleep.

There was silence, so I thought.

Boom!

Oh no, it started again!

How could this be? Why on earth was Pat snoring with me poking and jabbing at him?

With each roaring chord, I aimed for Pat's side with my hand. He in turn rolled from one position to another. My nerves were exploding by then. I was upset and quite irritated since I desperately needed some sleep in order to function the following day.

During this late hour, I was at wit's end. As a result, I took my pillow and popped Pat with one swift blow. In a flash, he sat upright. Not realizing what transpired seconds before, he mumbled something under his breath. At that exact moment, with the racket coming through louder than ever, I became aware it wasn't Pat who had been snoring. It was one particular cat—Rosie! Needless to say, I pretended I was asleep and just giggled under my breath. Shortly, Pat settled back down and quickly returned to his rest without ever realizing what I did.

Early in morning when we were fully awake, Pat complained about having some feline jump on him the night before. I maintained a straight face as I looked at him. Having total surprise in my voice, I asked if he knew which one it was. He said he didn't have a clue. Biting my lip, I tried very hard not to laugh and just give sympathy. Never once did I acknowledge what really occurred.

Now if there is a moral to this story, it is to never assume the one believed guilty is really the culprit of the deed. Even more importantly, never confess to be the one who popped the other with the pillow.

To this day, I have never explained what transpired that night. I assume Pat still believes a cat jumped on him while he was deep in sleep. There is also a good possibility I may never set the story straight either!

Cat Hair . . . Never in My House!

I am owned by a number of feline hair contributors in the constant production of fur.
Does that suggest cat hair can be acquired inside my house?
You jest!
There isn't any means possible such a thing can be found . . . especially in my house!

I comb and bath cats, run the vacuum 24/7, and use special air filters.
Is it very feasible cat hair can still be obtained inside my spotless abode?
Silly you!
That's most improbable . . . especially in my house!

If my husband happens to be wearing black shorts,
And I notice layered over his bottom is cat hair,
Can it be conceivable he received the pelt inside my stately manor?
You must be terribly mistaken!
There isn't a slight chance such a thing could ever happen . . . especially in my house!

Apparently, I have a well-established fur factory.
Hair is shed round the clock,
And a hairball or two can be found on a daily basis.
Can it be the reason you think cat hair is inside my pristine domicile?
Surely, you imagine way too much,
Since I believe it is inconceivable to locate cat hair . . . especially in my house!

Come by for a visit, then sit down, and sip some cool tea.
It is slightly probable you might notice cat hair floating on the ice.
Can you really be sure what you see?
Keep in mind it may be unfortunate vision with your eyes playing tricks on you!
Truth be told, cat hair does not exist . . . especially in my house!

Now if by chance you meet me at a store or a restaurant,
And I puff a cat hair or two,
Never give it a second thought what you may detect.
Most emphatically, please remember one thought.
Cat hair is never ever found . . . especially in my house!

A Special Moment

A special moment in everyone's life occurs when a touching gift is bestowed. At times it has very little monetary value, although it is priceless and irreplaceable to the one who receives it. For the human, the gift can be a teddy bear, doll, train, baseball, piece of crystal, book, ring, quilt, or anything imaginable. For the cat, it can be a toy, collar, blanket, or any prize the feline treasures. It really doesn't matter what it is because to the feline, the gift is, definitely, as equal in importance as the one the human receives.

Often the gift remains a part of the recipient's world for a lifetime. It is then passed to the next generation with the history of its past. The cat's perspective is quite different. After he has been honored with the special gift, the cat lacks any concept of what might happen to it in the future.

Sadly, the gift is sometimes lost and vanishes into memory. Even if words aren't spoken, regret still tugs at the human's heart, realizing it is gone forever. This is true for the cat, too.

Once in a while, another gift is presented with the expectation it might fill the empty spot of the missing treasure. It is not the original, and it will never take its place. Yet it is much more significant. The gift is a keepsake, given to help heal the heart. Both the human and the feline accept it as such.

Strangers to Each Other

Max was a little silver Persian who belonged to a dear friend, Noni. The day I met Max, she was almost sixteen years old and still feisty as a youngster.

Early one Friday morning around 6:30 a.m. a few years later, Noni called to tell me Max wasn't walking very well. She asked if I could come over and help. Wasting no time, I flew over to find out what was going on with her kitty. After watching Max unable to take more than one step and then stumble, I definitely was alarmed, fearing she might have had a stroke. I scooped Max up and took her into the clinic when it opened. Noni proceeded to a local school where she taught fifth grade since it was a school day.

When x-rays were taken, it was determined Max developed a growth inside her chest. Unfortunately, it could not be removed or treated. Max was dying. Because she wasn't in any distress, I wanted to contact Noni and explain the situation before facing a difficult decision.

I took Max home with me and called Noni. With a heavy heart, I related to Noni what was going on with her precious little one and that she should think about letting Max go in peace at the end of the day.

Noni immediately left work. She came and sat with Max for the last time as my cats watched and gave comfort to both of them.

Strangers to each other they may be, but this is never acknowledged.
As each kitty quietly approaches, tender greetings are exchanged.
In feline fashion, gentle nuzzles are given to the pretty little Persian.
Silent good-byes are softly rendered.

Tears fall, knowing the little Persian will soon leave.
Purrs sung now give comfort to the loved ones all around.
Wishes for a future fade into hopes for an easy departure.
Rest comes as the last reward here on earth.

With the gift of nurturing, the young Maine Coon keeps watch.
He guards the mom while she sits beside her little one.
The young Cooner's heart breaks, sensing an end will shortly arrive.
Nevertheless, he refuses to leave their sides.

Songs from heavenly kitty angels can be heard singing to the little Persian.
The little one's sister also comes from the heavens and stays with her.
Carefully lying beside the little Persian, Callie whispers how much she loves her.
Soon both will be together once more.

Eternal sleep quickly approaches, and one life passes into the next.
Sorrow fills the hearts of the loved ones left here on earth.
Now great joy begins thundering from the clouds beyond.
The little Persian is now a heavenly angel.

Another Black Cat

Ever since my husband and I moved into our current home, many cats have been abandoned around the country club down the street from us. Ultimately, quite a few of these new arrivals managed to make their way to our residence, which apparently includes a cat haven known throughout the cat kingdom. More than likely, the old-time felines at the club passed the word to the newcomers about this safe place. If not, they definitely posted signs giving directions to the feline sanctuary. Such happened to three black cats who magically appeared at the same time.

In the fall of 2003, a number of black cats were discarded in the subdivision. It didn't take them very long to find their way to a particular safe haven, my feline sanctuary. I was pretty sure they used their feline GPS systems to guide them if they either failed at getting directions from an old-timer or missed the postings by the club.

Pat maintained a routine of watering the potted plants in the backyard early every morning. As usual, he went outside to get the chores done. Over the following days, he kept noticing a black cat crouched inside one of the flower beds or sometimes walking about the yard. Since none of the neighbors were owned by a black cat, it was a pretty sure bet the new face was another drop-off.

One evening Pat asked me to come out in the front yard. There inside the flower bed was a very tattered and skinny black cat. He was talkative but skittish and pulled away if Pat attempted to move toward him.

Sitting on the flower bed wall, I softly talked to the black cat. He tried approaching, except he couldn't and remained at arm's length. Meanwhile, the two of us carried on a conversation; but he would not let me touch him. He wanted the company, although he was unsure of my intentions at the same time.

I instructed Pat to go and get a can of the smelliest fish cat food, open it, and bring it back. Pat did precisely as I requested and handed it to me. He then stepped back, allowing me the opportunity to catch the cat.

For what seemed like forever, I sat, holding the can of food. The black cat was hungry and wanted it, but he couldn't get over his uncertainty of the situation. Shortly, hunger got the better of him and he couldn't resist the temptation any longer. He came close enough to lick the food. The instant he realized my hand was clutching the can, he backed away.

When the black cat started to leave, I flipped a piece of the fish in his direction. He gobbled it down in nothing flat. He cautiously came in my direction, stopped, and turned away. I stretched my arm out as far as possible to allow another lick of food. Afterward, he again moved a few steps out of reach.

Trying to get close enough to grab the black cat, I was then on hands and knees so as not to intimidate him. I was positive I could catch him if given a chance to get a hold of the back of his neck, but obtaining a grip was another story. Even though I was definitely running into great difficulty in accomplishing the feat, I was definitely determined to succeed.

Inch by inch, I crawled across the street almost within a hand's reach of the cat. To my frustration, he kept just beyond my grasp and walked in the direction of a neighbor's house. It took me a few minutes to edge my way across the cul-de-sac and into the neighbor's side yard with the cat just maintaining an arm's length away from me.

Given a stubborn streak as great as a feline's, I wasn't about to quit. Slinking along, I diligently followed the black cat into the neighbor's flower bed. As it turned out, the bed was under their bathroom window. I kept a finger crossed and took a deep breath, praying they didn't see or hear me. It would be hard to explain exactly what I was doing, especially to a sane person!

Finally, the black cat surrendered and came to me. He wanted the food more than he feared me. At that point, I scooped him up without a struggle and proceeded back home at a quick pace. Pat opened the front door as I carried the bundle to the guest bathroom and closed the two of us inside of it.

I arranged the room for the exhausted cat and offered him a large bowl of cat food. After eating, he settled down on a soft blanket on the floor and soundly slept. The next day I took the cat to the veterinary clinic and had him checked.

The black cat was an older feline. He wore scars and a few ear nicks from previous battles. He was thin from having missed more than a few meals, and he was also wary. Other than that, he checked out with flying colors.

A good friend, Noni, adopted him and gave this tom the name of Harley. It took quite a bit of love and even more TLC before Harley trusted people. With time, he lost this uncertainty of the human race. For Harley, life on the golf course faded into a memory. He settled into his new home and savored the benefits it offered, especially food!

Pleased with the accomplishment, I thought the problem of noticing a stray black was over and put to rest. This only lasted until a certain husband, after watering the potted plants, came in and informed me he saw another black cat.

Annoyed with the announcement, I looked at Pat but didn't say a word. Whenever Pat reported he spotted a stray cat, he expected me to rescue and deal with the feline. I didn't mind, except I was the one required to catch the cat and then take care of him. I was just able to find a limited amount of homes. If I couldn't find a suitable one, the cat then lived with us. I realized that with another soon-to-be-caught stray cat, I would be adding another one to a certain thundering herd, my feline crew.

This time, the petite young black cat wore a little white in her coat. The kitty loved sleeping in the flower bed amid the daisy chrysanthemums. I tried ignoring her and hoped she had a residence where she belonged, but a little voice inside my head kept telling me a different story.

One afternoon, as the second black cat walked down the driveway, I snatched her up in my arms. After a month in isolation and two health checks, Miss Daisy Mae made her debut in the main arena (the back section of my house). She joined my domestic group of pampered felines. At last I felt for sure the problem of stray black cats was finished.

Well, not really!

One evening after dinner, Pat and I were sitting inside the garden room. We enjoyed the opportunity of relaxing and watching the setting sun after a long day. In the distance on the fairway, we noticed golfers finishing their golf game. Then without warning, Pat said, "Look, that's the black cat I've been seeing every morning!"

In total disbelief, I snapped my head around and noticed a young juvenile taking a long drink from the fountain at the far end of the room. Half under my breath, I asked Pat what he expected.

Excitedly, Pat said, "Catch him of course!"

Somehow I was not in the least little bit surprised. I was quite accustomed to the request by then. Once again, I walked over and nabbed the third black cat.

The young tom was feisty and wasn't particularly fond of me holding him, except I didn't give him an option. After passing two health checks and the obligatory isolation, the adolescent, like Daisy, joined my growing number of feline residents. I named the third black cat Angus for obvious reasons.

I did sternly explain to a particular husband not to tell me about any more black cats. I made it quite clear he would have to deal with the feline without my help.

Unequivocally, I declared, "The cat hotel is full!"

I also knew if Pat spotted another stray cat, even a black one, I would not turn my back. I'd be out trying to catch another one. He was also fully aware of this, too. Except at that particular moment, he didn't acknowledge it to prevent me from killing him!

Ah . . . here I go yet again!

Guess who came in and announced he spotted a vibrant calico kitten hiding in a flower bed out front?

Incidentally, I caught the young destitute kitten and placed her with Noni after a bit of arm-twisting. Magie, she was named.

As for Pat, he remains alive—barely!

The Street Ambassador

Early hours are a much-loved interval of the day for me and a time in which I accomplish the most tasks. I find it refreshing to hear birds singing, notice small lizards on the hunt for delectable bugs, and see lawns sparkling from the watering—the fairy dust—received the night before.

Every other Sunday morning, I stopped by a friend's home to clip some kitty nails. During each visit, I looked forward quite a bit to a particular activity—watching the neighborhood cat from across the street. Stepping out of my car, I would glance around and observe a lone feline in the distance. The kitty was Mr. Regal, and he was out on his daily ritual.

Kermit was the cat's given name, although I feel Mr. Regal seemed more appropriate. It was a name bestowed upon him long ago by my friend Marilyn. He definitely thought it was a worthy title and responded with the pride of a lion at the mention of it.

Mr. Regal was a cat of middle age, but this was hardly noticeable since he carried his years rather well. His stature maintained the handsome lines of a young tom. Sunshine bounced off his soft, long fur while he stretched in its warmth. Nothing missed his keen eyesight. I smiled as he pretended not to notice things he deemed unimportant to his feline senses.

I have to say neutering Mr. Regal at a young age certainly did not deter him from his tomcat ways. He "purrsisted" in marking his territory in "purrfect" male cat fashion.

This handsome feline ruled his domain as top cat and proclaimed to any roaming tom to keep a distance. Because of this attitude, Mr. Regal was a cat who fought a few battles during his time. With advancing age, he became more the street ambassador to his human friends than the terror he once was to his feline counterparts.

Each day Mr. Regal followed a "purrdictable" path that led him to certain houses, allowing him to visit the occupants. He religiously sought out their company with exceptional feline decorum.

I grew accustomed to greeting this stately cat and always enjoyed our conversations together. Mr. Regal's voice came from the long line of Siamese cats, and he unquestionably used it to get attention with his opinions.

Years passed and my schedule remained the same as did Mr. Regal's routine, though I noticed Mr. Regal's weight was a fraction of what it had been in the past and his fur undeniably had thinned. Each step he took appeared much slower and even more deliberate. I realized Mr. Regal was no longer in his prime, and old age had taken hold of his stately body. I saw an elderly cat. Somehow I sensed he viewed himself as the young tom of his youth. I too preferred thinking of him that way.

It was once again early morning, and I dropped by my friend's home simply to talk this time. Stepping out of my car, I looked about and sensed a quiet I never felt before. Mr. Regal wasn't anywhere around. Sadly, he left this earth the night before and returned to the heavenly home.

I stared at one of Mr. Regal's resting places. Unrealistically, I wanted to catch a glimpse of him once more. I suddenly noticed his choice bush move. Surely, a soft breeze must be stirring it! From the distance, I then softly heard Mr. Regal's distinctive Siamese call. I told myself it was not possible because I was looking with my heart and not my eyes for the street ambassador.

From somewhere inside me, a little voice whispered Mr. Regal's spirit did momentarily return. His life did not end with death, but continued. Deep down within my soul, I believe Mr. Regal returned to say good-bye in that early morning hour on the street he dearly loved.

Twinkle

On a beautiful clear evening, I was standing on the top of a mountain in the hills of West Virginia. It was the land upon which my husband and I were in the midst of building a home. The temperature remained slightly crisp since winter tried holding on to the weather, although it was quickly fading into spring. The sweet smells of new life were definitely emerging. The sky above was as black as coal. At the same time, it glowed with hundreds of twinkling stars. Due to this phenomenon, it was awesome to be able to see for miles on end even in the darkness.

Suddenly, a star began falling from the heavens. I intently watched as it raced for the earth below. It appeared to be headed for the exact location where I was resting. I promptly extended my hands above my head and cupped them tightly together. The twinkling star landed inside them with complete grace and absolute elegance.

The twinkling star was quite young and ever so pretty. I smiled as she nested down in her human cradle. I drew her close to my face. She then purred a song of total pleasure and contentment. I looked into her dark blue eyes and felt it was love for both of us. I explained to the twinkling star she would always be my little Twinkle. Somehow I sensed it was the Lord Father's gift at a time when I would need it. The Lord Father sent her to be Cackie's, my blue point Siamese cat, long sought-after kitten a few weeks before Cackie returned to the heavenly home.

Twinkle grew tall and slender. She was wise and, sometimes, much too intelligent. It didn't matter that Twinkle loved everyone she met since she was loyal to just one person—me! We traveled around the country together and lived in many places. Throughout every new challenge, Twinkle always stayed by me, giving comfort during the sad times and laughing with me in happy ones.

Regrettably, the years passed too quickly. Twinkle and I had grown older with neither of us noticing it. For the first time, Twinkle's light started to fade. She heard the heavens calling her back home. At first the song was merely a whisper, so she ignored it with all her might. Swiftly, it became quite loud that I too was aware of it calling for her. It was then she had no choice but listen to the message.

It was a mild spring in the month of March 2004, the same month in which my twinkling star was born on earth. In the early hours of a Sunday morning, I rested on the bed alongside Twinkle. Softly stroking her head, I told Twinkle how much I loved her. I cried, knowing she was about to leave. Even though my twinkling star's light was almost gone, she looked at me once more with her sparkling blue eyes. They were as clear and beautiful as when I first held her. While purring her last good-bye, she rested her head down and returned to the heavens from which she had come seventeen years earlier.

Days passed one by one, and I could hardly believe my twinkling star was gone. I had such a deep emptiness in me that I couldn't shake because of it.

It was a Thursday evening and a dear friend had come over for dinner. The hour was late, and Betty was ready to leave. I walked Betty out to Pat's car and helped her get settled inside on the passenger seat. Then I leaned over and gave Betty a hug. At the same time, Betty looked at the sky and remarked how funny to see only one star out on such a clear night and not any more. She asked if I knew which one it was since it was quite bright.

Staring at the star, I said without one once of uncertainty, "Venus."

Satisfied with the answer, Betty wished a good night and closed the door. Pat backed the car out of the driveway and drove Betty home.

After they left, I turned and slowly walked toward the front door. Once more, I glanced up at the bright star. At that exact moment, it twinkled. Tears filled my eyes as I suddenly realized the star I was watching wasn't Venus. It was my little twinkling star—Twinkle!

She Was My Youth and Innocence

From the time I was fourteen years old, my life had been dominated by a Siamese cat. The first one was a beautiful blue point with crossed eyes. Her name was Cackie. Cackie was a special gift from my dad. She ruled me with complete feline devotion. In her final days, she was blessed with an adopted kitten. I named the kitten Twinkle for the reason that the kitten was the twinkle from the heavens in Cackie's eye. Twinkle was a seal point Siamese with sparkling blue eyes. She was all ears as a tiny baby, and I wasn't sure she would ever grow into them, but she finally did.

Cackie was my youth and innocence. She guided me through my teenage years and many of my adulthood ones. She was my rock, stability, and confidant. She always remained with me in both good and bad times. The day I said good-bye to her I lost complete focus on the things around me. The world I had been quite comfortable in was lost, so I thought.

Twinkle followed in Cackie's paw prints after Cackie went to the heavenly home, and she carried on with Cackie's treasured ways. She was a rambunctious kitten who helped me deal with the loss of Cackie. This tiny Siamese was Cackie's gift to me just as Cackie was a gift from my dad. I felt Cackie possessed a sixth sense that told her how much Twinkle would be needed to help guide me when she would no longer be there for me. Out of love, she passed her wisdom to Twinkle as Dad had passed his wisdom to Cackie.

Days slipped into weeks and weeks into months. The months then passed into years. I found myself as an alleged mature adult. Twinkle also matured into an adult cat and maintained the bond Cackie once shared with me. Twinkle, like Cackie, was my rock, stability, and confidant. She was my prime of life as Cackie had been my youth and innocence.

Once again, many things happened along the way that I didn't consider. I know I took it for granted that Twinkle would always be with me. I should have been more perceptive, possibly more realistic.

It was March 4, 2004. Early that morning, Twinkle left me and joined Cackie. It was around 2:00 a.m., and Twinkle slipped quietly away. For the first time, I was without the loving companionship of a wonderful Siamese cat. The bond that had been formed and passed on, starting with my dad's gift of Cackie, was gone. I felt lost. At that moment, I made myself a promise of never having another Siamese cat because it would never be the same. The love Dad gave me was sustained through his gift of Cackie to me and then through Cackie's gift of Twinkle to me. The bond had ended. Nothing on this earth could bring my dad or my cats back and rebuild the bond. I believed I would have to wait for the day when I too would follow to the heavenly home to renew life with them. Until then, I asked Dad if he would take good care of my heavenly kitties, especially two Siamese angels.

Bells Ringing

A season slowly emerges and quickly disappears into the following one. A living being also has a time to live and then must pass on to eternity. Deep sadness comes when a soul who should still be enjoying the prime of life departs.

During a Christmas holiday, when joy and laughter were shared throughout the world, in a very small section, tears were falling for the loss of a gentle soul.

Pepper, the sparkle of her human mom's eyes, left us two days before Christmas. She was a tiny little bit who ruled the world with her independence and willingness to reach for the moon. Life for her was marvelous, full of fun and wonder. She adored it tremendously and her special loved ones, especially her human mom, Betty.

It's been said that when a heavenly angel receives a pair of wings, loved ones on earth hear a bell ringing. The singing bell is proclaiming the wonderful event. Very shortly, we would realize this marvelous blessing.

My husband and I, along with Betty's daughter, stepped into the coming night just moments after Pepper flew to the heavenly home. Singing through the air from the distance, the bells of a nearby church rang out loud and clear. With tears covering our faces, Noni and I looked at one another and smiled. Words weren't required. We fully understood the bells were declaring Pepper had been given some wings. It was difficult letting Pepper leave, although a feeling of peace came to us as the bells rang out the news of Pepper's new heavenly gift.

Pepper was part of our lives for such a short time. Unfortunately, nothing could change the course of Pepper's illness and keep her with us. She then became an angel in heaven.

Months earlier, Betty called one night. She was worried Pepper was having a seizure. Pepper, a tiny black-and-white Persian cat, was her special joy. Saying it mildly, Betty was more than a little frantic at the time.

I flew over to Betty's and brought Pepper back with me to keep a close eye on her through the night. The next morning, I took Pepper to the veterinary clinic and had her thoroughly checked for the cause of the head tilt and rapid eye movement. It turned out Pepper acquired a disease that couldn't be cured. It was controlled until the progression created health issues, ultimately causing her body to shut down.

What happened to Pepper wasn't fair.

Pepper was barely seven when she died. She was in her prime and full of life; and she reminded me of a bouncing ball of fur as she ran about with great joy, except she harbored a virus she probably received at birth. The hidden demon remained dormant until she was a full grown-adult; it raised its ugly head and took her precious life. This tragedy was something I never anticipated or wanted for Pepper. More than anything, I never wished this misfortune would come to pass for her human mom, Betty.

One Old and One Young

Mollie was one of the prettiest cats I ever met. She was a vibrant longhaired calico with white. I have to say it was her zest for life that absolutely stole my heart, not just her beauty. She was my little country girl from West Virginia, who always loved to play and snuggle. Her purrs were quite loud they could be heard throughout the house. Sometimes she possessed the fire of a devil, yet she never ceased to have the devotion of an angel at the same time. Mollie was also a fighter for life from the first moment I laid eyes on her over seventeen years previously; and she never stopped, not even for a moment. She never gave up on living and beat odds that would have conquered someone else.

Clover was the kitten I loved from the first instant I cradled her in my hands at the veterinary clinic. I gave Clover a name created from one I bestowed upon Shamrock, a cat who had passed on years before. With it, she most definitely received the personality of her namesake. Clover was my baby and remained as such when she entered into adulthood. She also never failed to remind me of it. Clover was vocal and opinionated. She was also shy—occasionally—but she always found her way to the front of the line for a tickle on the chin. She was ever so gentle and tender, too. Nonetheless, to a few in particular, Clover could be explosive and full of vinegar.

Mollie grew older as Clover matured, and both were dealt destinies they could not change. Mollie followed Clover and walked the path that took them to the heavenly home. Sadly, they became heavenly angels much too soon.

With Mollie's advancing age, I knew the day would come when her life would end. In contrast, when Clover died in her youth at the age of six without a warning from a hidden heart condition called hypertrophic cardiomyopathy (HCM), it came as a complete shock.

I have been told it is easier letting go of someone who is old than someone who is young. For me, it has never been easy in either case. I have to admit that's the reason I found it incredibly difficult to let go of either Mollie or Clover.

The Second Home

There was a time I was sitting at my desk watching Shasta. I could not help but think back through the many years to the moment I met this pretty kitty. I smiled, remembering how she decided she would leave her home next door and move into mine. It was because of Shasta and her twin sister, Tammy Fae, a strong friendship developed between her first caregivers and my husband and me.

Shasta was a pretty little feline with short silver hair. She was definitely nurturing of her special ones and always enjoyed sharing her affections with them. Even though Shasta could be lighthearted and very kittenish, she was most definitely very serious about life. If I asked Shasta what was troubling her, she disclosed long stories, insights, and opinions with me.

As a rule, Shasta stayed in the background, although she was never far away. I cannot think of a time Shasta would not quickly forgo the simple pleasures of stretching out in a sunny window, cuddling on a soft blanket, or sitting on a comfortable lap if another cat wanted it.

In Shasta's elder years, she took on the responsibility of teaching the young juveniles in the feline family much-desirable manners. I called her the enforcer for the fact that she was quite headstrong and determined with the duties of etiquette.

From all of Shasta's wisdom, I cannot forget a very essential lesson she taught me. In Shasta's very feline way, she imparted that the most important element in life is to care about those around us. Shasta accomplished it by not only reaching out to her feline family but also reaching out to four humans in her life. Shasta never forgot her first home. Through Shasta's own special quiet way, she extended it into her second home.

To Have Faith

Shortly before the second half of the nineties, my aunt had aged into a very elderly woman. She was in her late eighties and suffered from a number of health problems. Incredibly, through everything, she was still feisty and fun loving, very much like my cats.

I escorted my aunt to see her priest who was a longtime friend. I think she knew this would be the last outing there since she was well aware that her days of driving a car were over. She found that getting around was hard to undertake, even with help. She also knew I would not be available for chauffeuring after I returned to my home in another state. In the future, Monsignor would have to call at her home.

My aunt enjoyed a nice visit with Monsignor. They exchanged a number of pleasantries, both new and old. Monsignor served coffee and oatmeal raisin cookies. Long ago, he discovered my aunt's choice candy; so he never forgot to include Tootsie Rolls to take along as she was leaving. This always brought a laugh and, definitely, a thank-you. In about an hour, my aunt decided it was time to return home and said her good-byes.

We were preparing to depart when my aunt turned her head in the direction of the new priest standing inside his office. Noticing my aunt watching him, Father asked us to come and have a seat. He had been with the diocese for barely a few days and wanted to introduce himself. Slowly, my aunt made herself comfortable on one of the large wingback chairs. In my usual manner, I stood beside my aunt.

After a brief conversation, my aunt began to leave but stopped. Without any wavering in her voice, she said, "Father, I have a question. I am not afraid to die because I will finally be rid of my health problems and this old age. It seems I am not completely sure what comes afterward, and it has me a little uneasy. What will happen?"

I was dumbfounded my aunt would ask the young priest such a question. I was also confused given that she was a devout Catholic and never showed any doubts in her faith. I thought, more than likely, she was pulling his leg and testing him since he was new and quite young. Subsequently, I let Father take a breath before replying.

Very quietly, Father responded, "I don't know!"

This time, I thought Father was the one pulling my aunt's leg. I waited to see what would ensue next before questioning his answer.

Surprised and dismayed, my aunt looked into the priest's eyes and said, "You don't know? Father, you are a man of the church and you answer in such a manner?"

While contemplating my aunt's concern, Father went over to open the door. Sounds of scratching and meowing were coming from the other side. Actually, it was ruthless banging and merciless pounding on the unfortunate door as well as very loud complaining. When Father opened it, a cat sprang into the room with loud purrs after some scolding that was directed at Father for his misdeed of having a closed door. Then the kitty rubbed Father's legs, showing great happiness and satisfaction.

Turning toward my aunt, Father said, "Did you notice my cat? She's never been in this room before and didn't know what to expect. This inquisitive cat only knew her caregiver was inside, so she sprang in without the slightest fear as the door opened." Continuing with the analogy, Father said, "I know little of what is on the other side of death, other than I understand my caregiver is there and that is everything I will ever require."

Satisfied with the young priest's answer, my aunt nodded in agreement and we started to leave. I looked back at Father, smiling with gratitude for the way he handled my very spirited aunt. Father winked back at me.

I guess Father was pulling my aunt's leg with his reply since I had a sneaky feeling he used the analogy or a similar one in previous lectures. I also think Monsignor related how much I liked cats because I suspect it wasn't the first time the kitty was inside the office. Without a doubt, it gave Father the perfect opportunity to apply this knowledge to his example. I have to say that by the manner in which Father presented it, the analogy was better than the numerous sermons I sat through during mass on many past Sundays.

What's more, knowing my aunt's sense of humor, I feel this outspoken lady had fun by testing the young priest on his beliefs. What she never realized was that the priest also had fun by answering the question in an unusual manner and giving her something to think about.

My aunt died at the age of ninety-two, content in her faith. I believe she is now with the heavenly caregiver.

Remembering the Simple Things

Whenever I saw my best friend's mom dressed in a particular pretty casual outfit, I felt pink was most definitely Carol's color. On the occasions she wore it, she glowed.

Carol loved cats, especially one in particular. This special kitty was little Miss Frick, a Domestic Shorthair who wore a tortoiseshell with white coat. I enjoyed quietly watching Carol and her feline companion. They had been together for over twenty years and maintained a relationship that was tender and strong. They rarely said words to each other. There wasn't a need since they seemed to read each other's thoughts.

There never came a time Carol wasn't thrilled to receive roses, even a single rose, seeing as they were her much-loved flowers. Whenever she looked at them, they brought back the fond recollection of the rose bush she once planted outside the home she had lived in for many years. Not wanting to part with the roses, she kept them way past their prime.

As for Miss Frick's choice enjoyment, catnip topped the list of this kitty's pleasures. This kitty always treasured its aroma and welcomed the silly side effects. She constantly rolled in the dried leaves and nibbled them until she drooled with complete satisfaction.

Way too often, lives are lived and then forgotten. By remembering the simple things Carol and her kitty loved, somehow their memories remain a part of this life.

I became acquainted with Carol and Miss Frick when they moved to the town where I reside. Carol wanted to live close by Cheryl, Carol's daughter. Since Cheryl and I were best friends, I helped with the care of her mom and her mom's kitty whenever a need arose. It was sad to watch one leave and go to the heavenly home with the other one to shortly follow.

Now both are together, enjoying each other's company as I remember the simple things they enjoyed.

Who's Blind?

I never gave a bit of consideration that the smallest cat in my house, Sunshine Katie, would turn out to be one of the biggest felines. If not in stature, it was definitely in "purrsonality."

Sunshine Katie had been blind her entire life, although it was never a deterrent for this kitty. Katie was a little eight-pound pit bull who could back a twenty-two-pound Maine Coon cat, Miss Pansy, out of a cat bed if she sought to sleep in it. Katie could climb any cat tree she wanted to scale and descend without falling. Plus, it never mattered how high the tree was since Katie never lost her footing.

It was remarkable to watch Katie run through the house and never hit a piece of furniture or any other stationary item during a flight for the reason that she remembered where everything had been placed. It was also an advantage having whiskers longer and thicker than normal that allowed Katie to use them as a guide cane and, most assuredly, as a sonar detector during the many races.

The inability to see made Katie's other senses quite acute. If Katie heard a pin drop on the other side of the house, this little dynamo knew what it was. Catnip could be sealed in an airtight jar; and she was able, without a doubt, to smell it. Nothing passed beyond the realm of possibilities for Katie because of her heightened senses.

Katie was a longhaired calico with indications of Siamese in her background. Maybe it was Katie's blue eyes or the markings that gave the hint. It was the Siamese part that made Katie headstrong but never mean. This little powerhouse let everyone understand rather quickly she was the one in charge and no one else. On the other paw, she was gentle and loving to everyone this kitty cared about within her world.

Occasionally, Katie sought a pound of flesh if startled and took a bite out of just about everyone around at one time or another. It was a self-defense mechanism stemming from the lack of sight. One and all stayed aware of this fact, thereby keeping fingers and hands safe.

Never once did traveling to new places ever throw Katie. She thought it was an adventure and enjoyed exploring unknown surroundings. She was incredibility curious and quite outgoing.

Katie received a very loud Siamese voice and used it for communicating opinions. She could maintain a dialogue on any subject. She never failed to ask questions or give an order when she sensed it was necessary.

On Katie's last day, I was sitting on a wingback chair with my legs extended upon the bench in front of it. Katie climbed up, stretched out, and snuggled in for a siesta. I gave Katie combs. She purred and purred, thoroughly content. We took a short nap together. Funny, I never gave it a thought it would be for the last time. In a few hours, Katie went into heart failure and then became a heavenly angel.

Sunshine Katie was my little kitty for almost nineteen years. During those years, I never saw Katie's blindness. It wasn't an issue or problem. Throughout Katie's life, she lived as if she was given perfect vision. Possessing this aptitude made me wonder who was really blind—Katie or the rest of us who have the ability to see.

Just Have to Wonder

I always look beyond the logical to discover possibilities that may not seem real for someone else. I admit I have been doing this my entire life and find I cannot change. Naturally, I could be viewed as if I live inside a fantasy world for having this outlook. I assume if this certifies me as different from the rest of the world, then so be it.

Sometimes I do step back and question my sanity, although I still view life with this unusual approach. For this reason, I mostly keep many thoughts inside my head and say very little to anyone about them.

One event in particular, wherein I verified how I observe things, occurred two days before I lost Sunshine Katie. I have a special litter box for my cats. It is made up of two parts. The bottom section holds cat litter, and the top piece covers it. Down the middle of the top is a slit that lets the cat do his business while his feet are straddling on either side of this opening. The waste then falls into the bottom half of the box and into the litter. With this ingenious approach, the cat never touches any filler while inside the litter box.

The one cat in the household to ever use such a box was Shasta. She hated any type of cat litter for bathroom duties. To Shasta's satisfaction, this type of litter box worked out "purrfectly!" It definitely was a very unique solution for her fussy preferences.

Because of an unforeseen and unknown medical condition, Shasta died in December 2004. I had a very hard time dealing with the situation. I blamed myself after Shasta's heart gave out during a thyroid scan, and she died shortly afterward in my arms. After that incident, a part of me never completely forgave myself for putting Shasta under the stress that ultimately caused the fatal heart attack. Even though I have been told by the experts it was unfortunate and totally unpredictable, I could not accept it. I felt I had been irresponsible and failed my pretty kitty.

Since I was unable to come to terms with what occurred, I did not put Shasta's special litter box away after she died. With it ready for my pretty kitty, I could keep a part of Shasta with me. I felt comfort having the box accessible for her bathroom duties. I realized I was being silly, but it didn't matter. It was the only way I could cope with what happened.

A little over two months passed after Shasta died and Shasta's litter box remained in its spot. During that time, no other kitty ventured near it. Perhaps it was out of respect for Shasta or the fact that none of the other cats liked that particular type of box.

The Friday before I lost Sunshine Katie, I walked past Shasta's litter box and noticed it was dirty. It puzzled me at first since I did not observe any of the cats near it. I cleaned the box and went on with other chores. The subsequent day the same thing took place, except this time I had been watching to catch a glimpse of the cat who decided this novel box was the bathroom of choice. Even though I was watching, I didn't see any of them even close to it; I again scooped it and went on my way. Out of plain curiosity, I kept an eye out for the kitty who did the act.

On Sunday, Katie was rapidly losing her battle with kidney failure. Late that afternoon, her heart was starting to fail. Early in the evening I let my littlest kitty quietly return to the heavenly home.

After Katie's death, Shasta's special little box has not been soiled. As the time passed, I was still unable to stop thinking about those two days when it had been occupied. Finally, the thought occurred to me, I knew the likely party all along.

Ever since I saw Shasta's litter box soiled, a voice inside of me kept whispering Shasta was the kitty. She returned and guided Sunshine Katie when Katie set out on the journey to the heavenly home. Because of Shasta's nurturing nature, Shasta wanted to direct Katie through an unfamiliar time. By using this special box, I felt it was Shasta's way of letting me know she came to help Katie.

I believe Shasta recognized how much assistance Katie required. In Shasta's wisdom and unending love, she was Katie's eyes through her final hours and then the guiding angel on Katie's path to heaven.

Shasta's litter box has been kept in its place. Many years have since passed before another cat decided to occupy it. Possibly, the kitty might be Shasta coming for a visit!

Sometimes I wonder if what I perceived actually occurred. Conceivably, it was an overactive imagination at work at a time it was needed. There is a good chance I will never have an answer to what exactly transpired during Katie's journey to the heavenly home, and it really doesn't matter. Deep down in my beliefs, I don't want to consider any other explanation.

How to Open a Door

Some months after Betty died, Betty's daughter decided to purchase my dear friend's home from the estate and move into it with her husband and kitties. When I heard the news, I was undeniably thrilled beyond words for a number of reasons. Following Betty's passing, many of her possessions were either sold or given to others. I was greatly saddened to see the things she cared about leave. I couldn't bear the thought of Betty's home put on the market and bought by strangers, and so it meant a great deal to have Noni acquire the house. I felt a part of Betty remained by keeping something that was definitely important to her.

While Noni and her husband were in the midst of moving into the new residence, their felines came and camped at my home. This kept them from getting upset from the turmoil, lost in the process, or very likely, packed inside a box!

Harley was an older black cat. He was the abandoned cat I nabbed after crawling across the street and through a neighbor's yard a few years earlier. Magie was a homeless pretty calico I captured in my flower bed and persuaded Noni to adopt by means of a little arm-twisting. Scooter was a solid blue Domestic Shorthair and had been with Noni since she was a kitten. Major was a young tom. He was rescued as a juvenile around Noni's old habitat. The last one was Junior. At one time he was a skinny, forgotten stray Noni fell head over heels for but wasn't sure about adopting. With some more arm-twisting and a few added bribes, I talked her into taking on this redhead just a few weeks before she moved.

The five cats were sequestered inside my husband's office, the study. Later in the evening, I made sure both entry doors were closed before retiring for the night.

At least, I thought I did!

Sometime during the night, the office door to the hallway by the dining room mysteriously opened. Then the cats decided to investigate the house.

In the early hours of the next morning, Pat discovered the office door wide open. Of course, there wasn't a feline seen inside the room. Panicked, Pat called me to *immediately* come. He wanted my help to round up the missing cats.

Major was quickly located. He was crouched upon the staircase, making his way toward the second floor. I found Harley stretched out and sound asleep on the couch in the living room. Scooter was comfortably settled on a bed upstairs in a guest bedroom, with Junior curled in a ball beneath it. As for Magie, she was still missing.

Immediately after rounding up the four escapees and returning them to the office, Pat and I went from room to room and methodically searched for the misplaced little girl. We looked everywhere, but Magie wasn't to be found.

Assuming Magie somehow escaped outside, I was on the verge of alarm and feared I would never locate her. The probability of that happening was zero. On the other whisker, if she couldn't be found, where else could this kitty be hiding?

I hated the thought of telling Noni I lost her cat. With great determination to find the kitty, Pat and I decided to systematically go through each room one more time looking for the last feline in all corners and crevices.

I started the hunt inside the office, checking the cabinets, every nook and cranny, and underneath the furniture. Astonishingly, I located the runaway right behind the fax machine, where she was crouched down and hidden from sight.

I couldn't believe it!

Magie had been in the office the entire time and was never spotted. Clearly, both Pat and I were relieved to finally lay our hands on the wayward kitty.

Finally, with the five cats safely back inside the office, I wondered about the escape. I was baffled and kept running through my mind about the conceivable method these cats "purrcisely" used to open the door. Neither Pat nor I had been in the office after I checked on the cats before retiring for the evening. Then how on earth did the door get opened? No matter how much I tried to figure it out, I was unable to find a clue about the breakout—at least momentarily!

A little while later, I was standing outside the office entrance by the pantry hallway when I detected a rattling noise coming from inside the room. I opened the door just in time to watch Harley. He was standing on his hind legs and leaning on the other entry door. He was also pulling the door's handle with a front paw. It took him a few tries before he managed to sufficiently work the lever to release it. He then pulled the door ajar with his other paw. Harley succeeded and was about to make another escape until he realized he was caught.

Since Harley was quite adept at accessing the door handles, locking them did not help because these levers unlocked when pulled downward. For that reason, I placed heavy books against the inside of the front hallway office door. Harley could work the door handle, but he was unable to open the door because the books were too heavy to move out of the way. Any attempts at exiting through the door were completely foiled.

I had one slight problem.

These wannabe escapees still had to be cared for during their stay, which meant I had to access the room by the other entrance. Preventing any future plans Harley thought about escaping on the pantry side, I tied the handle to a hook, secured, in the woodwork. Much to Harley's dismay, this prevented him from opening this door, too!

Complicated?

Yes!

Despite that, it worked!

I then decided if ever a door was required opening, Harley could easily meet the challenge. Without question, he definitely demonstrated the ability.

A cat is quite intelligent and clever. The moment I think he isn't figuring out a situation, then I am the one who is foolish. Even though a cat appears totally oblivious to his surroundings, it is because he has already assessed the situation and deemed it is something that should be ignored.

The Christmas Gifts and Joseph's Song

Joseph was my magnificent Maine Coon cat. He was strikingly handsome with his long, square muzzle. His fur was shaded red, and he received the biggest golden eyes that danced with tremendous life inside them. He was, undeniably, a very large cat since he descended from the breed of gentle giants. This made Joseph's feet quite huge. Just one of his paws was as big as the palm of my hand; so I teased him about their size, calling them "mugwaws."

I believe Joseph was also a miracle cat for the reason that he overcame a tremendous handicap and never lost his tender nature along the way. Joseph's wonder of life captured my heart with a love affair that has never stopped and never will.

Joseph was born with a paralysis in his lower back. The lack of ability to move his hind limbs prevented him from walking on his rear legs or, for that matter, lifting his tail. When he was about ten days old, Joseph's littermates used their back legs for crawling; but Joseph wasn't able to accomplish this milestone. The only means by which Joseph could go anywhere was by pulling himself with his front legs.

I feel that since Joseph was born with this paralysis, he received an exceptionally gentle and loving heart. This was quite evident from the moment Joseph was minutes old. If any of Joseph's sisters wanted to nurse, Joseph quickly backed off and gave up his spot. The problem meant that this tiny baby required close monitoring and needed supplementation of kitten milk from a bottle for nourishment in order for him to thrive and develop.

As this gentle giant grew over the passing months, it was apparent Joseph possessed the sense of feeling in his back legs. Even with feeling, Joseph could not use them for walking in any manner. He basically stumbled and dragged his back end.

During Joseph's first summer, my neighbors were away on vacation. I was taking care of their cats, house, and pool in their absence. For me, it wasn't work in the least. I already loved their cats, and having access to a swimming pool throughout the hot days of East Texas weather was absolutely a big plus!

There wasn't a doubt I adored my neighbors' feisty cats, Tammy Fae and Shasta. They were very independent and loving felines. Tammy was a Domestic Longhair and Shasta a Domestic Shorthair. Both wore silver fur. Shasta was the worrywart and the very sensible one, while Tammy was the flirtatious, outgoing, and sassy one. They followed me everywhere in my neighbors' yard and mine. Given the chance, these two girls never missed a chance to instruct me accordingly.

It was late afternoon, and I finished cleaning the pool. I was hot and sweaty from the heat. Quickly, I dove into the warm, clear water and swam a couple of laps when the idea hit me about enlisting the pool as therapy for Joseph. I thought about how people benefited from water therapy and wondered if it would also profit my little boy. Joseph was about three months old. He was old enough to be walking, but he had trouble with it because of poor balance and the lack of strength in his back leg muscles.

After jumping out of the water, I ran home to retrieve Joseph. I scooped him into my arms and took him to see if he would be comfortable in the pool's water with me tightly holding him. I wanted Joseph to use the muscles in his rear legs without having his entire weight on them. In doing so, I was betting they would become sturdy enough and permit Joseph to finally walk.

Slowly, I entered the shallow end of the pool with Joseph clinging on me for dear life. At first he was petrified of the water and barely moved. I kept reassuring him everything was all right and that I would never let go of him. He still wasn't buying it.

When Tammy Fae and Shasta caught wind of what I was up to—that is, taking a protesting and terrified cat into the pool—these two cats headed for cover under nearby bushes with the speed of light and watched the proceedings at a safe distance. They made quite sure they were not the next victims in such shenanigans.

While holding Joseph in the doggy-paddle position, I encouraged him to move his back legs. Having quite a bit of trust in me, he relaxed—somewhat— and slowly paddled his legs, mostly to get out of the pool as fast as possible. Realizing I might be onto something, I repeated this a couple of times a week during the summer. Near the end of August, Joseph was walking, clumsily, but really walking for the first time. He didn't know where his back legs were at all times, but they were essentially working. As for his tail, Joseph dragged it behind him. I wasn't sure if he would ever lift it or, for that matter, if he would even move it. I felt time would tell if it could ever be a possibility.

The next challenge Joseph faced was learning to use a litter box. Joseph maintained erratic feeling in his back end. Consequently, he couldn't tell if his bladder was full or empty. This usually resulted in Joseph waiting too long before voiding and then having an accident on the floor. Eager to prevent this in the future, I trained Joseph to go to the potty box on command. Inside the box, I expressed his bladder. Soon it developed into a game, and Joseph took tremendous pleasure in playing it. Joseph actually asked me to follow him whenever he headed for the box. He enjoyed the assistance, even if his bladder was completely empty at the moment.

On Joseph's first Christmas, Joseph gave me a gift I have never forgotten. It was such a great gift and has remained as such to this day.

Christmas Eve arrived with its usual festivities. My husband and I invited a houseful of friends over to celebrate the holiday. Joseph was relishing every bit of attention he could command from the guests with his head bobs and chirps. I called Joseph to come for a treat, and he came running with his tail held high above his body! Stunned, I stood frozen in my steps and watched the great victory. I was indescribably surprised and almost couldn't believe my eyes!

After obtaining some composure, I remained elated beyond words. Naturally, I couldn't help myself; I grabbed Joseph and circled my arms around him. I just wanted to hug and kiss him for his amazing achievement. I looked into his big eyes and thanked him for giving me the best Christmas gift ever imagined.

My little boy wasn't sure what the commotion was about. He wiggled in every direction, trying to escape from my hold. Nevertheless, he unquestionably savored the attention I, along with everyone else, showered on him that night for the wonderful deed.

I have to say Joseph's most tender side was the strong attachments to his loved ones, and Joseph always demonstrated how he felt about them. Joseph loved both people and other cats. I think his heart was as big as his stature. When Joseph adopted a kitten, it wasn't a surprise to me. Since Joseph had a tremendous love for her, I never stopped considering she belonged to him.

Nellie grew into an independent adult. It didn't matter—I kept seeing

Nellie as Joseph's kitten because of my little boy's devotion and dedication to this pretty calico Cooner. As expected, I always referred to Nellie in this manner.

Each time my best friend visited, Joseph followed Cheryl everywhere. He recited long stories and played his prized game of "whop whop" with her. This pastime began when Joseph was a tiny kitten. First, Cheryl moved her fingers around her legs when she sat on the floor. Joseph then tried catching them to whop them with his paw. There wasn't any question that as a result of the affection Cheryl showered upon Joseph, he never liked when she left and greatly protested every time.

One of Joseph's greatest attributes was his affinity to any cat or human harboring a problem. I felt it was Joseph's way of informing them that they too could conquer their difficulty, and it didn't matter what it might be. Joseph spent many hours nurturing anyone he felt required help. Frequently, I was the one he comforted.

Through the years, Joseph took on the responsibility of kitty nurse. If one was sick, he centered his complete focus on that particular cat and alerted me if something necessitated any assistance.

Betty was a dear friend of mine. Tragically, she lost a leg in a terrible car accident. This made it hard for Betty to do the simplest things she once enjoyed. Sadly, she soon found it almost impossible to care for her very senior Persian cat, who she named Kotzen.

Kotzen developed arthritis in his lower back. This condition caused him to have a great deal of trouble when using his rear legs. He was also starting to have some loss in kidney function. Both situations required constant management. Out of desperation, Betty asked for my help. The old man then joined my thundering herd of felines.

Kotzen was a small cat compared to the other felines. This old man wore a long, flaming red coat. Sometimes his personality matched it, too!

From the moment Kotzen arrived, Joseph and Kotzen became inseparable. Given that both retained problems with walking, a close friendship was created. Joseph turned into Kotzen's protector, and Kotzen was Joseph's leader.

Joseph and Kotzen shared many special moments, but the one that I can never forget was the way Joseph sang with his old man.

The ritual started with Joseph and Kotzen facing each other, nose to nose. In a low voice almost undetectable, Kotzen chanted to Joseph. Excitedly, Joseph responded by bobbing his head and then singing to Kotzen. It was beautiful to hear in view of the fact that their voices were very melodious. Mesmerized, Kotzen intently listened to his best buddy while lifting his head high into the air. Kotzen closed his eyes with total contentment and slowly bobbed his head to Joseph's tune before he returned the chorus. Their duet was definitely captivating! After finishing, both boys butted heads and cooed. It was a ceremony celebrated, exclusively, between the two of them and never changed. It ended when Kotzen left this life, or so I thought.

The years flew by after Kotzen died, although Betty often came over to spend time with Joseph. They also formed a special bond. Possibly, it happened as a result of Joseph's love for Kotzen. Betty was hindered in walking, very similar to both boys. Maybe it was why she visited. Somehow I imagine it was for the two reasons.

I also was very fond of Betty. I cared about her as a friend, mentor, confidant, and definitely a second mom. Over time Betty's health began to fail, and I became her caregiver. The morning Betty died I was devastated. What I was not prepared for in the least possible way was that five months after Betty's death I would lose Joseph, too!

Throughout the weeks following Betty's death, I was involved in settling her estate. It was overwhelming and mind boggling. At the end of many long days, I was exhausted both physically and mentally. Sometimes I sat on the kitchen floor and talked with Joseph about my troubles as he stretched out in his bed after finishing dinner. My little boy intently listened and then butted my head, telling me everything was all right. He definitely possessed a way of easing stress and sadness when it was needed.

It was during that time Joseph initiated something that undeniably caught my interest. Joseph stood in the same spot where he sang with Kotzen, unaware I was watching him. Methodically, Joseph initiated the ritual he and Kotzen shared with each other. Joseph sang his beautiful song once more. It was as wonderful as when he sang it with Kotzen years earlier. I dearly loved hearing the melody again. If I asked Joseph what he was up to, he would stop, run to me, and act as if nothing occurred.

On a Monday in September, not unlike any other Monday, I was in the midst of grooming the cats. I gave Joseph his bath as usual. He always maintained very poor grooming skills, which meant he required a bath each week and, many times, in between. Afterward, I towel-dried my boy while he squirmed to get away. Finally free, he raced to his playhouse and hid inside of it. This was Joseph's means of punishing me for inflicting such horrendous torture upon him while putting himself back together.

Later, around 5:00 p.m., I called Joseph to come for dinner. He charged at top speed and jumped into his bed where he "purrferred" to consume his meals. I set the food dish down and gave him the afternoon meds. When he began to chow down, I turned my concentration toward the TV. I wanted to watch some news before Pat returned home from the office for the evening.

Joseph started coughing.

Somehow I felt something wasn't right and looked over at my little boy. I noticed by the expression on his face, he was having trouble catching his breath. Without a second thought, I flew to him! I assumed he swallowed some food and it became lodged inside his windpipe. I checked his mouth and throat. Both were clear. I quickly performed the baby Heimlich in case he did have something wedged.

Nothing!

Joseph didn't respond.

I was starting to panic, but I remained calm enough to perform CPR.

Again, *nothing!*

At that point I was frantic, although I maintained the CPR, except it wasn't working.

Joseph was gone!

How could this happen?

I held Joseph's limp body ever so tightly next to my heart. I still didn't believe it! Joseph wasn't sick. It wasn't possible!

Nonetheless, I kept pleading with the Lord Father not to take my little boy. Sobbing uncontrollably, I also begged Joseph not to leave me. Unfortunately, the words went unheard. Joseph, my little boy, was gone and there wasn't anything that could change the situation.

All night I didn't stop crying. Even with a houseful of cats and a caring husband, I felt alone and very upset. Joseph was gone, and I felt my world had just crumbled.

As for Maine Coon cats, I understood a certain heart disease ran in the breed. I also realized Joseph had a history of the heart disease since it was prevalent in his direct family line. Joseph's dad collapsed and died of it at the age of seven. I had hoped that with Joseph well over ten years of age, the old demon of hypertrophic cardiomyopathy (HCM) would spare my little boy.

It didn't!

This disease grabbed hold of Joseph and took him without a warning. Even if I was aware of the extent of Joseph's condition, the outcome would not have changed. There was no cure. I knew all this. Still, I couldn't help but consider I was somehow responsible for his death. In an unrealistic way, I felt I should have done something more to help him.

Over the coming days, the pain and anger set inside my thoughts as the shock of Joseph's sudden death wore off. I kept these feelings hidden. I didn't want to share them with anyone because I was afraid if I let my guard down, I would break into a thousand pieces and never find a way back. I recognized I couldn't allow this to happen for the reason that many cats and people depended upon me. As a result, silence was my best friend.

In order to deal with daily activities, I shut my thoughts off from the magic I sustained inside me. I no longer wished to see or hear the special things I believed in. I stopped letting the so-called fairies, the magic of imagination, be a part of my world. At least, I presumed I accomplished the deed.

Christmas season was quickly approaching, and I desperately tried to ignore the holidays. I wanted them over with as quickly as possible. On the outside, I participated in the festive rituals. Inside, I felt little enthusiasm for anything since it was the first Christmas without my dear friend and my little boy. Right or wrong, I didn't care about the coming holidays without Betty and Joseph.

I don't know for sure if Betty foresaw the turmoil I would be facing after she died; or possibly, Betty was aware of it from heaven—maybe both. Somehow with Joseph's guidance, Betty managed to reach out and help me on that first Christmas after they went to heaven.

It started with Betty's Christmas gift she artfully arranged for me.

Whenever I think about the present Betty purchased months before she died, I still marvel at the whole thing. I also can't help but be in awe of the way she placed something special inside the gift box. What's more, it amazes me how she managed to have the gift presented on the first Christmas after her departure from this life.

Betty bought three designer cat dolls. One was for Noni, her daughter; one for Erin, her granddaughter; and one for me. These dolls remained at Betty's longtime friend's house until early morning on Christmas Eve, when the friend delivered them to Noni's home. They had been gift-wrapped with instructions indicating which package was intended for whom.

Later that night, Noni brought this special gift to Christmas Eve dinner. She presented the package to me after we gathered in the living room to open gifts. Noni then explained the details. Staring at mine in amazement, I noticed there was more inside the box than just a cat doll. The doll was standing on an antique lace snowflake.

Not only was I startled by the gift, I was more taken aback by the snowflake since I realized it didn't come with the doll. Without hesitation, I asked Noni, "Who put the snowflake with the doll?"

Noni definitely didn't have any idea what I was talking about. The blank expression on her face revealed the lack of knowledge in regard to the snowflake. When she spoke, she stated both her doll and Erin's didn't have one. It appeared just mine came with a snowflake, and she absolutely had no clue who put it there.

Looking at the doll, I knew exactly what the snowflake meant. I remembered telling Betty my story about snowflakes some time ago. Sitting on the floor in silence, I stared at the doll in my hand while my mind drifted back into time.

Years earlier during a snowstorm, I had been resting on the couch in Betty's family room and was gazing out the window at the dancing snowflakes as they fell to the ground. Betty noticed I was quiet and deep in thought, so she asked me what I was thinking.

Almost in a trance, I explained I was watching the life of a snowflake and said, "A snowflake is similar to each one of my cats because the flake is very unique with no two ever alike. Each flake is beautiful and precious. If I hold a hand out, the flake will stay for a brief moment and then be gone. Unlike the delicate snowflake, my cats will forever be in my heart."

Betty laughed and said I was seeing fairies. She always referred to the way I viewed the magical aspects of life as my fairies.

While staring at the doll, I knew Betty did not forget my story of the snowflake. She wanted to remind me of the tale on that particular Christmas Eve. I speculated it was Betty's way of telling me she also resembled a snowflake—here for a short time and then gone. Similar to my cats, she too would always be in my heart.

Obviously, I kept silent and didn't say a word to anyone about what I was thinking. I wasn't sure I would have been believed; and I didn't want to be teased about having an overactive imagination, especially at that particular moment.

It was late evening and everyone had departed. Pat was upstairs, watching some TV through his eyelids. At the same time, the cats were snuggled in their chosen spots for a good night's sleep. It was a quiet time for me after finishing the cleanup and putting the last of the dishes away. I was tired, except I was unable to unwind. As a result, I sat on the living room floor, sipping from a glass of wine and looking at Betty's gift once more.

Remaining confused and mystified, I stared at the cat doll and the snowflake. I also passed through my mind the likelihood that Betty realized the snowflake would allow me to open my mind to my fairies, the magic of imagination.

Then it happened!

Unexpectedly, I thought I heard Joseph and looked across the room. There by the front door, Joseph sat and stared at me with his big eyes. The moment he obtained my attention, he did his head bobs and chirps. I froze and told myself this was just a wishful dream, although at that moment I didn't care. I really hoped the magic would come back.

Without a doubt, Joseph acted as if he wanted me to approach him. Dutifully, I rose, walked over, and gently petted his head. He motioned for me to open the door. I complied. Joseph then rotated around and walked outside. He turned his head, making sure I was coming. I obediently followed my handsome Cooner.

My beautiful little boy was "purrfectly" walking with his tail held high! I was thrilled beyond words, watching him strut down the sidewalk.

Before long, I became aware Joseph led me to Betty's house. Joseph was rather excited while he circled around my legs. He asked me to hurry and go inside. When I reached for the door's handle, the door opened. There stood Betty. She hugged me and invited me to come inside for a visit. I was delighted to observe Betty walking exactly like Joseph, perfectly and with both legs. She was whole once more!

It was undeniably Betty's house, but I felt something else. Right then I couldn't put a handle on what it was. Then it dawned on me what I was sensing—my kitty angels! My heavenly kitty angels began to appear everywhere I looked.

I could also see down the hall into the family room. The room was beautifully decorated for Christmas, with the most magnificent Christmas tree placed in the center. When I entered, Joseph raced past me and took his place next to Kotzen. They nuzzled each other and watched my every move quite intently. Both gave me kitty winks.

Betty motioned for me to come and sit with her on the couch. When I sat down, I perceived something more in the shadows. I could feel their presence, but I couldn't actually see who they were.

Mystified, I asked, "Who are they?"

Betty quickly responded, "Your loved ones."

I further questioned, "Why can't I see them?"

Grinning, Betty responded, "You will one day."

Extremely confused, I asked, "Then why can I see my kitty angels and not anyone else, except you?"

Betty cheerfully pointed out, "Even the Lord is unable to keep your heavenly kitty angels from coming to see you when you need them. As for me, it is the gift I had gotten for you this evening. It allowed you to find your way, find the magic of seeing beyond reality. In doing so, you can see me tonight!"

Cackie, my first Siamese, jumped on the couch and curled close by my legs. She purred as I tickled her chin. I looked around the room and observed my other heavenly kitty angels. They were happy and beautiful. One by one, each cat came and greeted me with "purrfect" catly manner. I had the best time hugging and kissing everyone in turn. All of a sudden, I realized one was missing. I asked Betty, "Where is Twinkle?"

Betty instructed me to look at the shining star on top of the tree and then cup my hands together. I did exactly as directed. Then the star flew off the treetop and landed in my hands. It was my Twinkling Star, the pretty little Siamese with the sparkling blue eyes.

Stunned, I looked at Betty and inquired, "How did you figure out that's how I see Twinkle . . . a twinkling star in the heavens?"

This time, Betty happily explained, "I now understand your magic and see it, too!" Betty placed her hand on my arm and continued, "Never stop seeing your fairies. It is the magic inside of you that makes you special. I know I teased you about your outlook in life. I shouldn't have because the magic you shared with me has always been special. Please never let it go. I now love sharing in it along with your cats. Try to remember the magic is there to help face the difficult times and to find joy in the good ones that will come."

I sat speechless for a moment and then sheepishly promised to keep my fairies, the magic of seeing life beyond reality—the wonderful imagination.

The evening passed before I realized it, and Betty announced I must go. I didn't want to leave. I wanted with all my heart to stay. Betty smiled and said, "Not now." In almost a whisper she explained, "You need to continue to take care of the ones who depend upon you."

Betty leaned over and gave me a kiss on my forehead. When she did, my Twinkling Star returned to the top of the tree. In the background, Joseph was singing his beautiful song with Kotzen. For the first time, it dawned on me why Joseph sang during the weeks before he died.

I turned toward Betty and said, "Kotzen came back to Joseph as Joseph began his journey to heaven. That explains why Joseph once more started singing. Since Kotzen's love for Joseph is truly timeless, Kotzen stayed with Joseph throughout those weeks and then guided Joseph home after he died.

"Even though Joseph's song is a song between Joseph and Kotzen, somehow I know that the next time I hear Joseph singing, he will be sharing his song with me, too. My beautiful little boy will come and walk with me on my journey to heaven and then reunite me with my heavenly kitty angels."

Smiling like a Cheshire cat, Betty nodded her head in agreement. Out of the corner of my eye, I noticed Joseph also nodding his head in agreement.

As I stood, Joseph came toward me. He asked me to follow him one more time. I reached down and petted my little boy. When I looked up, I saw the cat doll and snowflake Betty had given me in my hand. I was back sitting on the living room floor.

It was the first time in months that I cried, really cried. The tears were not of pain, but of relief. The magic, the gift of seeing fairies, returned. Betty accomplished the feat with her present on a special Christmas Eve.

Why?

Betty loved me and realized I needed help.

I am not sure if the Christmas vision was real or a dream. Conceivably, it might have been a very active imagination on a night of surprises; or perhaps it was just a means of coping with life. Whatever the reason doesn't matter; I want to hold on to this ability of seeing fairies, keep participating in this magic, and never stop believing that wondrous possibilities really can happen.

As for my beautiful little boy, my Joseph, the Christmas gift of lifting his tail high into the air remains one of my most treasured presents. The love affair that began at his birth lives on in my heart and will be with me forever. The wonderful song Joseph once sang with Kotzen will always be my much-cherished melody.

CHAPTER 11

NEVER STOPPED LEARNING

The cat finds contentment
by enjoying
today.

The moment I allowed the lost fairies back into my thoughts, they changed. They matured. I also discovered my outlook on the world around me somewhat altered. In some aspects, I was more accepting of many situations I didn't have any control over. This might be because I am simply getting older and view certain aspects of life in a different perspective than I did during my younger days.

Once again, I participated in the magic of imagination; but I kept it more to myself. I also noticed it turned quite mellow, much more so than it was in my youth.

Finally, through the different events that transpired throughout my life, a change occurred within me. I started to actually understand the person I think I was intended to become.

The Muffin Man Manual on Feline Diabetes

Muffin Man was a very tough, almost-impossible-to-regulate diabetic cat. His sugar was, unquestionably, a challenge from the first moment I met him and remained as such throughout his entire life. When I say challenge, I mean his sugar swings were all over the place. For this reason, I used a human blood glucose meter to obtain readings to remain, barely, a nose ahead of his condition. There was no question this tool helped figure out how much or how little insulin he required.

In point of fact, I believe Muffin Man read the chapter in my veterinary medical book on feline diabetes and decided to write his own thoughts on the entire subject. After finishing, the valuable knowledge was published so other diabetic felines could read it. This instructional handbook gave explicit information on ingenious methods of avoiding glucose control. By integrating this data into their lives, diabetic cats could then drive their caregivers to tears and almost crazy whenever the caregivers tried to regulate the cat's blood sugar.

In the years after Muffin Man became a heavenly angel, Buddy entered my life. He, like Muffin Man, was a very handsome black-and-white tuxedo feline. The big difference was he wore a shorthair coat while Muffin Man was dressed in longhair attire. Buddy, like his predecessor, was a diabetic. The problem happened when Buddy located a copy of *The Muffin Man Manual on Feline Diabetes* and read it from cover to cover. Buddy then acquired the techniques necessary to keep me on tiptoes. What was even more frustrating, Buddy used the newly acquired knowledge every chance he found and added his own very creative techniques on the subject.

Unlike Muffin Man who was an imp, Buddy was well behaved, except when it came to controlling his blood sugar! Then he categorically turned into Muffin Man reincarnated.

Without the use of the glucose meter, Buddy probably would have made countless visits to the veterinary clinic with diabetic crises. This single tool was definitely an aid in dealing with his sugar swings, thereby preventing emergency hospitalizations.

Since Buddy discovered the Muffin Man manual quite helpful, he figured it should be put online. He also decided to introduce further instructional hints he developed and then inserted these innovative techniques into the edition. Completely unaware what he was up to when I was sleeping, Buddy snuck into the family room and entered the text on his Web site by means of my computer. It took him many nights to achieve the goal. The moment the task was completed, Buddy turned into an instant celebrity in the feline kingdom!

Diabetic cats from everywhere read the new revised text and integrated many of the ideas found inside the chapters into their lives. Soon caregivers, along with veterinarians, were baffled and alarmed by the diabetic cats' poor glucose regulation. It positively never occurred to anyone, especially me, Buddy was the culprit until I noticed him on the computer.

After finding out about the Web page, Buddy just looked at me and grinned. Whenever I caught him smiling, I felt it was because he was pleased he shared the methods of keeping caregivers at a cat's beck and call by developing erratic sugar levels in more of his diabetic feline counterparts. Plus, Buddy was much more satisfied he could reach out to a growing number of diabetic cats with this valuable knowledge.

During Buddy's lifetime, friends informed me their diabetic cats found Buddy's revised edition and practiced the innovative suggestions. One good friend who was living in Indiana at the time e-mailed me that Moocher, her senior cat, used the computer and found the manual. He then tested my friend's sanity by sending his sugar in every direction. Both Sir Fluff and Geoffy also found the manual and quickly learned these step-by-step methods. Then they also tested their caregivers. This categorically pleased Buddy to no end the moment he heard the news.

A couple of years after Buddy became a heavenly angel, Scooter, another friend's cat, went online and came across Buddy's revised publication. Out of curiosity, she read it from beginning to end. It impressed her so much she executed its renowned and successful information in her life. Then she too was an expert in making her caregivers cringe when they attempted to control her sugar. Somehow I can picture Buddy and Muffin Man grinning from heaven with delight because the new improved copy of Muffin Man's manual was passed on to another diabetic feline, namely, Scooter.

I have to confess I can't seem to stop Muffin Man's edition from passing around in the feline kingdom, particularly Buddy's online revised version. I guess as long as there is Internet, diabetic cats will forever read Muffin Man's instructions with the added bonus of Buddy's groundbreaking techniques. After thoroughly studying the information, they too will utilize the knowledge to their advantage and to the dismay of the caregivers and, least forgotten, the veterinarians.

Over the years I have worked with many diabetic cats. It's been both a frustrating challenge and a tremendous reward with each one. I also learned discipline as well as compassion from these experiences. Even though the required care took quite a bit of time, I absolutely loved helping every one of them. What's more, I still find great gratification when I engage and assist another diabetic kitty.

My Monarch Butterfly

Su was a princess. She came from royal lines of Maine Coon cats and was well aware how special this made her. Su never attained the center of attention her sister, Miss Pansy, achieved since Miss Pansy was the queen puss. Unlike Miss Pansy, Su was a quiet princess. Su was very content to remain out of the limelight and away from center stage.

I perceived this princess to be similar to a Monarch butterfly. Like the Monarch, Su was a gentle giant and her beauty was breathtaking. Spreading her wings, Su enjoyed life to the fullest. She was also fragile, much like the Monarch.

In many ways, Su took after her mom, the queen mother, Nana. Su definitely acquired Nana's qualities of lovability and tenderness. I have to say Nana's royal heritage never went to her head. She much "purrferred" to have a tender morsel for munching on and a tickle on the head than be venerated. This was also true for Su. She also loved a tickle on the head. In contrast to her mom, Su and food were not the best of friends. Unlike Nana, Su ate to live while Nana lived to eat.

Even though Su did share some of her sister's traits, Miss Pansy realized the benefits of a queen's position and wore a crown with total regal pride. She believed all others were put on earth to adore her. Su also thought she should be worshiped, with one exception—Su wasn't as forthright in this demand. Because of this, she wore a slightly smaller tiara.

This striking beauty was dressed in long, flowing cream hair, which later in life turned quite wavy. That's why I teased Su and called her curly top. Without an ounce of indecisiveness, Su set me in my place with a stern look, telling me never to refer to her as such—ever again! Su reminded me she was a princess. Therefore, I must always remember proper manners and admire her position in the future. If I failed to do as instructed, I would suffer the consequences of a cold shoulder.

Living a wonderful life of crowned heads, Su believed it was her right to govern the kingdom of the bedroom. She proclaimed to the royal subjects of the realm she would allow certain ones the luxury of sleeping on the bed at night. This included a particular husband. If he snored or tossed in his sleep, Su did not hesitate to dole out swift and fitting punishment. She leveled a good whop with her paw, scolded, and finally insisted he behave or leave the room, immediately!

Su was fond of taking naps on a small antique sofa during the day. Regrettably, as her arthritis afflicted her more and more, she no longer could hop on it. A step stool was placed in front of it to aid in the task, although Su decided the small antique doll bed suited her better. Su never felt words were required with the other felines in the bedroom to make her wishes known about the bed. Recognizing it belonged to Su, the other cats never once challenged Su about trying out its comfort. They respected and allowed Su the first choice of anything she wanted, even though Su didn't ask very much. It just appeared to those who didn't know her very well.

One would have thought that Su was domineering and stubborn, but she was actually quite different. Su's attitude was a cover for a very tender side. By seeing through the pompous airs to what she was really like inside, it was easy to recognize Su was gentle and caring. She often demonstrated great tenderness by intently listening to those around her. Su possessed a deep understanding of their thoughts and always offered a comment to ponder.

With advancing age and health issues, Su grew to be quite delicate. Gradually, she was unable to take pleasure in many things she previously enjoyed. Su accepted many limitations and never once gave into them. She certainly wore her tiara with dignity because of the ability. Sadly, similar to the Monarch, Su's life here on earth was too short.

Su will always be the beautiful princess who was also a fragile butterfly in many ways. Now if I ever see a Monarch butterfly wearing a tiara around the garden, I will know it is my princess popping in for a moment to say hello.

The Last of Her Line

One of the most difficult tragedies I ever had to face was finding out that most of the Maine Coon cats in my care were afflicted with a genetic disease. It was a disease that eventually took these kitties' lives, except the last of their line, Penelopie—Nellie.

My best friend raised Maine Coon cats until it was determined Cheryl's line had a disease called hypertrophic cardiomyopathy (HCM). The moment this time bomb was discovered, it was too late. Cheryl already lost her foundation tomcat, Beau, to this syndrome; and others eventually followed his path. Regrettably, I eventually faced the same outcome with the ones who received the condition since I was a caregiver for a number of Cheryl's Cooners.

Nellie's heritage came about long ago. Her grandparents were a handsome red boy by the name of Beau (Cheryl's foundation tom) and a pretty little girl by the name of Arial, also known as Nana, the queen mother. Beau and Nana produced a number of kittens together, including one by the name of Miss Pansy. Miss Pansy was the queen of East Texas and became Nellie's mom. Nellie's dad was a New Orleans Maine Coon tom and was quite a man about town.

When this little Cooner was born, Nellie was the only girl in a litter of eight boys. Obviously, she grew up tough; yet she always stayed the cute talkative kitten. Nellie developed into a beautiful blue calico with large eyes and feet. She never received enough tickles, excluding ones on her tummy. That was one place in particular this pretty little girl never tolerated touches.

Nellie was still a young kitten when she joined my established household of felines. The second my shaded red Maine Coon little boy laid eyes on Nellie, he decided to take this young Cooner under his wing and raise her. Joseph was Miss Pansy's brother, making him Nellie's uncle. It didn't matter to Joseph. He thoroughly believed he was Nellie's dad.

Joseph was handicapped. He was partially paralyzed in his back legs. This condition never mattered to Nellie. She adored Joseph, and Joseph in turn loved his Nellie. Joseph guided Nellie and watched over her as she became a beautiful adult. Even when she was full grown, I never ceased for a moment referring to Nellie as Joseph's kitten.

It wasn't hard to see that Joseph was devoted to Nellie. Joseph taught her the etiquette of how to be a well-mannered cat. He also kept a close eye on this kitty and always knew where she was at all times. If, for any reason, he could not find Nellie, he became upset and searched until he located her.

One afternoon I took Nellie over to Cheryl's home. I returned while Nellie stayed for the day. In the meantime, Joseph recognized I left with Nellie in tow and came back without her. He then glued himself by the door calling for her. I realized Nellie was coming back home in a couple of hours. For Joseph, there was nothing that would appease him or make him understand that she would shortly be home. He wanted his Nellie, and he wanted her right then. The moment Nellie returned, Joseph was thrilled. He ran circles around her, gave her kisses, and repeated over and over how much he missed her.

On the day Joseph left Nellie and went to the heavenly home, Nellie was heartbroken. She followed me everywhere, insisting I must bring him back. I wished I possessed the power to perform the act, except I didn't. I knew Joseph received the heart disease that ran throughout his line, but I did not anticipate Joseph would die so suddenly from HCM since his condition was the milder form. Tragically, he succumbed in "purrcisely" the same manner as his dad did years earlier.

Each one of my Maine Coons, not counting Nellie and one other from another line, followed Beau's and Joseph's paths in a short period of time. There was nothing on earth available to stop the outcome of the disease.

The Cooner girls developed complications from HCM and ultimately lost their lives because of it, while the boys dropped dead without a warning. I felt extremely helpless since there wasn't a thing that could be done to prevent it.

Nellie was lucky. She was spared from inheriting HCM, although not from the misfortune of losing someone she cared about to the disease.

Today as I sit petting Nellie, I look back and think about my Cooner cats who lost their lives to HCM. I admit many mixed emotions run through my mind because of it. With every tragedy, I asked the question "Why?"

I never found an answer.

Beyond a shadow of a doubt, I loved each Cooner lost to HCM and was thankful to have them with me for as long as I did. Still, it was devastating to realize each one carried a time bomb just waiting to go off. HCM certainly didn't have an ounce of mercy when it took over. At the same time, I wondered if I would ever have accepted these special Cooners into my life even after knowing about HCM.

There is only one conclusion. Yes, I would have opened my arms to these cats even realizing what HCM could do to them since they already stole my heart at the moment of our first meeting.

I also question myself if in the very beginning I would have permitted Beau and Nana to be bred together, recognizing they could pass on to their future generations this deadly form of heart disease.

No, there wasn't any way I could stand by and allow such a potential tragedy to occur. It would have been better not to have bred these cats if it was recognized that there existed a potential for passing a lethal genetic disease to the offspring, even though I'd never have known and loved Nellie along with many others.

I believe the Cooners made my world a better place. They were blessings given by the Lord Father; and for that, I am eternally grateful. Nevertheless, these wonderful Maine Coon cats were put in my care for such a short time before they had to go back to the heavenly home. I confess that has been the hardest part to understand and accept.

My heart was torn into many pieces when I lost one Cooner after another. I was devastated and wasn't sure I had the strength to pull myself together and carry on with my chosen path, but I did. Somehow I managed to work through the grief and live with the losses. I overcame the heartbreaks. I also remind myself that if Beau and Nana were never bred and didn't have kittens, I would not be sitting here today petting my wonderful Nellie.

I only wish the price that was paid for Joseph's kitten wasn't as high as it turned out to be. I also wish the Lord Father could have found a different plan on giving me fortitude to handle such adversity, the misfortune of losing many wonderful cats to HCM.

Bottom Pats

Windy was a blue-gray tuxedo cat with white who had the biggest green eyes. She flashed a smile that absolutely melted the hearts of those who took notice. Given the chance, Windy curled her tail to make it appear exactly like a candy cane when she danced on her tiptoes. Nevertheless, what Windy loved more than anything else in the entire world was pats on her bottom. The longer it was carried out, the more she enjoyed it. I never met a cat before or after who liked to be patted as much as little Windy relished this gesture.

Many times I would sing to Windy,

Where is Tippy Toes, Tippy Toes, with the tail curl?

The second I recited this short verse, Windy came and performed a little dance, the marching two-step. She then turned around, pointed her back end in my direction while looking over her shoulder, and asked, "Well, aren't you going to pat my bottom?"

Of course, I patted Windy's bottom as requested!

Windy responded by singing,

Pop, pop, please give me more!
I like it, I like it, please don't stop!

In Windy's teenage years, she developed a malignant tumor inside her chest. It was the same cancer her twin sister, Feathers, died from a year earlier. Windy showed no signs of having anything wrong until her last day on earth, when she suddenly developed difficulty with breathing.

It was an early Thursday morning in January 2008, and I rushed Windy to the veterinary clinic. She was having what seemed an asthma attack. The doctors checked Windy, ruled out heart failure, and treated the obvious, asthma.

Gradually, as the morning progressed, Windy improved. But the moment she was taken out of the oxygen chamber, Windy's breathing rapidly deteriorated. After more tests and finally x-rays, the growth was discovered. It was inoperable, and there wasn't any other viable treatment option.

I sat with Windy all day, inches away from my baby. I maintained high hopes she was going to get over the asthma attack and come home that night.

I was wrong.

Windy was dying.

With tears flowing down my cheeks and my heart breaking in half, the hardest thing I did that day was to let go of my little Tippy Toes who loved her bottom pats. Right before the gift of peace was administered, I gave Windy bottom pats and whispered my short verse. Windy purred back one last time with her song.

A cat retains the uncanny ability to hide a health problem until the issue has become full blown and, more than likely, already in the final stage. This behavior can be devastating to the cat's caregiver and leave the caregiver wondering if something was missed. It is a remarkable skill the cat inherited that allowed the cat to survive in the wild. However, this ability is a determent for the cat's well-being in domestication since treatment can be delayed or never given. Even if the problem is discovered during the early stage, the outcome, quite often, is the same seeing as there may not be a treatment for the condition. The huge difference is that the caregiver is provided a chance to accept the situation before the final outcome.

The Book about a Siamese Cat

A few years ago, I attended an antique show in the town where I currently live with two good friends. Passing by a book dealer, I happened to notice a table upon which old cat books were displayed. One book in particular caught my attention. The book's jacket was orange with a Siamese cat picture on the front cover.

After stopping to get a better look at the small hardback, I then lifted it off the table and smiled as I flipped through the pages. The book was about the adventures of a Siamese cat. But it was not just any book of a Siamese cat. It was a copy of one my dad had given me when I was around ten years old. The moment I started turning each page, my thoughts tossed back to my youth.

When I was a child, my dad was employed by the US Post Office within the motor vehicle division in the city where I was raised. Over the years he worked his way up to the supervisory position of that particular section. His drivers made daily stops at mainly large businesses, including the printing plants of the book publishing companies around the downtown area and in the industrial park.

The main offices of the publishing companies were in New York City, with a number of the printing operations located in my hometown. Often inside the warehouses of these printing plants was a stack of books that were discarded for one reason or another. The management regularly let either their employees or the men from the post office have any of the rejected books at no charge.

One day Dad attended a meeting at one of the printing plants. When it was over, Dad was preparing to leave but hesitated. From the corner of his eye, he noticed a small book with a cat on its front cover in the reject pile. He carefully reached for the book and looked at it. Nothing seemed to be wrong with it. Naturally, Dad asked the foreman if he could have it for his daughter since she loved cats. The foreman said he could have it along with any other book he wanted from the pile. Dad only took one, the book about a Siamese cat.

Later in the day, after arriving home from work, Dad gave me the special find he stumbled upon during his visit to the plant. He figured I might enjoy reading about a Siamese cat.

Dad was right. I did enjoy reading the story. I loved the book and reread it many times. I kept the treasure in my bedroom, hidden inside a dresser drawer with other prized possessions.

The book was my introduction to Siamese cats and the reason for my fascination with the breed. Because of it, Dad later helped me acquire a blue point Siamese cat at the age of fourteen.

I don't know whatever happened to the special treasure. It disappeared into time and became a memory; even the memory was forgotten until one particular afternoon, when I was passing by the dealer of old books at the antique show.

Thrilled with the find, I bought the one in my hand. While I was paying the elderly dealer, I explained it was a copy of the one my dad gave me when I was a child. Sadly, it had gotten lost long ago; and I was elated to find another one.

The dealer then asked, "What part of the country were you raised in?"

At first I thought how odd to ask that question, but I replied anyway. I said, "In the Northeast, Pennsylvania to be exact."

The dealer stated not many prints of this particular book were ever published. What's more, they were only sold in the New York area. That's why he was curious to find out where I lived. He thought it never would have been feasible for anyone residing in Texas to come across a copy when it was printed, and that was the reason he was interested to know the region where I was raised.

Living within the New York metropolitan vicinity was an advantage for the dealer. It allowed the opportunity to periodically investigate bookstores in both New York and New Jersey. The dealer discovered the one he sold me at an old bookstore going out of business in New Jersey. He was pretty sure there were about a couple dozen copies still existing.

Further elaborating, the dealer related he made the circuit of antique shows from the East coast to the West coast each year with this particular one in Texas on his list. Apparently, he wasn't interested in selling the book at previous shows, even though he had been at numerous ones before hitting Texas. For some unknown rationale that afternoon, the dealer suddenly decided to put it out for sale, just minutes before I came by and picked it up and looked at it.

Standing there and listening to the elderly dealer's tale, I was dumbfounded. I wondered if perhaps he was giving me a good storyline but figured he was telling the truth by the sincerity in his voice.

Hearing the discussion, one of my friends leaned over and whispered into my ear, "Do you think this is your book and it was meant for you to find today?"

I mulled over the possibility that the book belonged to me. The likelihood was definitely conceivable but unlikely. It didn't matter. I had fun considering the idea. If nothing else, the book was then mine.

Ever since that afternoon at the antique show, I have thought about coming across the book and wondered if it occurred by chance. Perhaps it was just meant to happen. Without saying, I found the whole idea intriguing and still do.

I placed the prized find in my library. It sits next to a special kitty doll. Periodically, I reread the story. After finishing, I sit there and think about the book, Dad, and my Siamese cats.

When my first Siamese of almost twenty years and the next one of seventeen years went to heaven, I was ready to let go of that part of my life and move on to a new chapter. I didn't want another one any more. Everything changed when I stumbled upon the book that created my love affair with the Siamese breed.

I wondered if it was Dad's means of helping me cope with the sorrow of losing two wonderful Siamese cats and allow me to consider another one someday. Because they were a special connection with Dad, it's very probable he wanted me to preserve the bond we shared and not let it end.

I am not sure if it was plain luck I saw the copy at the show or something more. Feasibly, it could have been Dad's sneaky way of reminding me he maintains an eye on me from heaven. It is also quite plausible Dad wanted me to consider sharing my life, once again, with another wonderful Siamese kitty.

Subsequent to stumbling across the book, I now have doubts about the decision on closing that period of life. I award Dad the honor of accomplishing the deed by the best means possible—returning the Siamese cat book back to me.

At least, I now tell Dad I will reflect on the resolution and possibly consider being owned by another wonderful Siamese cat.

Finding Courage

If it is not present at birth, courage can often be developed through quite a bit of hard work. Sometimes courage can be found or tripped over without even knowing it.

Luke was a cream colored Domestic Shorthair with white. He wore long legs and a tail that curled in every conceivable position. Luke was quite shy and was definitely a loner. He never asked for anything and always stayed in the background. This outlook absolutely changed on the day Luke found his courage.

Even though this kitty actually belonged to both my best friend and me, Luke lived with Cheryl. He had been part of the rescue cats we cared for in her garage apartment. During operation, Cheryl supplied the food and utilities while I furnished everything else. We equally looked after and loved every one of these once abandoned cats.

When caring for the rescues, I went over to Cheryl's house every morning to partake in the cleanup, feeding, and grooming of the apartment felines. Eventually, we were able to adopt a few into good homes. As the number gradually decreased, we soon found less and less suitable caregivers for the remainder. We then decided to place these kitties into each of our two homes. Afterward, I remained the other caregiver to the ones residing with Cheryl.

It was the day after Christmas in 2000, and a severe ice storm hit the area where I lived. My home lost power for a few hours, but Cheryl's place lost power for about a week.

Cheryl made the best of it by barely keeping one area of her place warm enough for the crew with the fireplace for the first couple of days after the outage. When she was away at work, my husband stayed at the house for safety reasons, making sure the fire remained lit since it was gas. More importantly, although there was a screen in front of it, he kept a watchful eye on the cats and the bird so they didn't get too close to the fire.

In a few days, the power was slowly restored in most of the city, except Cheryl remained without any electricity. With no end in sight, I talked her into coming over to my home with her menagerie.

Some of the cats were settled in the library and the others were quartered inside the sewing room accompanied with the necessary amenities. The bird and his cage were placed in a guest bedroom with Cheryl.

At some point during the first night's stay, Luke managed to open the door of the sewing room and make a break downstairs. He was very proud of the fact that he accomplished such a feat. In no time, he sat on a step in the middle of the staircase. Then with a smile on his face, he proclaimed with a sturdy voice, "I am king!"

There was one slight problem in Luke's adventure. He still had to return to the sewing room for the duration of the holiday. As soon as Cheryl's power returned, I loaded her crew in my car and returned them to her place.

Luke discovered courage because of the visit. For the first time ever, he put a paw forward and claimed his rightful throne. He remained vocal and opinionated from that day forward. He no longer lingered in the background. He turned into a lion king and finally demanded his fair share of adoration and respect.

Periodically over the following years, Luke made numerous visits to my home. Each time his courage grew stronger while in my care. When he returned to Cheryl, Luke was even more outgoing and loving.

Sadly, Luke was struck with cancer in his senior years and required special attention. Cheryl's work schedule didn't allow her to tend to Luke's special needs. Cheryl and I agreed that in Luke's best interest, he should spend his last weeks on earth with me.

The courage Luke found years ago helped him face his final battles. He met each challenge the cancer threw his way with great inner strength and fortitude. Luke left this life as the proud lion he became years earlier.

A Walking Litter Box

In general, a cat's concept of a bath is something thought up by a crazed and demented human in order to inflict horrendous torture on an innocent and unsuspecting feline. A bottom wash given to rectify the quandary of a walking litter box comes in second to this act of ultimate feline humiliation.

Apparently, I never found it difficult to guess what cat came down with the problem of a messy bottom; and I still don't. Upon entering the room, the afflicted cat has always been the first one to greet me on my arrival.

One time in particular, this unfortunate situation of a condemned and overpowering messy bottom occurred to Blueberry, a pretty blue-gray Domestic Longhair with green crossed eyes. The best way of describing this kitty: she was a very odorous walking litter box.

The pungent fumes emanating from Blueberry's disastrous bottom more than filled the entire house, and a gas mask totally failed to prevent the tears from forming in my eyes. Since it reached that point, Blueberry definitely refused to clean it and "purrferred" not to acknowledge it even belonged to any part of her body.

The first thing I told myself: *Don't React!* I was quite eager to prevent Blueberry from catching on to what I was about to execute. I learned, long ago, the art of surprise works best with felines. By not thinking about the strategy, I was optimistic I might possibly keep Blueberry from reading my mind. My intentions were to stop Blueberry from heading for the nearest bedroom and attaching herself "purrmanently" to the carpet located dead center under the bed. This devious tactic of mine would also hinder Blueberry from running at warp speed and painting every wall with a much-polluted tail on the way to a safe zone.

I prepared the laundry room that has a large sink with a crucial water sprayer attached to the faucet. I piled a stack of towels on the counter and placed the shampoo bottle within arm's reach. I made sure the water was the right temperature before I casually headed for the walking litter box.

Nonchalantly, I bent over and gently stroked Blueberry. Trying hard not to choke or pass out, I hoisted this kitty with my hands and swiftly headed for the awaiting sink while holding her at arm's length. Unfortunately, my cover was rapidly blown and Blueberry was determined to get out of my grasp. Given that she acquired a black belt in kitty karate, Blueberry sought to utilize her knowledge of the martial arts. She did this with the intention of inflicting injury on any part of my body she could latch on to with her talons or jaws of life in a desperate attempt to free her body and then flee. I knew, as long as I did not relent in my grip, that Blueberry couldn't escape. With a little luck, I figured I would not receive too many life-threatening wounds by the time I was finished.

Blueberry maintained dilated eyes and a look of total shock as she demonstrated the ability to turn inside out in her frantic efforts to get away, but I held a firm lock-hold on her. Water was sprayed in every direction; and amazingly enough, it essentially hit the targeted area! Buying shampoo by the gallon definitely helped since it took about that much to clean Blueberry's bottom while simultaneously applying it to the sink, countertop, walls, cabinets, floor, ceiling, and me.

Then Blueberry tried another maneuver she learned at kitty defense class. She screamed blood-curdling cries at the top of her lungs. Wishing I owned a pair of industrial-strength earplugs, I relentlessly carried on with the scrubbing and tried ignoring Blueberry's ear-piercing, four-letter kitty cussing.

After the final rinse, I grabbed the towels and quickly dried off the fresh-smelling, clean kitty as best as possible. Still remaining quite saturated with water, Blueberry lunged through the laundry room door and soared to the exact center of the kitchen table. She deliberately did this to groom her much-rumpled and water-saturated fur while concurrently destroying the table's finish as a just reward for such unspeakable actions.

It merely took an hour to mop up water covering the laundry room floor, wipe down countertops, scrape shampoo off of almost every imaginable surface, and do a load of laundry. I finished by retiring my shredded jeans and shirt into the garbage.

Without saying, I was exhausted but pleased at the same time. I felt successful since I obtained a spotless kitty and a fresh-smelling house. In addition, I just needed a dozen Band-Aids to cover the nonfatal wounds. My hearing began to come back within the hour and completely returned by the next day. I then placed a call to the furniture refinisher. The best part, it would only cost $250 to have the table restored!

Later, as soon as I completed dinner preparations, I turned on the TV to catch the evening news. On the local coverage, it was reported that a loud noise was discharged in my area earlier in the day. The reporter stated it sounded as if one of the city's disaster emergency alarms malfunctioned, although the city's maintenance workers were unable to locate the actual source of the problem but were still investigating it.

Grinning, I looked over at a very relaxed and contented Blueberry curled inside a warm bed and purring. She was wholeheartedly enjoying herself because she knew the exact source of the unknown noise. I chuckled as I watched her. I greatly suspected Blueberry, the once very dirty walking litter box, was "purrcisely" the cause of the commotion in the city a few hours previously with her ear-piercing and blood-curdling cries.

A Cat with an Attitude

One of the greatest challenges for me has been dealing with a cat with an attitude. When I say attitude, I mean a cat getting aggressive to the point of inflicting bodily harm on others around him the moment he is set off and out of control.

There have been times that it took a few weeks to penetrate the aggressive cat's defenses. Sometimes it was years before I accomplished the endeavor. In a few cases, I established a compromise with the cat, although I eventually found a way to reach the cat's good side if given enough time to locate it.

My caring ability or, more than likely, the stubborn part of me never let me give up on an aggressive cat. I constantly tried locating the crack in the cat's resistance so I could find the good side. After I achieved the breakthrough, the cat turned into a loving "mushmallow." I was also very aware that the aggressive side remained below the surface and could possibly reappear at any second. If the attitude emerged, at least I learned the means to appropriately deal with the situation.

Buttons was adopted as a very young kitten by two good friends of mine. I assisted in her care from the day she entered their home, and I carried on with it throughout her life. This longhair kitty was a vibrant calico. Since Buttons was dressed in flaming colors, perhaps she acquired the personality to match it.

This pretty little kitty was raised with two Maine Coon cats, a loving cream-colored boy and a headstrong white lad with bicolor eyes. This striking white Cooner was also deaf. Buttons ruled her gentleman cream brother and was constantly teased by the white-thunder one. For this reason, Buttons learned how to both give and take; but this did not help improve her "purrsonality" in the least little bit.

The one thing could undeniably be said about Buttons: she definitely enjoyed having a pound of flesh whenever the mood hit her. On the other side of the tail, she could be the most loving little girl. I like everyone else around her was never really sure what attitude was ever at hand. Therefore, I presented the nickname of "Pudding" seeing as this creamy mixture has the potential to contain different consistencies. Alas, so did Button's "purrsonality."

Throughout the years, I shuttled Buttons into the veterinary clinic for routine health checks and other procedures. At first Buttons was terrified and froze. I treasured it because I was allowed to hold and hug this kitty without calling 911. She in turn hugged me back, "purrsuming" I would save her from the cat-eating doctors. The behavior lasted until Buttons overcame her fears of the clinic and she turned into a holy terror to everyone there and to me as well. Then the muzzle came out to protect anyone she came in contact with during the appointment.

Every two weeks, I trimmed Button's nails with a muzzle safely surrounding her jaws of life and another person wearing my mad kitty gloves on both hands while holding her. It was quite amazing to witness how powerful a fourteen-pound cat could get when agitated.

On many occasions, I babysat Buttons and her brothers when their human parents were away on trips. Sometimes these kitties visited for as long as a month. During the long stays, I did break through and find Button's good side, only to see it fade away the moment she returned home.

There was never a time I wasn't patient with Buttons, and I positively never scolded her. I treated this kitty with kindness and, absolutely, with a tremendous amount of respect. I constantly reinforced the positive and ignored the negative. Regardless, the most frustrating thing was that Buttons just wanted to see me jump off a short pier and, preferably, into a dry lake bed!

When this kitty developed other medical issues that had to be addressed at home, I was the one to help. In Button's senior years, it was daily ritual. Despite that, Button's attitude didn't alter. Buttons tried to nail me every chance she found and accomplished it twice. Amazingly, I survived, much to her dismay.

Button's attitude toward me improved as she was about to enter her super senior years. It was then she mellowed. I was no longer "purrceived" as the evil witch sent to torment her. I was finally able to retire my mad kitty gloves, blanket, and muzzle, which prevented mass destruction to everyone concerned when handling this very headstrong cat.

One of the most joyous times happened when Buttons, at the age of fifteen, allowed me to touch her at home without any protective gear on my body. From then on, Buttons was my "mushmallow." I find that the biggest thrills come after patiently waiting many years for a breakthrough, and this definitely was one of those times.

Sir Fluff was another kitty with a very aggressive attitude. I also needed to win him over to his good side in a very short period of time because of health reasons on his part.

This handsome white cat with longhair became unbelievably hostile the instant he lost control since he maintained a high level of fear. The one person he trusted to handle him was his human mom, yet there were some instances she also had to back away from him.

The aggressive side of Fluff completely took over if he was afraid. He literally went into a frenzy in which he recognized no one, not even his human mom. He was then out to inflict major damage on anyone who tried to come close and, above all, attempted any touches!

Sir Fluff was a diabetic for many years before I entered into his life. Because of it, he was required to make many trips into the veterinary clinic for sugar checks. In the early days, before the diabetes, he was easy to handle. He just froze in place, but this was short lived after he developed diabetes. To get the needed blood sample for a glucose reading, blood was drawn from his leg. It hurt. He felt threatened. For this reason, Fluff's fear escalated to the point that his aggressive side took over. He literally was deadly to anyone coming in contact with him, including his human mom.

Fluff's attitude deteriorated so badly at the clinic that the only way the staff could work with him was with sedation, and he was out cold. Since it had to be accomplished in such a manner, Fluff's sugar elevated significantly. Therefore, trying to get an accurate reading was almost impossible to achieve at the clinic. It was then decided that home checks of blood sugar were required to have any kind of success with controlling Fluff's diabetes.

This is where I came into Fluff's life.

Fluff's doctor asked me to teach his human mom how to check his sugar at home. Fluff's mom was a good student and learned the technique very quickly. She was then able to track the sugar, and Fluff's doctor could then adjust Fluff's insulin accordingly.

The following Christmas after I taught Fluff's human mom how to use the glucose meter, this kitty did a major nosedive. He crashed and required extended medical attention. I stepped in and offered my services. Under the directions of the doctors, I became Fluff's visiting home nurse.

While Fluff was quite ill, I was able to accomplish anything, except that quickly passed. Fluff pulled through and returned to his normal untouchable self. At that point I religiously worked on winning his trust because I had a feeling I would remain a big part of his life.

For months, I tried every trick in the book I knew on behavior to alter Fluff's attitude. From giving treats, playing with toys, to sitting in the same room with the untouchable cat—nothing worked. There was no doubt in my mind Fluff wanted very little to do with me, although I was persistent or possibly plain stubborn in my efforts. Each week, I visited and tried my best to breach his distrust. I made small steps, but they were not enough to permit me into Fluff's world for any length of time.

It was during Fluff's first visit with me when his human mom was away on an extended trip that things went from bad to total disaster. Handling Fluff was impossible to begin with, and Fluff's aggression escalated while in my care.

Since Fluff was a diabetic, he required insulin twice a day. That meant I was obliged to touch him for about five seconds to give the injection. This was certainly not in Fluff's agenda, and he was not going to let me administer it without a fight. To accomplish the goal, I pinned him to the floor with mad cat gloves on my hands and a blanket thrown over the front part of his body. I could then give the injection in his butt. There was no other option without having the luxury of time to find his good side. Fluff required insulin, and it was the best way to succeed at giving it.

The doctors would either have to pin Fluff or knock him out with anesthesia to give the insulin if he was boarded at the veterinary clinic. In my opinion, that was not a very good alternative. I believed it was up to me to figure out a solution.

Each time I faced the Great White to give the insulin, I dreaded it. I hated wrestling with Fluff to inject him. I was never mean, just very firm. There was no choice that it was administered in such a manner since it was a matter of safety for me.

Rather quickly, I felt like Captain Ahab struggling to capture Moby Dick every time I harpooned Fluff with the insulin syringe. While carefully wading through rough seas, I attempted to overcome the Great White. With each encounter, I was unrelenting and the Great White was merciless!

Between the wrestling matches, I tried everything from sweetly talking, playing soothing music, doling out treats, offering tempting toys, using aroma therapy to simply sitting with Fluff. I desperately searched for his good side. Fluff's attitude throughout those times was civil—nothing more. Unfortunately, he never allowed any touches.

After a few days, the situation did not improve. When it came to insulin time, Fluff waited, ready to impart bodily harm on any section of my body if given the opportunity.

Frustrated beyond words, I did not admit defeat. However, I was at the bottom of the bag of tricks to alter his behavior. I decided to turn to medication instead. It was the last resort because I never liked using it if there was another alternative. Not having the option of time on my side, I had to quickly do something and find some alternative. I preferred not making Fluff sick. I also didn't want to get hurt. As a result, I turned to Fluff's veterinarians to prescribe a drug that would calm Fluff's fear. If nothing else, I was optimistic it would stop the aggression at least long enough to give him the insulin without a major battle.

Luckily, I was able to trick Fluff into ingesting the drug by mixing it in his food. I was fortunate Fluff savored moist food and gobbled everything down in no time without ever realizing anything extra was added to his meal.

In a few days, the medication took effect. Fluff's fear started to diminish. As it weakened, I broke through and found his good side. He no longer saw me as the insidious whaler on a mission to destroy him. Fluff's fear faded, and he stopped the violence. I finally received the five seconds needed to give the insulin without a struggle. I then had time to use behavior techniques to keep the good side present. Toward the end of the fourth week, I weaned Fluff off of the drug. To my total delight, Fluff finally became my "mushmallow!"

The drug provided me the ability to work with Fluff without having to grapple this kitty to give the insulin. As a result, the cycle stopped. Fluff finally saw me in a different light. He accepted me into his world, and I could touch him. He realized I was there to help and love him in his human mom's absence. Fluff turned into my Sugar Baby and was no longer the Great White to be harpooned twice a day.

After my big step forward, Sir Fluff still suffered from fear aggression with one big difference—I was at least allowed to reach him without resorting to medication since I finally gained his trust. What thrilled me more than anything was that Fluff continued to be my Sugar Baby after he returned to his residence. He also remained my sweet boy each time he came back to my home for a visit.

Anger aggression is hard enough to deal with as in the case with Buttons, but Fluff's fear aggression is one of the most difficult and complicated to manage. A cat with either type cannot be reasoned with when the cat loses control of reality and turns hostile. It is a dangerous situation to anyone around the cat.

As long as I never forgot that the dark sides of Buttons and Fluff were always present right below the surface, I never found a problem in dealing with either of them. I fully understood they retained the ability to go from docile to deadly in a moment's notice. For this reason, I always was alert around them.

Undeniably, I wholeheartedly cherished the good sides of Buttons and Fluff. I loved giving these kitties scratches on their heads, tickles under their chins, and kisses on their noses!

Catching a Tiger

Over the years, I have caught a few tigers, including a two-and-a-half-pound black-and-white kitten abandoned on the golf course behind my home.

It may be said I have things completely wrong . . . the domestic feline is not a wild tiger. Nevertheless, this cat can surely be one! The hunt may be on a less grand scale. Even so, the thrill of capture is exactly the same.

In the early morning hours before sunrise, my husband was outside filling the bird feeder. He accidentally dropped some seed on the driveway due to the poor light. After Pat walked over to hang the feeder on its hook in the yard, a tiny kitten appeared and ravenously ate the fallen seed. The kitten was starved; and the seed was, probably, the only thing he could find that was edible.

Pat tried getting close to the baby. As he approached, the kitten ran through the iron fence and took cover under the bushes in the neighbor's yard. Shortly afterward, Pat came rushing in the house. He excitedly related the saga about the very tiny and famished kitten. He then asked me to come and catch the baby. I opened a small can of cat food and followed Pat back outside.

Slowly, I went over and sat on the driveway adjacent to where the kitten was hiding. I set the can of food down and waited. The kitten came out and began to eat. I reached over and tried to grab him, but he was fast. He squirmed and turned in every direction, escaping from of my grasp. He then flew at the speed of light across the neighbor's yard and into the darkness.

Over the coming days, near dusk, the kitten continued to appear, looking for something to eat. Each time I took food out and placed it down in the same spot for the tiny bag of bones to consume. I remained at a distance and quietly watched. I wanted the kitten to realize I was the one bringing his dinner since my motive was to win his trust and ultimately catch him. The kitten devoured the feast under the condition I did not approach him. The second I attempted to move in his direction, he took off and disappeared.

Before long, I decided the only way to capture the kitten was by means of a humane trap baited with cat food. Having previous experience in this area, I was aware the kitten was too small to set off the trigger. If I wanted the door of the trap to close, the trigger had to be booby trapped.

Early one evening, the kitten appeared for some dinner "purrcisely" on time. The big difference was that the feast was sitting inside the humane trap.

I fastened one end of a long string to the trap's trigger and sat about twenty feet away, holding the other end of the string. After making sure I was not anywhere in the vicinity of the food, which was tantalizing his nose, the kitten slowly approached the trap and entered.

Not moving a muscle, I waited until the kitten was crouched down and eating before pulling the string. The trigger quickly released, and the door slammed closed. Amazingly, the kitten never came up for a breath of air and "purrsisted" to chow down. He was totally unaware there was no longer an exit.

By having the patience that Job would be proud of, I sat motionless and just watched the kitten eat. Pat failed to notice I set off the trigger and didn't understand the kitten was safely secured inside the cage. Consequently, he became impatient with me.

Annoyed, Pat snapped, "Pull the string!"

Turning my head around, I grinned. Then pointing at the trap, I demonstrated I already accomplished the endeavor. The kitten was definitely locked within the cage.

Pat asked, "Why didn't you tell me you caught him?"

Smiling, I explained, "I wanted the kitten to finish eating before making a sound or a move in the direction of the trap."

After a few minutes, both Pat and I approached the trap. It was at that point the kitten became aware there wasn't a way out. He tried desperately to escape but couldn't. He bounced off the walls in every direction.

Pat carried the trap into the house and proceeded to the guest bathroom. With doors tightly closed, I slowly and carefully reached inside the cage. I gently lifted the kitten out, and he went limp in my hand. He started purring, as I cradled him next to my heart. I was pleased the tiger was finally caught.

As it turned out, it was a good thing the kitten had been snared because late the following day, the skies broke loose; and terrible storms hit the area. There was a good possibility such a small kitten could not survive that kind of weather, even a kitten as agile and determined to stay alive as this tiny bag of bones.

What did I name the tiny black-and-white kitten found on the golf course?

Tiger Woods, of course!

Two Friends and Their Cats

End-of-life care is challenging. I understand how taxing the situation can be because too many times I have been in that very position when the life of one of my cats began to fade.

The nursing part of the end-of-life care is time consuming and demands a tremendous amount of physical attention. The amount of required work can also be bone tiring. Furthermore, the fact that a life is about to shortly cease is mentally exhausting, often taking a tremendous toll on the person with the direct responsibility.

End-of-life nursing for a cat is an area in which I am particularly good at providing. For me, this care can be the most rewarding work I do. After it stops, I know everything in my power has been done to provide the cat with the best quality of life until the moment arrived for the little one to return to the heavenly home. This responsibility can also be the most heartbreaking time since I realize there is nothing on earth that can change the ultimate outcome.

I definitely recognize that caring for a dying loved one is a tremendously difficult task for a caregiver. The load is somewhat easier when there is a support system around. Whenever a friend's cat enters the last phase of life, I walk with the friend and assist with the nursing of the kitty in order to help both.

A few years ago, I helped a pretty little Tonkinese cat of elder years by the name of Purcilla. She belonged to Charlotte, who was devoted to this tiny ball of energy. Under the instructions of my friend's veterinarian, I managed Purcilla's medications so she could live with quality in her life. I showed Charlotte how to syringe-feed and give oral medicines in Purcilla's food. I shared many helpful techniques for Purcilla that made life easier as her illness progressed.

Purcilla was adorable. She sported gorgeous blue-green eyes. This petite kitty wore a pretty lilac coat. She was quite dainty and sweet. She also gave the best hugs and loved to bury her head under anyone's chin when held on the shoulder. However, Purcilla could also be a little spitfire. As a result, I nicknamed her Hisscilla.

I knew Purcilla from the moment Charlotte adopted her. She grew up with a big brother, Clarence, a Tonkinese as well. In Clarence's last year on earth, I stepped in and helped with his nursing care. It was during the visits to treat Clarence that I became well acquainted with Purcilla.

During Purcilla's mid teenage years, she developed kidney failure and later cancer. I couldn't believe it at first. In my mind, I never understood how Purcilla entered the elder years. To me, she was still a young kitten and never changed.

Purcilla is now in heaven with Clarence. I sense she remains the sweet little kitten I grew to adore and, possibly, the little spitfire if the mood hits her.

Meowie was an Abyssinian. She belonged to a different friend who moved to another part of the world. In reality, the location was a northern state. For me, the move might as well have been China since years sometimes passed between visits. This never really mattered because we stayed in touch, and Carol never failed to send pictures along with the numerous tales of Meowie's ongoing ventures.

When visiting, Carol was accompanied with Meowie. Traveling around the country never bothered Meowie. This passion for adventure was definitely in her blood. She turned into a trucker cat with Carol and her beau. I think Meowie journeyed to every state because of Mike's job as a driver of a fifty-foot trailer truck. For this reason, staying in my guest bedroom was not a problem for Meowie in the least.

Meowie modeled a flaming red coat and a tuff of hair on the top of her head I called a horn. Anytime this kitty lost her temper, I swear this hair stuck straight up exactly like a horn. It always tickled me whenever the cute tuff appeared.

Like Purcilla, Meowie grew to be a senior cat. In her teenage years, she developed lymphoma. Throughout the course of the diagnosis and treatments, I walked with Carol. I guided my friend during the difficult times until Meowie also returned to the heavenly home.

None of these cats belonged to me, although in a way they were mine. I cared about them, as I care for my own cats. They stole a piece of my heart in the same way my cats have also captured sections of it. Needless to say, I was saddened to say good-bye to them.

I think what bothered me about losing both Purcilla and Meowie, along with Clarence, was the fact that time passed quickly and I never was conscious of it. Even though these cats turned into seniors right before my eyes, I never saw the transition. This lack of sight happened because they never acted as elder felines but as kittens. Then the day arrived, and they went back to the heavenly home.

Braveheart

A cat can be born without any fear. At the same time, another one tries to conquer fear throughout his life. The feline demonstrates great inner strength if he can master control over this state of mind. He also must work extremely hard at keeping the fear from returning and consuming his whole world.

It seems that as with a human, a cat also struggles to defeat an imperfection such as retaining fear of the unknown. Many times the cat arrives at a compromise and lives with the problem, just like Spot did.

Spot was an extremely tender and gentle cat who tried to overcome his fear of anything new and different around him. It was extremely difficult for Spot to keep this specific anxiety in check, but he managed to deal with it through the encouragement from his special humans.

This kitty was a handsome Siamese mix, though any more similarities to the Siamese breed stopped with Spot's coloring and blue eyes. Spot also wore a mark shaped like a heart in his fur. Obviously, I called him Braveheart because I wanted Spot to find strength from the name.

Whenever I addressed this handsome tom as Braveheart, Spot unquestionably enjoyed the idea. By the gleam in his eye and a flick of the tail, I felt he relished the possibility of possessing the boldness of a lordly lion to take on the world, especially overcoming his fear of the unknown.

In many ways, Spot controlled his fear. As Braveheart, Spot could keep the emotion in check. By accomplishing this, he steadily relaxed, accepting many new and different things. With the triumph, Spot's fear faded into a memory.

Wouldn't it be nice if everyone could find strength in their names to overcome the unknowns and then conquer them?

Gentle Soul Cali

I believe a gentle soul is exactly that—a gentle soul. I have an idea the Lord Father allows a special angel to come to earth disguised as a gentle soul, so the rest of us can see the wonders around and yet to appear.

A gentle soul cat is likely to be very quiet, frequently staying in the background and never demanding very much from anyone. This cat loves the attention received but seldom steps forward to ask for any. The gentle soul is definitely caring and very loving when given the chance to share these gifts with others.

Sometimes I think the rabble-rouser cat, the troublemaker, misbehaves for the mere fact that he realizes he will be noticed even if the reward for the act is punishment. In my home, it is usually timeout inside a playhouse with a lecture from me. For the cat, this just means naptime with Mom talking to herself again. In contrast, a gentle soul never causes any trouble; maybe that is why he doesn't stand out enough to receive his fair share of attention.

From Mini, Annie, Windy, Tail Chaser, Bloomie, Nana, Joseph, Su, Tigger, Spot, and Cali to many more, I have been fortunate to have been owned by many gentle souls throughout the years. The gift of tenderness these cats shared allowed me to perceive how wonderful everything can be with them in my life. Their gentle hearts unquestionably made their places on earth a little bit of heaven.

Cali Cat was a longhair dilute calico. She stole my heart with her soft ways. I never had to look for this kitty since she always remained close, especially near my husband. Cali adored Pat and thought the sun rose and set upon his shoulders. She also believed he could accomplish anything with a wave of his hand. In no time, he became her "purrferred" person.

With a "purrcise" inner clock, Cali knew the exact moment Pat came home from the office and always met him at the door. She followed Pat everywhere just to be close. Cali adored Pat, although she allowed the other cats to come first for attention before she requested any for herself. Cali never made a fuss over the position either. She was always tolerant while quietly waiting for her turn to receive a tickle on the head.

At mealtime, Cali was the last to partake. It never bothered her in the least since Cali recognized she was never forgotten. She remained quite patient when waiting for a bowl of delectable food to be offered. Slowly eating, Cali savored every bite with appreciation.

This sweet calico enjoyed sunshine through a window, except she willingly surrendered the spot whenever another cat asked her to move. Selfishness was something Cali knew very little about because that sort of attitude was never part of her nature.

When nighttime came, Cali slept at the foot of the bed by my feet. If I was restless, Cali took it in stride. She was never bothered by how much I tossed and turned. Cali rode the waves with gratitude and never with a grumble. Cali realized how much Pat and I loved her.

Even in Cali's fight with cancer, she never lost her gentle way. Throughout Cali's short life, she definitely showed the simple wonders at hand and the ones to come if I open my eyes and heart to see them. Cali was a gentle soul, my special angel here on earth.

Did You Say Chicken Broth?

Geoffy was a handsome cream-colored Maine Coon cat. He lived with his white thunder brother and persnickety calico sister at a friend's home. I was quite attached to Geoffy, along with his siblings, and thought of him as one of my extended thundering herd of pampered felines. I was also part of Geoffy's health care team and visited daily to help with his medical therapy in his elder years.

When first pilling Geoffy, I filled a syringe with water and gently administered the fluid one drop at a time into the side of his mouth to help flush the pill down his throat. Geoffy loved having the water squirted into his mouth. Trying to get a little more liquid into him, I suggested chicken broth be substituted instead. The idea to use chicken broth struck me because Geoffy always loved his bowl of grilled chicken, and I figured the broth would also be a hit with him.

Throughout the years, Geoffy never failed to relish chicken and almost turned inside out to get his fair share of this flavorsome treat. Later, he expanded his gourmet taste to include a new love, chicken broth. This wonderful liquid certainly wasn't the kind purchased at the grocery store. Obviously, it was homemade. Plus, the broth was prepared to Geoffy's exact specifications.

Marilyn, Geoffy's human mom, bought the finest chicken breasts. Each piece was cleaned, placed in a large pot, and then covered with purified water. There was never one drop or pinch of seasoning ever added to the premium mixture since Geoffy was a true purist.

The chicken was simmered on the stove until the meat arrived at the point of falling to pieces. Then the juice was drained into small individual containers and frozen. One by one, the scrumptious liquid was taken out as needed and then defrosted. It was most important that the broth remained as fresh as possible for a particular five-star connoisseur!

Well?

Not only did Geoffy love the broth, he considered the liquid to be absolutely delectable. He rated the broth a number ten on a scale of one to ten with ten as the best. Subsequently, he assumed that whenever I did anything to him, I was required to accompany these actions with a syringe filled with chicken broth as a well-deserved treat. Each time Geoffy sat at complete attention and announced in no uncertain terms he must be given the broth—*presently*—and I should immediately stop dragging my heels about the matter! The moment Geoffy thought I possibly failed to move fast enough, this connoisseur pawed me with his very large feet, displaying impatience with the delay.

Geoffy cocked his head to the side the second he caught a glimpse of the nectar of the gods. He allowed the broth to be placed, drop by drop, into his mouth. As each mouth-watering trickle touched the awaiting taste buds, Geoffy smacked his lips in pure ecstasy. The instant the syringe was empty, Geoffy smiled and quickly demanded *more* of course!

Snuggle Buggle

A snuggle buggle is a specific cat who loves sleeping with me at night. Not just sleeping next to me, but this is a certain one who climbs on top of my chest and falls into a deep slumber. She then takes total pleasure in having me struggle for each new breath of air. I am always in awe of how such a small ball of warm fur can turn into a dead weight equal to a ten-ton truck when I try to sneak some rest for a few hours.

Missy, a small and dainty almost twelve-pound feline dynamo, is feisty and cute. I have to say she absolutely received a voice and the intelligence of a Siamese cat. This kitty is a blue-gray tuxedo with white. She is a headstrong Domestic Shorthair who knows she is pretty and adorable. She was given golden eyes and bats them at any human in a flirtatious manner every time she finds the opportunity. This little dynamo categorically loves attention and demands more than her fair share of it. Furthermore, Missy is also quick to bat another cat with her paw who mistakenly crosses her path when coming between her and a tickle on the head or a pat on the bottom.

At night, if I am not ready for bed in a reasonable time, Missy never misses the opportunity to lecture me. She follows my every step and tells me she needs her beauty rest, except she cannot get any until I am tucked in the bed.

The instant I finally hit the bed, Annie, a sweet calico, softly tiptoes and settles beside my arm. This lasts until Missy flies up and demands Annie must immediately depart or face a pop on the head with her paw. Through the art of intimidation, a huff, and a raised paw, the small powerhouse doesn't waste a moment's notice in sending Annie to the bottom of the bed. Annie settles on the farthest corner just to stay out of harm's way. Triumphantly, Missy then assumes her rightful spot.

While I lay in bed with Missy happily purring on top of my chest, I think about those who have breathing disorders. As the minutes tick away, Missy's weight gets heavier and heavier. I then understand how the poor souls feel having to struggle to take air into their lungs. I definitely have gained a tremendous amount of empathy for their efforts because of this snuggle buggle.

If I dare move, Missy scolds me. She categorically states she is comfortable and I must stop disturbing her rest. I then try to explain how essential it is to occasionally take in at least a few breaths of air. Missy looks at me in absolute sheer wonder. It seems that is my problem and she couldn't be bothered by such complaints. If I begin to turn blue and roll over on my side out of absolute necessity, Missy stomps over to the pillow and falls down close by my face in utter disgust. Now I must struggle to get a breath of air with this heavyweight trying to smother me.

Will I ever change my nightly sleeping habits with this eleven-pound-plus powerhouse?

Never!

Why?

Remarkably, I am still able to intermittently receive a breath of air at night, even with a ten-ton truck parked on my chest or covering my face. Missy is my snuggle buggle, and I wouldn't alter her sleeping habits in any conceivable way!

The Austin Cats

Way back in the early nineties when my best friend and I rescued a number of abandoned cats around Cheryl's neighborhood, we made a cat room for them inside her garage apartment. Bloomie and her son were two of the cats in this group of felines. Bloomie was a beautiful black-and-brown classic tabby with white. Sal was the spitting image of her except much larger.

Eventually, Bloomie and Sal were adopted by a couple in the area. After these kitties moved into their forever home, I continued to assist their new mom with their care. In no time at all, Sandra and I became friends. Then whenever these kitties' human parents went on vacation, Bloomie and Sal came and stayed with me. They quickly fit in with my thundering crew.

After a few years, Sandra and her husband with their two adorable kitties moved to the Austin vicinity. This didn't alter our relationship in the least since Sandra and I kept in touch. Often Bloomie and Sal came back to stay with me anytime Sandra and her husband took extended holidays. I always loved the opportunity to be the kitties' sitter. I really enjoyed these two cats reentering my life, and I enjoyed spending some time with Sandra as well. It was fun visiting and catching up with what was new for Sandra when she brought the kitties to me and upon her return to take them back to Austin.

On a Saturday in June 2008, I was working in the garden room when the phone rang. It was Sandra. She called to ask if I was available to sit her two precious kitties once more. Delighted and without a second thought, I said, "Yes, of course, I will!"

Not having seen either the kitties or Sandra in some time, I was more than pleased to help out. Still, there was something else in Sandra's voice. I definitely felt it was bothering her, but I didn't ask right away. I gave Sandra time to explain.

Sandra slowly related the reason she hadn't been in touch very much since

Christmas. During the previous months, she had been feeling ill. Finally, the doctors pinpointed the problem and scheduled surgery the following week to remove Sandra's spleen. The doctors were positive it was cancer, except they didn't know the type at the moment. The pathology performed afterward would determine exactly what cancer it was and then what treatment, if any, would be recommended.

Following surgery, Sandra wanted to take a couple of weeks of vacation with her husband at their special retreat to have time for recouping and getting some strength back. Depending on the results of the pathology and the doctors' plans, they would either stay at the retreat the entire planned length or cut the trip short if required. Sandra stated the cats would have to stay for about two months and asked if it was a problem.

I never had a single reservation about the required length of time these kitties would stay. Without any hesitation, I said, "No, it isn't a problem! I am thrilled to have them come, and I am looking forward to the visit as always. They can remain as long as needed."

Sandra's husband drove Bloomie and Sal to my home. Pat and I briefly visited with Ted before he departed back to Austin. I sensed he felt uncomfortable leaving Sandra for very long, even with a sitter.

It was fun to observe Bloomie and Sal. These two kitties remembered everything from the last time they came, although four years had passed. They did find a couple of new friends to adjust to but quickly acclimated to the latest additions. Bloomie was my sweetheart as always; and Sal was the apple of my eye, my Baby Biggs.

About a week after Sandra's surgery, the pathology came back. The results weren't good. The cancer was a very rare type, so Sandra chose to let the oncology doctors at MD Anderson in Houston treat it. A few weeks later, Sandra underwent strenuous chemotherapy.

Before starting the chemo, Sandra called and asked if Bloomie and Sal could remain with me permanently. Sandra realized she would never have to worry about them if they were under my watchful eye. Amid so much chemotherapy and an uncertain future, she especially wanted her two precious kitties to be safe and loved in her absence.

Heartbroken for Sandra and fighting back tears, I responded, "Most definitely, Bloomie and Sal can remain. I will care for them with all my heart until the day comes you can resume. They will always belong to you. In the meantime, I will watch over them until you're health returns. Then they can go back to you."

Sandra cried. She was relieved and grateful. She thanked me over and over again. After I hung up the phone, I too cried. In the back of my mind, I had a terrible feeling my friend, more than likely, wasn't going to get better. Sandra just wanted to make sure her two adorable kitties would always be cared for if she was no longer in the position.

It would have been impossible for Sandra to part with her cats under normal circumstances. For Sandra to give them up because she faced a cancer that was going to take her life was extremely distressing. I was saddened beyond belief. I certainly never wanted Bloomie and Sal to come back to me under such conditions.

Three years later, after living longer than the doctors' expectations, Sandra decided she didn't want any more chemo. She wished to live the rest of her time with life in it. She definitely did not want to just exist and deal with the horrendous side effects of more experimental treatments with very little to no promise for a future.

Sandra said this *Bible verse* helped her through the many trials and tribulations she had undergone after the diagnosis:

> *Thus says the Lord . . .*
> *"I have heard your prayer and seen your tears, I will heal you."*
> —*Isaiah 38:5*

I fully believe the Lord Father did this for Sandra so she could enjoy some precious time here on earth and then receive complete health in eternity.

There was never a question about stepping in and caring for Sandra's adorable kitties. Saying good-bye to someone I cared about to have Bloomie and Sal live out the rest of their lives with me was absolutely something I never expected or wished to ever happen.

The Neon Sign

If you are an abandoned feline and quite homeless,
Welcome to my home!
If you are a starving feline and totally famished,
Come in and have a meal!
If you are a forlorn feline and ever so lonely,
Think about staying!
If you are a destitute feline and choose to be adopted,
Definitely ring the doorbell!

Somehow this neon sign appeared on the roof when my husband and I moved into our present home during the spring of 1991. It has remained in place through every kind of weather and has never changed. Much more frustrating, the sign was never removed, even though two new roofs have been installed since the house was constructed.

The sign is seen for miles around, but only by cats! The feline population around town has also put out the message by having it printed on every sack of cat litter, can of moist cat food, and bag of dry cat food sold throughout the county, perhaps the entire state. While the print is invisible to a human, it can be read, quite easily, by every cat in search of a good home.

Many times I open the door to find a cat pleading for help after reading the message. Thus far, I have never turned one away. Some have remained and became one of my feline crew. Others were placed in very suitable homes.

In the summer of 2009, I was in the process of having the trees trimmed in the front yard when the doorbell rang. It was one of the workmen standing on the porch and holding a young black-and-white cat. The worker explained he picked up my cat and requested I keep him indoors. I looked at the cat and grinned at the worker. Politely, I made it clear the juvenile wasn't mine, as my cats were indoor felines. I closed the door and proceeded with my chores, thinking it was the workman's problem and not mine.

It wasn't very long before the doorbell rang again. The same workman was once more standing on the porch, holding the same cat. This time, he said the cat didn't have any fear of the equipment and he was afraid the cat would get hurt or killed by getting too close. The worker pleaded for my help. Needless to say, I took the tom from his arms and inquired if by chance he noticed the direction the cat came from. Quickly, the workman pointed at a neighbor's house across the street before he went back to collecting debris from the trees.

With the silly notion the cat belonged to the neighbor, I walked across the street and rang the doorbell. Shortly, a gentleman answered. I inquired if possibly the young tom was his cat. The gentleman smiled and said he never saw the cat before. He thought the kitty was a drop-off.

Muttering under my breath, I walked back home. I knew the cat was a drop-off. Why not? After all, where else does a stray cat come to when seeking help other than my house?

While the workers trimmed the trees, I approached and asked if any of them wanted a cat. One responded and stated he was allergic. The second didn't want a longhair cat, except the cat wasn't and there was no conceivable way of convincing him differently. Another absolutely didn't like cats in any shape or form. The last worker said his wife wouldn't let him have a pet. I thought to myself: *Sure!*

I looked at the purring juvenile in my arms and told him he was able to read quite well. I then stared at the roof and realized the neon sign was working better than ever. It had to be because it enlisted the aid of the tree trimmers to find this feline a good home.

Closing the door behind me, I walked to the powder room. I put the cat in the safe place until I could take him to the veterinary clinic and have him checked the next day.

Fairway completed the first round of medical tests without a hitch. He then finished going through the isolation time designated for every newcomer. After Fairway passed his final health check with flying colors, he joined my thundering crew in time for a two-year-old tom who also saw the neon sign and came asking for help.

Actually, this tom saw the sign and then followed me. He approached me when I was at a good friend's home tending the cats while she was away for the weekend with her husband. The cat explained how he "purrsued" the remote signal, which I seem to possess. Apparently, this signal sends the message on my neon sign.

Noni offered to foster the cat when I explained how he needed to be off the streets. He was named after the crossed-eyed lion, Clarence, for the reason that he was also slightly crossed-eyed. Clarence also passed the medical requirements and remained with Noni once she realized he could be tamed. It took some time before Clarence left his wild side behind, although it does occasionally rear its head. Noni has come to terms with this behavior and has worked hard to get the handsome tom to accept domestication.

The neon sign has faded over the years. However, the message remains strong and clear in view of the fact that Jack Nicklaus came asking to join my thundering crew after noticing the sign approximately two miles away and then getting Noni to act as a mediator!

Never Say Never

There is one thing I have unquestionably learned over the years. It is to never say never because the second I speak those infamous words, I will shortly end up eating them.

In 2010, I lost many kitties to a number of different diseases. Some were older, and some were too young to become heavenly angels, but they did. With all the sadness I went through during the year, I reached a point where I wanted to slow down a little and have some time for me. I definitely did not have any desire of taking on more felines in need of a home. I wanted to selectively choose to work with cats, except with one difference. I sought to do home health care for felines in someone else's home and not in mine. I really preferred helping cats belonging to others.

However . . .

First, Foxy Lady appeared on the scene.

Admittedly, I threw my resolve out the window and made an exception in Foxy's case. With some of my therapy cats advancing in age, I realized I would be retiring them in the coming years. Nonetheless, I wanted to continue working with cats in the program. After assessing Foxy Lady, I recognized she demonstrated potential as a future therapy cat. Needless to say, I adopted this pretty kitty.

Foxy Lady is still young, approximately a year old. She has to mature and slow down quite a bit before I will consider training her to be a therapy cat. She must also develop social skills along with manners. In the meantime, I will let her be a juvenile and enjoy terrorizing the rest of the thundering herd with her kitten play.

Second, Sweet William came into my life.

When the doctors told my friend in Austin she could have her cats back, Sandra decided after much soul-searching it was in their best interest that her adorable kitties remain with me. They came and stayed while Sandra underwent cancer surgery followed by years of chemo. Bloomie and Sal entered their senior years at the time and developed health issues. For many reasons, mostly because of her own health, Sandra was unable to meet the challenges these two adorable kitties presented in their care.

Ted, Sandra's husband, found a young shelter cat to bring into Sandra's life and give the comfort Sandra missed without Bloomie and Sal around to supply it. Willy (William) bridged the gap and brought joy into Sandra's life.

On Friday, April 8, 2011, Sandra posed a big request and one I could not decline fulfilling. She asked if I would take Willy. Sandra was dying, and she needed to know her third precious kitty would be all right after she was gone. I never had any reservations about accepting the responsibility. I felt the request was something that couldn't be turned down for any reason.

The following Sunday, my husband and I drove down to the Austin area so I could see Sandra for the last time and then take Willy back with us. I never realized how much heartache could be felt on that day, but it happened.

When I entered Sandra's bedroom, Sandra smiled. She was thrilled I came. Sandra was cheerful and witty, even though I could see she didn't look good. She was as beautiful as ever, except the cancer was taking the life out of her. Sandra thanked me over and over for coming to her rescue and helping out once more.

The moment I was about to leave, Sandra grabbed my hand. With tears swelling in her eyes and almost unable to speak, she whispered, "We will never see each other." I squeezed Sandra's hand back and replied, "We will see each other . . . one day."

Sandra looked at me with a surprised and puzzled expression, knowing there wasn't a possibility with time rapidly disappearing for her. Then it dawned on Sandra what I meant and she smiled with complete gratitude as I left.

Six days later, Sandra returned to the heavenly home.

In my heart, I now thank Sandra for allowing Willy to be a part of my life.

Obviously, I will not say *never again* to anything that I make a solemn pledge not to do. Apparently, very much like a cat, I will categorically perform exactly the opposite way.

I Believe

My forever kitties are the heavenly kitty angels. They will always remain a part of me, and one day I shall once again be with them.

I wrote this for a presentation I did on behalf of my heavenly kitty angels. Since that time, many more have joined the ranks.

I believe,
Although I can no longer hold you,
In my arms,
A piece of you will always remain,
Within my heart.

I believe,
Whenever I close my eyes,
You will come to me,
If nothing more,
Than one brief moment in time.

I believe,
Each time I look to the heavens,
I will feel comfort,
Knowing,
You have found peace.

I believe,
As long as I have faith in the everlasting,
I will remember,
You are forever
Watching over me.

Temporary Conclusion, Not an End

Throughout *Reflections of a Cat Whisperer*, I have shared selected segments from my life. This collection of writings contains a variety of my thoughts and adventures. At this point, I have reached a temporary conclusion, but not an end to my tales since the collection is far from finished in acknowledging every one of them. Essentially, I have established a foundation for many more to come by moving forward on a journey that will discover new horizons while revisiting old wonders through memory.

What greater gift to ever receive
than the love of a feline,
the domestic cat!

MEOW

CPSIA information can be obtained at www.ICGtesting.com
Printed in the USA
LVOW12s1648220713

344068LV00009B/1360/P